AMERICA

D1565732

*the text of this book is printed
on 100% recycled paper*

Johan Huizinga

AMERICA

A DUTCH HISTORIAN'S VISION,
FROM AFAR AND NEAR

Translated, with an Introduction and Notes,
by Herbert H. Rowen

HARPER ❦ TORCHBOOKS
Harper & Row, Publishers
New York, Evanston, San Francisco, London

TABLE OF CONTENTS

INTRODUCTION

By Herbert H. Rowen

In these two books on America in the past and America in his own times, the Dutch historian Johan Huizinga has an unusual angle of vision. He is an outside observer with a difference. When a foreign historian undertakes the study of the history of another country, he characteristically seeks to combine the native's familiarity with the outsider's freshness of approach. It is seldom that he can achieve the insider's full sureness of touch, but he can come close to it by dint of sustained study. His new thoughts may on occasion betray not novelty but naïveté, yet at his best he sees clearly and sharply things that the native in his very familiarity with the material takes for granted. His special advantage lies in writing for an outside audience, for he is less likely to attribute to it a knowledge of fact or interpretation that it does not possess. But these are precisely the qualities that Huizinga does not and cannot display in these essays, especially when, as in this translation, they will be read chiefly not by Dutchmen but by Americans. Huizinga was not a specialist in American history, and his essays, written for Dutch readers, will on occasion strike an American as stating the elementary and the obvious. Yet the value of these essays lies in Huizinga's unusual questions and the often unexpected answers they give rise to. These are to only a limited extent what one would expect of almost any European historian looking at America with his own national and continental assumptions and predilections. Much more are they the product of a highly individual historical mind.

Although with his younger contemporary Pieter Geyl he was undoubtedly the outstanding Dutch historian of the twentieth century, Huizinga was not a historian by training. Born on December 7, 1872, in the northern Dutch city of Groningen, he was the son of a professor of physiology at the university there; but his father had turned to a scientific career only after completing training in theology, ending the line of Mennonite preachers in the Huizinga family which was almost unbroken since the sixteenth century. Johan followed neither his father nor his earlier forebears in his educational pattern. His university training at Groningen was in literature, and his special subject was old Hindu literature. However, after receiving his doctorate in 1897, his first teaching appointment was in history at the secondary school in Haarlem, where he remained until 1905. Although he became an instructor in Hindu studies at Amsterdam university in 1903, he was called to the chair of Dutch history at Groningen two years later, thanks to the powerful support of his former teacher, P. J. Blok, who had already persuaded him to undertake studies in the medieval origins of Haarlem. In 1915, Huizinga was called to Leiden to take over Blok's own chair, and there he remained until Leiden university was closed by the German occupation authorities in 1940. During these years he rose to a position of eminence among historians not only of his own country but of the whole world. His most famous book was *The Waning of the Middle*

Ages (1919), a study of the cultural life of the Low Countries and northern France in the Burgundian period. His biography of Erasmus (1924) was also widely read. Huizinga's other writings were mainly in the field of Low Countries history, including the recently translated *Dutch Civilization in the Seventeenth Century* (original edition in German, 1933; expanded Dutch version, 1941). He also wrote several books on contemporary civilization, in which he was, as Geyl put it in a commemorative address, "the accuser of his own times." The two works translated in this volume are anticipations of the mood and thought of these later, larger works. Arrested by the Germans and sent to a concentration camp in 1941, Huizinga was released for reasons of ill health but sent into quasi-exile in De Steeg, a little town near Arnhem, where he died on February 1, 1945.

The first of these books on American history resulted from the task accepted by Huizinga during World War I of presenting a course in American history at Leiden university. It was based on printed materials only, for he had not yet visited the United States. The second book is fundamentally his travel notes from a trip to America in 1926, during which he journeyed in the Northeast, the Midwest and Far West, and the South. The specialist in American history will be able to judge for himself how far these two works illuminate the past and present of American civilization; but it would be well for him to do so with understanding of the shape of Huizinga's mind, which was European in its general cast and "cultural" in the broadest possible sense in its individual characteristics. It is difficult to imagine any fuller revelation of the individual spirit of a historian than is given in these pages.

Although influenced by the school of German historians and historical thinkers around Wilhelm Dilthey, Huizinga developed a quite individual approach to the content and form of history. From the very beginning of his career as a professor, he put stress upon the esthetic component of history. By this he meant not the literary qualities of historical writing (although he gave much attention to them, as we shall see), but the grasping of the past as "form," in a pictorial or even musical sense. When he spoke of the creation and contemplation of a "historical picture," he was not using the phrase in a more or less metaphorical way for an essentially philosophical idea, like the Diltheyans; rather he intended it quite literally, as the past seen and felt. He rejected the model of the physical sciences for history because he did not think in terms of theories, hypotheses, and proofs. For him, historical scholarship was the careful discovery of the past from the sources, illuminated by the historian's vision and sensibility, a truth of fact and a truth of feeling. For he also rejected the fanciful and irresponsible treatment of the past in the writings of the popular biographers of the twenties and thirties. He saw anachronism as the historian's cardinal sin, which violated not only the rule of literal accuracy but also that of rightness of mood.

Huizinga's subject, after his first (and only archivally based) work on Haarlem, was the history of culture, the forms in which society gives expression to its spiritual life and in which it takes account of itself. He was therefore deeply concerned with the moral and esthetic dimensions of the past, both for themselves and as essential aspects of the totality of human life. He looked at politics as a kind of applied morality and even, as in the studies of America, a kind of applied esthetics of the masses, much more than as the working out of social forces and purposes through the instrumentality of power. His ethical standards were complex. From his Mennonite background he inherited and preserved the principle of a forthright yet modest morality, which the individual sets for himself more than for others; thus he was able to escape the tortures of ethical dilemmas in a world of relativist diversity. He abandoned the formal dogmas of his inherited religion but not the deep sense of the mystery of man's existence and a broad responsiveness to all the rituals by which man embodies that sense. He claimed little knowledge of philosophy and less of natural science, but he was almost a philosopher-in-spite-of-himself, for his extraordinary critical powers when applied to the discipline of history revealed the workings of a coherent and even systematic mind. Yet he abhorred systematizing as the mechanization of the spirit and the death of creativity. But he also despised mindless sentimentality and the abandonment of reason.

These qualities give a special character to Huizinga's work. It displays an openness to a variety of ways of thinking and feeling but without the loss of the central integrity of the author, who retains his own thoughts and moods. It has a logic of flowing depiction into which are set islands of analytic judgment; but there are few definitions, hard, fixed and often illusory. Remarkably, Huizinga's characteristic form is the essay, not the narrative, the set piece and not the account of time's flux. Yet the ages that particularly attracted his interest were the times of change, when the old was passing but not yet gone and the new was being born but had not yet won.

Huizinga, who underwent in his youth the esthetic influence of the Dutch literary movement known as the *Tachtigers* ("Men of the '80s"), with its affirmation of an art-for-art's-sake doctrine, created a distinctive and personal literary style in his historical writing. He seldom lapsed into jargon, although the sections on economic developments in the first of the essays translated here are marred by just such standardized language; doubtless he was not at home with such material. Normally he writes in a style that combines strength and subtlety, rhythm and color, with a precise choice of word and an original turning of phrase. It is a taut style that should not be transformed by translation into limp Victorian English. Huizinga's allusiveness can taunt and betray the translator; in the few places where he writes not in his own way but like a German professor of the old school, he is difficult to convey in plain English, but where he distils his thought into a powerful image he often comes straight over into English, word for word.

In this work of translation, I enjoyed the critical assistance of my Dutch-born friend, Kees Schagen, who saved me from some slips; I did not adopt a few of his suggested improvements, at my own peril. The task of putting these essays into English was undertaken at the suggestion of my colleague and friend, Professor Warren I. Susman, whose vision of history is so much like Huizinga's. Some day he will perhaps put into print his own personal understanding of the significance of Huizinga, given to me in discussions which accompanied the progress of this translation.

A Note on Footnotes

Huizinga's own notes are given usually without identification, except where I have felt that further clarification was necessary. In that case, the initials *J.H.* follow Huizinga's text, and my own, *H.H.R.*, what I have added. I have not attempted to track down citations for which Huizinga gives no source, nor generally to verify his references; his bibliographical citations in the footnotes are left in his own form, although it is inconsistent and sometimes unclear. Here and there I have added some notes which are entirely my own, either to call attention to an error on Huizinga's part or to explain some word or concept which could not be adequately conveyed by translation alone; these of course are also followed by the initials *H.H.R.*

I

MAN AND THE MASSES IN AMERICA:

*Four Essays in the History
of Modern Civilization*

Preface to the First Edition

This book is the product of my studies for a course in American history which I gave during the past academic year at the University of Leiden. The first of these essays appeared in *De Gids* in July and August 1918, under the title "A historical contrast examined in the light of American history." The third is included in the *Verslagen en mededeelingen der Koninklijke Akademie van Wetenschappen, afdeeling Letterkunde*,[1] 5th series, volume IV.

We know much too little about America. True, many a traveler back from America sets down his impressions in a book, but by their very nature such writings lack the historical background necessary for understanding the present. This may serve as an excuse for an attempt by someone who has never been to the New World to fill in some of the background from the perspective of cultural history.

The history of America used to hold no attraction for

[1] "Reports and Communications of the Royal [Dutch] Academy of Sciences, Section Literature."–H.H.R.

me. I did not expect to find in it any of the things by which the grandeur of the European past holds us in its grasp. This changed when I began my studies, however, and I found myself stimulated and fascinated as seldom ever before; it was as if something of America's spiritual élan is transmitted to anyone who takes the trouble to understand the spirit of the country.

Another circumstance makes it a joy to study the history of America—the excellence of its organization of work in national history. This is not known widely enough. History as an organized scholarly discipline dates back no further than the establishment of the American Historical Association in 1884, but it was a sound beginning. Thus, although American history is badly underrepresented in Dutch public libraries, this difficulty is made good to some extent by the preeminently practical way that American aids to research are arranged. One is repeatedly struck by how well American historians understand that the task of historical scholarship goes beyond and differs in character from the production of knowledge for professional historians alone.

September 1918   *J.H.*

Preface to the Third Edition

This book was written in 1918, and revised in 1920 to be as up to date as possible. Therefore it would be even more difficult to make it accurate as of 1928 than to recreate a woman of the earlier time in today's image with the help of nothing but scissors. The author considers himself relieved of such a perilous duty for two reasons. The first is that these essays were always intended to be *historical* in nature, as the subtitle indicates, and the second that he published another book a year ago, *Life and Thought in America: Stray Remarks,* which in a certain sense is an amplification of this book.

In revising these essays, I have therefore aimed principally at heightening their historical character. Where feasible, however, figures for the intervening years have been brought up to date and those which no longer applied have been deleted.

Since 1920, American business has opened up so many new paths of development and displayed so many aspects that only a complete rewriting of the second essay [Chapter 2] would have brought it into line with the present. The very question underlying this essay has now taken on another shape. The reader interested in the economic developments of recent years may read Arthur Feiler, *Amerika-Europa, Erfahrungen einer Reise* (Frankfurter Societäts-Druckerei, 1926), and M. J. Bonn, *Geld und Geist: Vom Wesen und Werden der Amerikanischen Welt* (Berlin: S. Fischer, 1927).

The attention of all readers should be drawn to two excellent surveys of the whole of American history, both in two volumes: D. S. Muzzey, *The United States of America* (Ginn and Co., 1922–1924), and Charles A. and Mary R. Beard, *The Rise of American Civilization* (Macmillan, 1927).

January 1928 *J.H.*

Chapter 1

INDIVIDUALISM AND ASSOCIATION

Anyone who undertakes a study of the history of the United States of America for the first time may well have the feeling that he is looking through a telescope and cannot quickly bring it into focus. He lengthens it, shortens it, but the picture remains blurred. If you prefer a more elegant comparison, it is as if someone accustomed to the strict, transparent forms of classical music is hearing a modern composition for the first time. He does not immediately perceive the form that controls it, a form over which he too has control; instead, he is merely confused at first by the overpowering masses of sound and the unfamiliar harmonies. If we try to understand the history of the United States as a whole, it possesses in great measure this overpowering quality, this dissonance, and the confusing quality to which they give rise. We see exaggerated movements, passionate conflicts, and flagrant contradictions of words and deeds, but the reasons for the conflicts and the causes of the movements are not immediately clear. The lines of the picture will not come into sharp focus.

There will be nothing surprising in this if we are aware
how we come to possess our understanding of history and that
it is always an inadequate understanding. History, as the study
of the past, makes the coherence of what happened compre-
hensible by reducing events to a dramatic pattern and seeing
them in a simple form. Fundamentally there are only a few
patterns and forms at the service of historical thought. They
were conceived for the history of antiquity and medieval and
modern Europe. They have been elaborated by historical
thinkers over the centuries; Thucydides had his share in this
work, as did Augustine, Machiavelli, Voltaire, and Burckhardt.
It is this history of the Old World to which we are accustomed,
and we therefore tend to look for its patterns and its shapes in
the history of the largest community of the New World as
well. Why then should we be surprised to find that the old
forms appear not at all or only partly adequate for the New
World?

What I wish to do in these pages is to test against the facts
of American history two of the schematic forms through which
we are accustomed to understand history. The first of these
is the clash between the old and the new; the second involves
the conflict between the desire for personal independence and
the need for association.

Consciously or not, we have a strong tendency to see
history in the form of a struggle between the old and the new,
the desire to preserve and to maintain in eternal opposition to
the will to reform and to renew. Every great historical process
can be conceived in the form of this conflict, whether we are
concerned with intellectual or social developments or only
with the struggle for power. Events may almost always be
reduced to the resistance put in the way of the operation of
the new purposes and the new forces by the inertia of an age-
old social structure. It is obvious that this contrast does not

express the *meaning* of great events but merely indicates what the course of events actually was. Yet this principle of distinction between the old and the new in struggle which so largely dominates our historical vision holds a strong ethical component as well as a strong element of drama. It is drama because we always see the fated inability of conservatives and innovators to understand each other as a great tragic contrast between the blindness of the former and the hubris of the latter. It is ethics because we always pay our respects to what is dead and beautiful, and give our love to what is young and alive. If the spectator takes sides, then the conflict falls into place for him as an episode in the cosmic struggle between light and darkness, between good and evil.

This historical standard, by which we measure according to a scale set by our hearts, virtually fails us when we attempt to grasp the history of America. That we have a tendency to use it anyway is hard to deny. Who among us, in attempting to understand the party conflict between Republicans and Democrats, has not begun by asking the question, "Which is the conservative and which the progressive party?" The question at once proved of no use, for in America the line of division between the old and the new cannot be drawn so easily. In America, all forces are new; as a consequence, the factors that have dominated European history are almost wholly absent from American history. As soon as independence had been achieved and the Constitution ratified, there were no more attempts to bring about a new form of government in the republic, any more than there was a dynastic question. No stumps from a feudal forest remained, still rooted everywhere in the soil, as in Europe. There exists no problem of the relationship between government and religion, no question of the power of the church or its landed possessions. There exists no question of defence, no question of how to keep a political balance in the midst of neighbors, or how to establish dominance over them. There exists no question of national minorities, and for a long time there was no social question (the question of slavery is neither).

All this does not mean that old forces do not continue to exist in America which resist the growth of the new. Of course they exist: Every center of power, whether it consists in property, interests, or ideas, is constantly becoming old and inert. But in America the old forces are not bound together in the luster of age-old institutions, like church and crown, nobility and army, to which respect is paid because they rest in men's imaginations on deep traditions and prestige.

We find not a conflict between the old and the new forms of life within society, but an even more violent one between nature and man. The power whose inertia needs to be overcome is the power of matter. The conquest of the immense continent by work has been the commanding task the American people has seen before its eyes since the beginning. At bottom, every political and cultural question in America is an economic one. On America's virgin soil, which is free of old, strongly rooted social growths, economic factors work with a freedom and directness unknown in European history. Political passions in America are deliberately directed to economic questions, and these are not subordinated to a system of intellectual convictions which become for the man who believes them the content of his culture. Expressing this in the language of Marxism, we would say that economic factors operate to a much greater extent without a cloak of ideological conceptions.

By comparing the debates of the French Constituent Assembly of 1789 with those of the Continental Congress of 1776, we can get a good insight into the difference between American and European history. In the Constituent Assembly we find a love of mankind in general and a rational optimism which bubble like champagne; in the Continental Congress, a trenchant, businesslike tone, so that one would scarcely suspect that these Americans were also devoted to the same ideas of the Enlightenment . . . but it was only as *ideas*. We do hear these ideas in the Declaration of Independence, but a more sober attitude prevailed when the form of government was discussed. During the debate on the important question whether Congress should vote by states or according to population, John Adams remarked, "Reason, justice and equity never had weight enough on the face of the earth to govern the councils of men. It is interest alone which does it, and it is interest alone which can be trusted."

I do not know whether a blunter realist in social and economic matters than John Adams existed during the eighteenth century. He argued in Congress with the greatest impartiality that it did not matter whether one called workers free men or slaves.[1] No one could be more persuaded than he was of the inevitability of the class struggle. "In every society where property exists, there will ever be a struggle between the rich and the poor." He accepted a *Verelendungstheorie*[2] and did not trust religious principles to act as a brake on rebellion.[3] "It is interest alone which does it." "I know not," he once said, "why we should blush to confess that molasses was an essential ingredient in American independence."[4] And Adams was not the only one in his circle who held such ideas. Samuel

[1] *Journals of the Continental Congress 1774–1779* (Washington, 1906), vol. VI, pp. 1104, 1099.

[2] German for "theory of pauperization."—H. H. R.

[3] J. Adams, *A Defence of the Constitutions of Government of the United States of America against the Attack of M. Turgot in His Letter to Dr. Price*, 1787; see C. A. Beard, *Economic Origins of Jeffersonian Democracy* (1915), pp. 299–319, and the literature cited there.

[4] See A. M. Schlesinger, *The Colonial Merchant and the American Revolution, 1763–1776* (Columbia University Studies in History, Economics and Public Law, vol. 78. New York, 1918), p. 59.

Chase, a delegate from Maryland, spoke no differently in 1776: "We shall be governed by our interests, and ought to be."[5]

This is how things actually were. From the start the great economic interests and controversies stand in the forefront of American history as motives for political struggle. The question of paper money against hard money began to be debated even before the revolt against England and there was almost no interruption of the strong disturbances caused in the country by this controversy. The most serious threat to the existence of the Union and the prelude to secession arose directly out of resistance by the Southern states to protectionism, which served only the interests of the commercial and industrial states. It was purely on the grounds of this single economic difference that John Calhoun preached "nullification" about 1830, that is, the declaration by a state that a federal law was null and void, with its secession as an inevitable consequence. At that time the danger was still averted by President Andrew Jackson's vigorous Union policy. South Carolina, which had begun to put nullification into practice, gave way. Another passionate struggle arose at once with a pure economic principle at stake: Jackson's stubborn war of annihilation against the National Bank. A deep economic antagonism also underlay this struggle which had been vigorously waged ever since the bank was first established in 1791. The pioneer democracy of the agricultural West, which for the first time had been able to put its representative at the head of government in Jackson, was battling the rising concentration of capital.

Economic factors lie so close to the surface of American history that we repeatedly see the enactment before our eyes of the process postulated by Marx as all-controlling. This is

[5] *Journals*, p. 1080; cf. Jefferson, *Anas, Memoirs, etc.*, vol. IV, 456: "Hamilton . . . avowed the opinion that man could be governed by one of two motives only: force or interest."

the way in which the forces of production—which in the last instance are the technical and natural means of economic production—are able directly to define an entire historical epoch, with all its social, political, and cultural arrangements. Eli Whitney invented the cotton gin, a device to remove the cotton fiber from the boll, in 1793. As a result, cotton-growing became dominant everywhere in the South; and this brought about in turn a consolidation of the system of slavery, which had appeared about ready to die out. Commerce and industry were the products of the railways.

Even more striking in its brief course was the rise and development of cattle ranching in the prairie lands west of the Mississippi, the so-called cow country. In 1860 a wagon train became snow-bound in Nebraska. The travelers turned their draft cattle loose in the wilderness because they could not feed them. Expecting them to die of hunger, they found them again in the spring, well-fed. This was the start of the great cattle-herding industry in the prairies. Each year the "Long Drive" was held from Texas to Wyoming and Montana over completely unoccupied and ownerless land, in pure nomadic style. Within a few years the cowboy arose as a type, with his own brand-new romanticism, which still lives on in the movies. But meanwhile cattle-herding on the open range was gradually limited by a process of enclosure, in which land was fenced off as private property without any basis in law. This change in the legal situation and the economic relationships occurred because of the invention of barbed wire about 1870. A simple and cheap way of fencing in cattle suddenly became available in a country where no trees grew for thousands[6] of miles. It is the fence which creates property, not the property-owner the fence. This process of enclosure went so far that the ranchers

---

[6] Huizinga obviously has his geography off. This should be "tens" or "hundreds," of course.—H.H.R.

even blocked mail routes. By about 1885 the system of "free grass" and the "long drive" belonged to the past. When Colonel Cody—"Buffalo Bill"—organized his Wild West Show in 1883, it was already a piece of cultural history.

Developments did not rest, however, at the stage of illegal enclosures. The farmer followed on the heels of the cattle-rancher; the land which previously had been scorned as useless was now wanted for agriculture, but it could not be developed until the illegal fences were removed. In 1885 Congress passed a law authorizing the summary removal of illegal enclosures, and the homesteaders, as the small farming pioneers were called, went everywhere the soil permitted.

Cattle-raising now became standardized, but in its further history the forces of production continued to play a notably direct role. Three great interests were involved in the cattle industry: the cowmen in the prairie country, the meat packers in Chicago, and the railway companies; to these we may add as a fourth interest the barbed-wire trust. All these interests were now organized as great corporations. At first the cattle were shipped live to the slaughterhouses, and the railway companies, which had to provide large stockyards for which they could charge high rates, earned large profits. Next came the invention of refrigeration,[7] which caused slaughtering to be shifted to the districts where cattle were raised. For the railways, this meant that their cattle cars declined in value, since a slaughtered steer takes less room than a live one; they therefore resisted this shift and tried to prevent it by manipu-

---

[7] I have left out here Huizinga's comment that *koeltechniek* (his term for refrigeration, literally "cooling technique" or "engineering") is a Delft-style Germanism (that is, such as used at the Delft Institute of Technology) which he employed "without blushing." It is revealing on the one hand of his own primarily cultural orientation and on the other of his awareness of technology, which both fascinated and frightened him.—H.H.R.

lating rates. We see the industry rising during the period of half a century from the most primitive forms to become finally an economic organization of the most modern kind, involved in the most modern forms of economic combat.[8]

We cannot help seeing the idea of the social struggle in European history from the viewpoint of the perpetual struggle of the old and the new, which I presented before as one of the most elementary notions of our historical vision. We express the aspirations of democracy as a striving for new times, *rerum novarum cupido*. The linkage of this conflict to the sequence of old and new applies to a much smaller extent in America. This may be considered as one of the reasons why our picture of American history at first stayed blurred—we lack the ordinary pattern which, almost unawares, we had grown accustomed to applying to history.

The second historical pattern whose validity I wish to test against the facts of American history is the conflict of individualism and association. It is clear that this way of conceiving historical development has much more specific significance and hence greater scientific value than the conception of an eternal struggle between the old and the new, which is vague, ethical, and esthetic. The importance gained in historical thinking by this conflict between individualism and association, which we also call organization or collectivism, is obvious on almost any page of contemporary historical writing. The whole development of the civilization of Western Europe since the beginning of the Middle Ages can be schematized from this point of view as a great process of action and reaction. There is no doubt that such a general view is extremely one-sided, incomplete, and in many respects inaccurate; nonetheless it

[8] F. L. Paxson, "The Cow Country," *American Historical Review*, XXI (1916), p. 65.

continues to dominate our view of the history of civilization because we do not have anything better to put in its place. We are accustomed to seeing the Middle Ages as a period of predominant collectivism—individuals appear before us faintly, but organizations, the church and the monasteries as well as social and economic groups like the feudal order and the guilds, seem solid and alive. Then the great awakening of the individual man comes at the end of the Middle Ages. The great Swiss master, Jakob Burckhardt, taught us to see the essence of the Renaissance in the transition from medieval to modern times in this process by which the individual became aware of himself. No matter how much we may be convinced now that a revision of Burckhardt's ideas is necessary, we have not yet been able to break away from this idea that individualism is the hallmark of European civilization since the Middle Ages. All the great events in the history of modern civilization are easily conceived as forms in which the predominant individualism of these centuries is expressed. The Renaissance, the Reformation, the emancipation of business, absolutism, the Enlightenment, Romanticism, and liberalism—all lend themselves to an interpretation that considers them as workings of the individualist spirit. This is a spirit which we now fancy belongs to the past. We dream of a future that will be a new period of community organization in the state and in economic and intellectual life, a higher and more complete form of collectivism in which the intellectual element profits and the freedom of individuality must be absorbed into the forms of a new sense of community and protected by them.

Leaving aside the question how correct or useful we should consider this schematization of historical development to be, the concept of organization nevertheless represents on the one hand the original state of affairs and on the other the highest development presented to society; individualism, however, is presented as an intermediate and, so to speak, hypertrophic stage which civilization must pass through in order to move from the primitive to a higher form of collectivism.

How can we use these conceptions for understanding American history? This is how the situation appears from the standpoint of European history. If the spirit of a free and bold individualism ever spoke out during the Renaissance and the Reformation, it was when this spirit became reality with the establishment and development of the English and Dutch colonies in North America. The yearning for adventure and the grandiose plans of a Gilbert and a Raleigh, the quest of the Pilgrim Fathers for religious freedom, the drive of a William Penn and a James Oglethorpe to found institutions, the entrepreneurial spirit in all of them—these are so many expressions of the spirit of the new time. All this individualism was the ferment of America's creation. What is missing is the phase of primitive collectivism. While the foundations of state and society in Europe rest in the forms of the older sense of community, in America a population of individualist spirit was called to the task of winning an immense country and conquering an overwhelming nature.

Their spirit proved equal to the task, which was carried through. But if we inquire how this happened, how individualism revealed itself in American history, then we find a number of corrections which need to be made in the excessively crude conception of individualism that we brought over from European history.

We are accustomed to considering individualism, which for us is the essence of the Renaissance and the modern era, as a highly developed, free and positive attitude of spirit, an element of high and noble culture, and Leonardo, Erasmus, and Montaigne are the examples that come to mind. But the individualism which was at work in the establishment of the American colonies reveals itself as much more of a primitive, limiting, and negative force. The spirit that maintained and strengthened the Calvinist communities of New England was utterly old-fashioned. It was the spirit of strict, intolerant enforcement of religious authority and public morals within their own circle and resistance to any authority from outside. Ever since Ernst Troeltsch showed the way in his studies, we have become familiar with the notion that earlier Protestantism was essentially a continuation of medieval civilization.[9] Actually, this can hold true for the political and social conceptions of the Protestant bourgeoisie no less than for their religious standpoint. When they were left to their fate without strong intervention by the central authority of the modern state, as in America, we find that it was the ideals of the medieval city in which their spirit dwelled. Freedom meant for them the same thing that it meant in the Middle Ages—intolerance of interference. In their case we feel at once how much our connection of the concept of individualism with the idea of the Renaissance and modern civilization requires correction. America was won and maintained by the dogged and old-fashioned individualism of the small town—we could almost say by medieval individualism. It remains one of the most remarkable facts of modern history that a continent could be conquered by these principles, while the imperialist policy of the French crown failed to achieve the same aims in America, although its view of the geographical possibilities of the country was far broader than that of the English colonists, its activity far more fixed of purpose, and its plans much more vigorous and uniform.

The rebellion of the American colonies against England

---

[9] E. Troeltsch, *Die Bedeutung des Protestantismus für die Entstehung der modernen Welt.* (*Historische Bibliothek,* Band 24 [1911]; *Historische Zeitschrift,* XCVII [1906]).

arose out of the same individualism in a later phase of development.

Their rebellion had in common with the revolt of the Low Countries against Spain that it was in the first instance a conservative revolution—a struggle for the preservation of liberties more than for the conquest of freedom. But its ideals, coming two centuries later, wore a wholly different look—the spirit of the Reformation had been replaced by that of the Enlightenment. We can best define the character of the American rebellion by comparing it with the French Revolution on the one hand and the controversy over the Dutch Patriots[10] on the other. It becomes at once apparent that the American Revolution was more conservative than either of these others. There was no towering political and social structure to be overthrown, as in France. The Americans had long enjoyed such modest self-government as the Dutch Patriots sought. At first their purpose was purely negative—to destroy the control of the mother country—and was only the simple consequence of old-fashioned burgher individualism. The tone, the pathos, and the details of the American Revolution resemble those of the Patriot controversy as much as of the French Revolution, but were much more vigorous and vehement than among the Dutch. The spirit that inspired the American revolt was England's own old feeling for freedom, that is, for guaranteed protection of financial and mercantile interests, as it blended with the radiance of the new feeling for Freedom as an idea. Small, modest causes for complaints gave rise to grand passions and great words. About 1763, Virginia became agitated over the question of clergymen's salaries, which were customarily paid

[10] A political movement in the United Provinces during the 1770s and 80s, supporting the ideas of the Enlightenment and directed against both the stadholder's party (the Orangists) and the traditional republican party (the States party).—H. H. R.

in the form of a fixed contribution of tobacco. The colonial assembly, seeing no necessity to let the preachers profit by price changes, decided that in the event of a poor tobacco harvest their salaries would be paid in money; the poor men of the cloth would suffer therefore when tobacco prices were low but not gain any advantage when they were high. When the crown reversed this unfair measure, the colony continued to act as if it were still in force. The preachers then brought suit against the government of the colony. It was during this suit that Patrick Henry cried, "A king, by disallowing acts of a salutary nature, from being the father of his people, degenerates into a tyrant and forfeits all right to his subjects' obedience." That was what usually happened in those days—the intoxicating call for freedom was sounded on the occasion of what was only a paltry affair. It would soon ring out as a clarion call: "O ye that love mankind; ye that dare oppose not only the tyranny but the tyrant, stand forth: every spot of the old world is overcome with oppression. Freedom hath been hunted round the globe. . . . England hath given her warning to depart. O receive the fugitive, and prepare, in time, an asylum for mankind."[11] But while in the mature little country of the Dutch, where everyone enjoyed more security than any other country gave and thus everyone was accustomed to peace and quiet, the Patriot affair ended in nothing but grand words, the American passions were transformed into fierce action, in which old-fashioned individualist license was displayed—riots, interference with legal proceedings, the tar-and-feathering of Loyalists.

When it became necessary to organize resistance in a political body, it was the old individualism, in the broader form of state particularism, which conquered. When the Articles of Confederation were drawn up in 1776, the example

[11] Thomas Paine, *Common Sense* (1776).

of Holland was clear before the delegates' eyes. The short-comings of the Union of Utrecht[12] were well known from the writings of Abbé Raynal and others;[13] it was used as a warning that the new union should not be made powerless by granting each state an equal vote. Nonetheless the old particularism won out. "The colonies should in fact be considered as individuals," said a delegate from New Jersey, one of the small states. "They are now collected as individuals making a bargain with each other, and of course had a right to vote as individuals."[14] It was just like the habitual hostility of the Hanseatic towns toward each other during the Middle Ages or the stubborn re-fusal of the provinces in the Dutch Republic to accept any limitation on their legal jurisdiction. The result was that the Confederation, the only bond among the states in their difficult struggle against England, remained an inadequate and almost powerless instrument, "a rope of sand."

Ten years later the Americans did the great deed which the Dutch Republic had not been able to do in time—the com-plete transformation of the basis of the Union, the strong com-bination of the country's forces, internally and externally, by the Constitution. Was the power that overcame deep-rooted individualism in the years 1787 to 1789 a high sense of com-munity, to which incorrigible individualists came when pain-ful experience taught them wisdom? Not at all, for there was no such talk. The driving force in the drafting and adoption of the Constitution was the interest of the groups needing

[12] The treaty of 1579 among the provinces, principally in the north-ern Low Countries, still in rebellion against the king of Spain. It became a kind of constitution for the republic of the United Provinces in which the sovereignty of the individual provinces was strongly confirmed, and no effective executive power was created.—H. H. R.

[13] *Journals of the Continental Congress 1776*, vol. VI, pp. 1081, 1103 seq.

[14] *Journals*, vol. IV, p. 1103.

central authority and a stronger system of government—the big merchants and shippers of New England and New York, the bondholders, the land speculators, in brief, big capital. Although the contemporaries did not use the word "capitalism," they saw this clearly as the meaning of the struggle over the Constitution and said so, and it is therefore somewhat surprising to see the storm of criticism stirred up by the studies of C. A. Beard, in which the whole affair was set forth in strict scholarship for the first time a few years ago.[15] For it was quite well known who had been the advocates and the adversaries of the Constitution in the years from 1787 to 1789 and afterward, even before this historian brought all the material together in a synthesis of superb clarity.

"The contest over the Constitution," says Beard, "was not primarily a war over abstract political ideals, such as states' rights and centralization, but over concrete economic issues, and the political division which accompanied it was substantially along the lines of the interests affected—the financiers, public creditors, traders, commercial men, manufacturers and allied groups, centering mainly in the larger seaboard towns, being chief among the advocates of the Constitution, and the farmers, particularly in the inland regions, and the debtors being chief among its opponents."[16]

The advocates of the Constitution, declared a writer in the *Boston Gazette* of November 26, 1787, consist chiefly of "the noble order of Cincinnatus (that is, the officers of the army of liberation), holders of public securities, bankers, and

[15] C. A. Beard, *An Economic Interpretation of the Constitution* (1914); *Economic Origins of Jeffersonian Democracy* (1915).
[16] Beard, *Economic Origins of Jeffersonian Democracy*, p. 3; cf. McLaughlin, *The Confederation and the Constitution* (*The American Nation: a History*, vol. X) p. 279; MacMaster, *History of the People of the U.S.*, vol. I, p. 399; Bryce, *The American Commonwealth* (ed. 1914), vol. II, p. 9.

lawyers. These with their train of dependents form the aristocratic combination."[17] —"It is a singular circumstance," General Knox, the founder of the Order of Cincinnatus just named, wrote with some naïveté, "that in Massachusetts the property, the ability and the virtue of the State are almost solely in favor of the Constitution."[18] John Adams had spoken in a careless moment of "the rich, the wellborn and the able" as those for whom the greatest share in the functions of state had been set aside,[19] and this remark was picked up by the opponents of the Constitution as a taunt. Even in the *Federalist*, the famous series of pamphlets in which Alexander Hamilton, Madison, and Jay recommended the adoption of the Constitution, we can observe how carefully the suspicion is countered that it would result in a class government by the moneyed class.[20] Yet Hamilton was, as no one doubts, as deliberate a plutocrat as ever existed: in his judgment, the country could only be governed by those who held the largest share in industrial and commercial business.[21]

The vigorous opposition that made the ratification of the Constitution uncertain for some time and continued after it came into force was fundamentally the resistance of the agricultural interests, including those of the large planters of the South, against the moneyed class. But the ideological terms in which the struggle was waged were those of Freedom against Aristocracy, and the passion that inspired it was that of unbroken individualism resisting the menacing pressure of government. If nonetheless the Constitution was adopted, it was with the silent reservation that amendments would at once be added to it in which the old ideals and the beloved liberties

[17] McLaughlin, *The Confederation and the Constitution*, p. 289.
[18] Ibid., p. 290.
[19] John Adams, *A Defence of the Constitution* . . . (1787), preface.
[20] *The Federalist*, nos. 35, 57, and especially no. 60.
[21] Beard, *Economic Origins of Jeffersonian Democracy*, p. 318.

would be rescued and safeguarded. The framers of the Constitution had not considered it necessary to preface it with a
declaration of principles affirming the fundamental rights of
citizens, a Bill of Rights such as Virginia had put at the beginning of its Constitution when it was established as a state in
1776. That was an example the French Constituent Assembly
would soon follow in the Declaration of the Rights of Man
and the Citizen; but in the American Constitution its place
was taken in a way by the first ten amendments of 1789. They
contain in brief the concepts of the principles of liberty, both
the old English kind and the new general human type, in which
individualism saw its own safeguards—freedom of religion, of
speech, person, assembly and petition, the right to bear arms,
protection against arbitrary quartering of troops and against
search and arrest, the right to trial by a jury, the security of
property, in a word, the ideals of political individualism.

That individualism became the shibboleth in the party
division which occurred after the Constitution came into force.
The funding of the national debt and the establishment of the
National Bank were among the first legislative acts of Congress.
Both came out of Hamilton's mind and both were in the obvious interest of the moneyed groups, which Hamilton, who
wanted to make the new government strong, wished to bind
to it by bestowed advantages. The heavily depreciated debts
of the Confederation, dating back to the long critical period of
the struggle for independence, were funded at their nomi-
nal value, while the Union also took over the war debts of the
individual states. These measures and the centralization of the
financial system in a National Bank seemed intolerable favoritism toward the owners of capital, and elevation of an aristocracy, really a plutocracy, into the leading force in the United
States. It was resisted by those who felt themselves to be the
representatives of true democracy; as the Federal Republicans

they formed the first opposition party, in opposition to the group of Hamilton, Jay and John Adams, who called themselves Federalists.[22]

It was Thomas Jefferson who breathed life into the party of Federal Republicans. What he fought in Hamilton and his adherents was the endeavor to create a powerful central government in the hands of the commercial and financial forces in the cities of New England, New York, and Pennsylvania. He opposed this development in the name of a total political and economic individualism. A more extreme individualist than Jefferson is scarcely conceivable. The doctrine Americans call "Jeffersonian democracy," as distinct from the phase of "Jacksonian democracy" which followed it, ultimately meant that the only purpose of government was to assure fair play for the individual. The state might place theoretical limits on the activity of citizens but it might not act as a power itself. "The rights of the whole can be no more than the sum of the rights of individuals."[23] Jefferson conceived the difference dividing him and his party from their opponents as a preference for the legislative instead of the executive principle. This was completely in the spirit of the general ideas of the Enlightenment, of which Jefferson was one of the purest exponents: Man is by nature inclined to the good and does not need much more from the state than pedagogical guidance by means of wise laws; the executive authority, on the other hand, essentially arises out of evil. Applied to the practice of political life, this meant thoroughgoing local autonomy. Bryce describes this point of view as follows: "Jefferson's importance lies in

[22] It should be remembered here that the Federal Republicans of 1791 were the precursors and in a certain sense the fathers of the later Democrats, while the present-day Republicans, as a party born in 1854, have continued the tradition of the old Federalists, if not directly, at least from some points of view.—J.H.

[23] Jefferson to Madison, September 6, 1789. *Writings,* ed. P. L. Ford, vol. VI, p. 116.

the fact that he became the representative not merely of democracy, but of local democracy, of the notion that government is hardly wanted at all, that the people are sure to go right if they are left alone, that he who resists authority is prima facie justified in doing so, because authority is prima facie tyrannical, that a country where each local body in its own local area looks after the objects of common concern, raising and administering any such funds as are needed, and is interfered with as little as possible by any external power, comes nearest to the ideal of a truly free people. . . ." "An insurrection every few years, he said, must be looked for, and even desired, to keep government in order."[24] This has something of the ring of Whitman's democratic individualism:

> To the States or any one of them, or any city of the
> States, *Resist much, obey little* . . .[25]

Jefferson's whole political theory was supported by the rational optimism of his time, an optimistic trust in the wisdom and goodness of men, which made him say: "It is error alone which needs the support of government; truth can stand by itself."

In order to win acceptance for such a doctrine, Jefferson needed only to appeal to the old instincts of freedom in his own house and his own circle. Political individualism had its basis in a primitive attitude of dislike for all authority which has had such broad opportunity to express itself in American society. Franklin recommended, as a weapon against the unbridled freedom of the press, with its small-town delight in defaming name and reputation, the reestablishment of "the liberty of the cudgel," that is, private enforcement of honor.[26] As if Americans had not always enjoyed this right and made

---

[24] Bryce, *The American Commonwealth*, vol. II, pp. 9, 18.
[25] *Leaves of Grass*, p. 10. (*The Complete Writings of Walt Whitman*, ed. Richard M. Bucke, et al. [New York, 1902], vol. I.)
[26] *Franklin's Works*, ed. Bigelow, vol. X, p. 139.

wide use of it! The enforcement of one's own rights and the fierce violence only too frequent in the episodes of American history, which so shocked European visitors like Dickens in 1842, is nothing but the other side of the admirable independence, the self-help, that conquered the American continent.

This winning of the West was the most productive field for an energetic and primitive individualism. The occupation and utilization of the land west of the original settlements on the Atlantic Ocean was the work of the pioneers alone. Region after region was added to the inhabited territory; the frontier moved from the coast to the Alleghenies, to the Mississippi, and steadily westward until the Pacific Ocean was reached. Each region in turn became for a time a frontier zone which often passed very quickly through every stage of development from the most primitive life of hunting and fishing to intensive capitalism, with wholly commercialized agriculture, mining, and industry. The fur-trapper, the cattle-rancher, and the pioneer farmer literally came one after the other. During the eighteenth century the cattle-drovers held their drives[27] to Charleston, Philadelphia, and New York while the trader had already long since crossed the Alleghenies. When the trappers were climbing the Rockies, the farmers had gotten no farther than the mouth of the Missouri.[28]

American civilization until the last quarter of the nineteenth century therefore always represented at a given time not just one but a whole series of stages of civilization in descending order from east to west. There was a repetition of the process of development as each western district was reached. As long as there was a continued movement westward,

[27] Huizinga, in a rare slip, calls these "droves."—H.H.R.
[28] See F. J. Turner, "The Significance of the Frontier in American History," *Annual Report of the American Historical Association* (1893), pp. 199–277.

there was always a frontier where the white man's civilization was just beginning to grow out of primitive conditions. "American social development has been continually beginning over again on the frontier."[29] But what is important is that in each of these stages, whether that of the hunters, or of the trappers and fishermen, the squatters who squandered the soil, the nomadic cowboys, small-scale agriculture and trade and capitalist big business, the type of civilization always remained individualistic. Even where a semicommunism prevailed, as among the squatters, or private property in land was absent, as in the initial period of cattle-herding, the purely individualist character was not lost. Often the men who won the new land were old pioneers who traveled on; there were some who moved four to six times, always westward. The pure type of the pioneer is the man who cannot stand any government authority and flees the limitations of civilization. Such were the men who led the first great expansion to the West, the occupation of Kentucky and Tennessee, in the last third of the eighteenth century—Daniel Boone, John Sevier, James Robertson. In 1769 Daniel Boone left his home and family in Pennsylvania in order to build a fort on the Kentucky River with five comrades; then he brought his wife and children. He lived in a constant fight with the Indians, was taken prisoner and adopted by the Great Blackfish, and regained his freedom. In 1791 Kentucky was accepted as a state and his ownership of his land was challenged. So he traveled on to the Missouri, where he settled until his ownership was declared invalid, after the land became part of the United States by the Louisiana Purchase of 1803.

The lingering effects of this pioneer individualism are felt everywhere in American history. They appear in the lack of respect for government which characterized the American, at

[29] Ibid., p. 200.

least until recently, and in what may be called his exaggerated localism. The notable laxness in government operations as compared to the driving energy with which personal interests are promoted is a direct result of this pioneer individualism. It penetrated into the central government with President Andrew Jackson in 1829, succeeding Jefferson's individualism, which was always more philosophical in character. Jackson was the most perfect type of pioneer democrat, with all the romanticism typical of this free style of life. He was born in a log cabin in the wilderness on the border between North and South Carolina. At the age of thirteen, he fought in the War of Independence, and at the age of fourteen was alone in the world. He became a saddlemaker, a school teacher (although he never learned to write correctly), and then a judge in newly occupied Tennessee. But it was war, first against the Indians and then against the English, whom he defeated in 1814 at New Orleans, which made him famous. The romantic story of his life fuses wild chivalry, unbridled frenzy, and stubborn partisanship and violence; and he carried all these qualities into the political arena, where he was sent by the admiring people. He was the creator of the spoils system, that is, the practice of dismissing government employees on a change in administration. His intentions were the best, "simply to turn the rascals out." He poured into his fight against the National Bank all the temperament and energy of a man who has made his own way in life.

The essence of the new democracy of the West in that period consisted in this struggle against the bank. There had already been in Jefferson's earlier democracy an attitude of hostility toward big capitalism, and Jackson's hostility was even stronger. In America opposition to capitalism was in the first place the individualism of the pioneers, the old spirit of self-help and personal initiative. From the beginning of the westward expansion there was a conflict of interests between the capitalist interests in the coast towns and the new inhabitants of the Mississippi region. Even before the War of Independence there existed the difference which always divided the West from the East down to the days of Bryan's silver policy—the capital-short frontier districts in their first beginnings had a need for a means of exchange that could be easily expanded, and they favored paper money, or later the silver standard. Whenever a special Western party arose, first in Jackson's time and then as the Greenbackers after the Civil War, it was driven by this desire for "soft money."

At the end of the eighteenth century the money powers of the East were intent upon exploiting the West financially and at the same time holding it down politically. Entry into the Mississippi region should not be made too easy and the land sold too cheaply lest the westward movement depopulate the coastal towns and make labor expensive. Migration to the West meant liberation from debts and economic pressure; if this were prevented, it was asserted in Congress shortly before 1800, then one class was declared to be required by law to continue to serve the other for whatever wages it was pleased to give.[30] From the start two principles confronted each other sharply in the process of settling the West—the money powers in the Eastern cities established companies to carry on settlement on a capitalist basis, such as the Ohio Company of 1786, while at the same time individual pioneers traveled into the wilderness on their own authority and at their own risk in order to win it by their labors. Already in the days of the Confederation (1776–1789), the pioneers of Kentucky harassed Congress with petition after petition against the "nabobs" who took for themselves the lands which they,

[30] F. J. Turner, "Social Forces in American History," *American Historical Review*, XVI (1910–1911), p. 221.

the pioneers, had defended against the Indians with their blood without having the time to obtain legal confirmation of their claims.

Linked to the history of the Ohio Company is that of the first great swindle of land speculators—the Scioto Land Company, which did its unholy work from 1788 to 1792. It is a curious tale worth telling at greater length than the scope of this essay allows. In it there appears a poet-emigrant agent and a preacher-philanthropist-discoverer, and with them one of the first money magnates, William Duer, an entrepreneur and the prototype of the modern industrial monarch.[31]

The great contrariety of economic interests was clearly apparent from the beginning. Both sides saw the danger. The land speculator Robert Morris, a Philadelphia banker, one of the first men of very great wealth and one of the most powerful collaborators in the drafting of the Constitution, declared haughtily in 1787: "The busy haunts of men, not the remote wilderness is the proper school of political talents," and then added these frank words: "If the Western people get the power into their hands, they will ruin the Atlantic interests."[32]

In 1811 Henry Clay, "Harry of the West," had pointed to the National Bank as the great obstacle to the development of the West because it gave privilege to a few. Hatred for the National Bank became such a dominant motif in the political attitude of the West that Andrew Jackson devoted his presidency to the task of destroying it. An acute economic instinct lay at the bottom of this purpose, however crudely it was expressed and carried out. Although he may have been a backwoodsman who grew up in the wilderness, Jackson was the

---

[31] Cf. P. J. van Winter, *Het Aandeel van den Amsterdamschen Handel aan den Opbouw van het Amerikaansche Gemeenebest*, (1927), pp. 156 ff.

[32] McLaughlin, *The Confederation and the Constitution*, p. 256.

first to see clearly the threatening evil of the future—the concentration of capital.

There is some reason, therefore, to consider individualism as the very contrary of capitalism in their role as factors in American history, even if we are in the habit of considering socialism to be opposite of capitalism. Yet even this contrast is not absolute, for no one will deny that powerful individualist characteristics have always been typical of American capitalism. But if we attempt to formulate the fundamental conflict as one between individualism and organization, other difficulties arise. The principle of collective organization most certainly permeated the development of American capitalism, but it manifested itself just as strongly among the agrarian groups who opened up the land, and who were at the same time the most passionate individualists as well. These are all reasons to make apparent to us the inadequacy of such conceptual distinctions and to spur us to observe without prejudice the operation of these principles *in* history, with its variegated interweaving of forces, sometimes in apparent contradiction—and not to take this activity *out* of history.

Yet this much is certain, that in American history we are confronted by individualism as the preponderant, primary, and actively shaping force in society. The individualism of the American colonist, rebel, and pioneer has little in common with the state of mind to which we are in the habit of giving the same name in our idea of the Renaissance. American individualism displays itself on the one hand as the puritan sense of independence that created the communities of New England, and on the other hand as the primitive spirit of the worker in the wilderness that continues to be nourished as long as there is some part of nature still unconquered. These two forces produced the highly developed modern American individual-

ism, the spirit of the modern businessman who prides himself
that the old pioneer attitudes are still active in him. It is also
the individualism of America's greatest minds—Emerson and
Whitman, in whom extreme individualism passed over into its
opposite and took in the whole world.

What place remains then in American history for the impulse of civilized man which we are accustomed to considering as the opposite of individualism—the impulse of association,
social organization, or even sense of community? No one who
knows even the least bit about American history or American
life will doubt for a moment that this function of civilized
life also exercises an enormous effect in America. From the
beginning a strong sense of organization has been active in the
history of the various kinds of political and cultural life in
America. The distinctive thing is that this sense of community
has not abolished individualism but rather remains subordinated to it.

Just as with individualism, the social impulse displays itself
in America principally in a primitive form, that is, as a spontaneous and strongly emotional combination of forces for a
concrete goal, with a pronounced need for secret forms and
a far-reaching readiness to place personal energies without reservation at the service of the goal of the association, in brief,
in the formation of a club or the foundation of a fraternal
order.[33] We have an involuntary tendency to assume that the
sense of social organization is directly governed by objective
interests. But it is a question whether the history of civilization
does not have to take another primary factor into account at
least as much—the concentration of common activity for the

---

[33] Huizinga uses the unadorned term *ordestichting*, literally "foundation of an order," which would be used ordinarily for the creation of a
religious order, as the Jesuits by Ignatius Loyola.—H.H.R.

sake of the effect of fellowship, or to express it less barbarously, the enthusiasm and the energy which arise from the powerful feeling of striving together for any goal whatever. It is an irony of the history of civilization that it was precisely the country which did not tolerate any order of chivalry and forbade all noble ranks that has been and still is pervaded with the spirit of those who found orders and accept their discipline. In the America of the 1830s, Tocqueville was already impressed by the enormous number and vital importance of associations, and he devoted several chapters to this phenomenon.[34] "Americans of all ages, all conditions, and all dispositions constantly form associations. They have not only commercial and manufacturing companies, in which all take part, but associations of a thousand other kinds, religious, moral, serious, futile, general or restricted, enormous or diminutive. The Americans make associations to give entertainments, to found seminaries, to build inns, to construct churches, to diffuse books. . . . If it is proposed to inculcate some truth or to foster some feeling by the encouragement of a great example, they form a society."[35] Such was the America of 1830. If we are inclined, perhaps, to consider that this picture also fits somewhat our own European society today, we must not lose from sight that our customs, especially in the last twenty years, have been much more strongly Americanized than we ordinarily realize.

I have described both the organizational sense of the Americans and their individualism as of primitive character in the main. In this respect too, the forefathers brought important elements of civilization from the motherland with them. In any case, this connection of primitive individualism and the sense

[34] *De la démocratie en Amérique,* vol. III, chaps. 5–7, pp. 175–198. [*Democracy in America,* trans. Henry Reeve and Francis Bowen, rev. and ed. Philipps Bradley (Vintage Books: New York), vol. II, pp. 114–128.]

[35] Tocqueville, *Democracy in America,* vol. II, p. 114.

of organization belong to Calvinism itself. While still aboard the *Mayflower*[36] the Pilgrim Fathers signed their brief and sober agreement, in which they "solemnly and mutualy in the presence of God and one of another, covenant and combine ourselves togeather into a civill body politick, for our better ordering and preservation, and furtherance of the ends aforesaid (namely, the glory of God, the advancement of the Christian faith, and the honor of king and country); and by vertue hearof to enacte, constitute and frame such just and equall lawes, ordinances, acts, constitutions and offices, from time to time, as shall be thought most meete and convenient for the generall good of the colonie; unto which we promise all due submission and obedience."[37]

"Here the idea of the state is present in its entirety," says Émile Boutmy.[38] I would be more specific: that means the idea of the state as the core of politics, the notion of the state in its narrowest form, still conceived in a medieval, corporative way. For when we take American social organizations into consideration as one whole, it is clear that what is weak in it is just the real idea of the state, and what is strong, on the contrary, is the feeling of forming a social and moral unity.

The actions of the Pilgrim Fathers that gave rise to the Plymouth colony were not unique. Similar "compacts of government" and "plantation covenants," which used church organization as their model, were signed by the Puritans of Rhode Island, Connecticut, New Haven, and New Hampshire.[39]

Like Calvinism, the Enlightenment also introduced a strong

---

[36] Which Huizinga calls the *May Flower*, an indication of the newness of his familiarity with American history.—H.H.R.

[37] W. Macdonald, *Documentary Source Book of American History 1606–1913*, (1917), no. 4, p. 19.

[38] Boutmy, *Eléments d'une psychologie politique du peuple américain*, (Paris, 1902), p. 117.

[39] Macdonald, *Documentary Source Book*, nos. 9–11, pp. 36–45.

basis of association. The idea of a common humanity brought about a sense of brotherhood, expressed in the form of associations. The eighteenth century in Europe also experienced a rage for more or less secret societies with the noble aims of freedom and humanity. When, on the eve of the American Revolution, we find the work of resistance prepared by the Sons of Liberty and similar societies, we do not need to consider them as specific expressions of an American spirit; we can also see them as a general product of the Enlightenment. Or was Americanism already at work in the European freedom societies, which are for the most part of a later date?[40]

In any case, the function of these spontaneous nuclei of organization was then and remained more important in America than in Europe. There is an essential relationship between the eighteenth-century clubs and the immensely extensive and technically perfect organizations of the Republicans and the Democrats. Political life to this day retains many of the aspects of the primitive emotional character of spontaneous group formation. The major political parties still retain something of the character of fraternal orders, of (*sit venia verbo*[41]) friendly meetings on a vast scale. The various forms of American political association can be arranged to display a gradual transition from the secret club to the political party.

The caucus, the archetype of the private political meeting, of political organization in a club spirit, dates back with all its special characteristics to the period before the rebellion. See how John Adams in 1763 described the working of this institution in Boston:

> This day learned that the Caucus Club meets, at certain times, in the garret of Tom Dawes, the Adjutant of the

[40] On the mutual influence of European and American ideas in the eighteenth century, read the excellent work of B. Faÿ, *L'Esprit révolutionnaire en France et aux Etats-Unis à la fin du XVIIIe siècle* (Paris, 1925).–J.H.

[41] "If we may be pardoned the expression."–H.H.R.

Boston Regiment. He has a large house, and he has a movable partition in his garret which he takes down, and the whole club meets in one room. There they smoke tobacco till you cannot see from one end of the garret to the other. There they drink flip, I suppose, and there they choose a moderator, who puts questions to the vote regularly; and selectmen, assessors, collectors, wardens, firewards, and representatives are regularly chosen before they are chosen in the town. Uncle Fairfield, Story, Ruddock, Adams, Cooper and a *rudis indigestaque moles* of others are members. They send committees to wait on the merchants' club, and to propose and join in the choice of men and measures. Captain Cunningham says, they have often solicited him to go to these caucuses; they have assured him benefit in his business, &c.[42]

That was American party life in embryo. The Adams referred to is probably Samuel Adams, a distant cousin of John, who himself was later an envoy to the Dutch Republic and then president of the United States; A. B. Hart calls Samuel Adams the prototype of the political boss.[43]

The "organized disorder" the revolution began with in 1775 was the work of such caucuses. "The political world of Hamilton's time," says MacMaster, "was ruled chiefly by caucuses. It was through the agency of caucuses that the revolution was begun, that the first Congress was assembled, that independence was declared, that the Confederation was formed, that the war was carried on, that the way was made ready for the framing of the Constitution."[44]

We speak of a caucus when a part of a political group meets on its own authority and takes over the group's leader-

[42] John Adams, *Works*, ed. C. F. Adams (1850), vol. II, p. 144, in A. B. Hart, *American History Told by Contemporaries*, vol. II, p. 220.

[43] Hart, *National Ideals Historically Traced* (1907) (*The American Nation: A History*) vol. 26, p. 159.

[44] J. B. MacMàster, *History of the People of the United States*, vol. I, p. 528.

ship. But if this joint activity becomes official because some members of a political body or party are assigned to this task or are accepted in it, then we have a committee. The committee principle, which also played a very great role in the European revolutions and had extraordinary importance in the development of American history, can be called an American invention with good reason. In the years preceding the revolution, local centers of resistance arose everywhere, at first in response to special needs and with narrowly defined goals. As soon as these committees entered into relationship with each other, they became committees of correspondence. One of the proposals for a confederation of the colonies discussed in 1754 (that of Preacher Peters) rested upon the principle of such correspondence.[45] This form of correspondence was already in use in American church administration, business, secret societies, and in the colonial representative assemblies.[46]

It was Samuel Adams, the "party manager" of Boston, who forged the instrument of revolution from this principle. In 1772 he organized the Committee of Correspondence in Boston. Its purpose was "to state the rights of the colonists, and of this province in particular, as men and Christians, and as subjects." It arranged meetings, conferred with committees in neighboring towns, prepared political questions for the press, distributed newspapers and pamphlets, schemed, roused public feeling . . . and began to assume the powers of a legislative and executive council. By January 1773 Governor Hutchinson reported that there were such committees at work in eighty or more communities in Massachusetts. The heart of a revolutionary confederation had been created.

[45] These plans of 1754 are to be found in *American History Leaflets*, ed. A. B. Hart and E. Channing, no. 14 (Plans of Union 1696–1780).

[46] E. D. Collins, "Committees of correspondence of the American revolution," *Annual Report of the American Historical Association* (1901), vol. I, p. 243.

In Virginia it was the House of Burgesses itself which instituted a committee of correspondence in March 1773; this was therefore the link between the spontaneous committees and the official delegation of legislative functions to a committee. In North Carolina the committees chose seven of their members to act as a "committee of secrecy, intelligence and observation." "Committees of safety" were known in America long before the French Revolution incorporated them into its machinery of government.

The Continental Congress, the central organ of the Confederation of the states during the war for freedom, arose directly out of the committees of correspondence. And the numerous committees of the Senate and the House of Representatives, which now prepare legislative activity in all fields, are indebted for their great importance in American political life to the fact that the principle of entrusting special business to special committees was already rooted in colonial customs by the time of the revolution.

The committee of correspondence is merely the normalized form of spontaneous organization, which continued to exist alongside it in every kind of form, varying according to the scene where it functioned, the goal that it took, and the circle from which it arose.

In the New West of 1770, that is, in the settled territories of Kentucky and Tennessee, the act of the Pilgrim Fathers in creating a state was repeated. James Robertson, discontented with the government of North Carolina, which was in the hands of the merchants in the ports and served their interests, traveled west with his neighbors and settled on the Watauga in Tennessee. They lived there wholly on their own. The old Presbyterian leaven continued to work among them, and they entered into a "compact," an agreement by which their community was governed. When North Carolina incorporated the young settlement in 1776, Robertson traveled further west and established more new compacts. When the Eastern states endeavored to bring the new communities in the West under their authority, it was the preachers who kept alive among the pioneers the desire for independence and organization through "compacts."[47]

Whenever new settlements arose on the western frontier of the Union, this principle of independent political formation continued to be followed. It was present in the years from 1840 to 1850 in the "land clubs" or "claim associations" among the colonists in Iowa; their traces can also be found in Wisconsin and Illinois. The process was repeated a decade later in Colorado, where the "miners' laws" display very notable and highly varied types of political formation of this kind.[48]

The beginning of a similar development can be observed as well in the "rush" to Oklahoma in 1899, when 50,000 settlers who had camped on the border to wait for the day it was to be opened, flooded into the territory during the first day.

As an example, let us consider the land clubs in Iowa in somewhat more detail. National laws forbade settlement in newly opened territories until the Indian property claims, which were transferred to the national government by treaty, had expired and the territory had been surveyed by national authority. Nonetheless squatters streamed into the territory before the date of termination had been reached; ten thousand squatters, who had no status in law but only that of hard, honorable labor, had already settled in Iowa when the survey began several years after the purchase. Almost every group of

[47] F. J. Turner, "Western State Making in the Revolutionary Era," *American Historical Review*, vol. I (1895–1896), p. 87.

[48] B. F. Shambaugh, "Frontier Land Clubs or Claim Associations," *Annual Report of the American Historical Association* (1900), vol. I, p. 67; T. M. Marshall, "The Miners' Laws of Colorado," *American Historical Review*, XXV (1920), p. 426.

these settlers had its own "land club" or "claim association" to protect these self-acquired rights against each other and against the government, and to keep out the land speculators. They were full-scale political organizations, with a president, judges, and executive officers, with regular and special meetings, with self-decreed laws and a constitution in rather bad spelling. Anyone who did not obey the laws and decisions of the club lost his membership. "For the faithful observance and maintenance of all the foregoing laws we mutually pledge our honours, and subscribe our names here unto"—with these words, less pious than those of the Covenant of the Pilgrim Fathers, but in the same vein, the compact of Johnson County closes. A peculiarity worth mentioning is the clause in one of the miners' laws in Colorado that lawyers who settle in the district shall be whipped and driven out.

By their nature such organizations were capable of development. In 1861 the Union district in Colorado was in the midst of transformation from direct democracy to a representative system, when the federal authority cut off the further growth of the miners' laws by granting Colorado a territorial organization. If there had been no national government, then the seeds of political organization in Colorado would have developed along the same lines as the communities in New England two centuries before.

It was not only the old puritan spirit which created this form of political organization. The aforementioned Robertson and many of his comrades came from the hinterlands of the Carolinas, where the backwoodsmen were in the habit of adopting written agreements for the purpose of "regulating" horse thieves by summary measures, in the absence of regular courts, and at the same time of resisting the colonial officials in the collection of taxes which the backwoodsmen considered unlawful or excessive. There can be no doubt that these associations of Regulators were Robertson's immediate model when he founded his primitive political system in the wilderness.

In it we make the acquaintance of a form of organization which has held exceptional importance in American history. I call it the organization of the *Fehmgericht* type.[49] It is, in fact, a form which cannot be divided from the caucus and the committee of correspondence but is simply the wild offshoot of the same tree. The transition was constituted by the secret political societies, such as the Sons of Liberty.

In the more orderly and civilized East, the secret societies appear strongly permeated by the political romanticism of the eighteenth century. The first in the series were the Sons of Liberty in New York, the systematic organization of the artisans and the farmers called into existence by the aristocratic Whigs in their resistance to the Stamp Act of 1765. They escaped the leadership of the fathers at once; they established a committee of vigilance and a committee of correspondence, threatened with mob law anyone who used paper with a seal, considered a nocturnal attack on the fort on Guy Fawkes' Day, and by means of their committee of vigilance conducted a veritable inquisition into business transactions and private expenditures, income, and opinions. They called the tavern where they met "Hampden Hall," as if they emphasize their high political aims, while their kinship with the *Fehmgericht* type is obvious.

A sharp contrast to the Sons of Liberty is the society established by General Henry Knox at the end of the War of Independence in 1783 in order to hold together by a solid and solemn bond of friendship the officers who had served

---

[49] Irregular courts of medieval Germany, often sitting secretly and meting out judgments and punishments, including the capital penalty.— H.H.R.

in the war and their French allies. They took the name of "Cincinnatus," to tell of the old Roman civic virtue which they displayed on their return to civil life. But their civil feeling had an aristocratic hue. The Cincinnati were a social order in the full sense of the word. They would transmit the badges they chose for themselves, a blue ribbon with an eagle that the artist managed to make look a little comical, by heritage to their descendents. At the same time they formed a political society. They would regularly consider in secret the welfare of the nation; in fact, during the first twenty years of their existence, they conducted a far-reaching political activity in the spirit of the plutocratic Federalists, forming as it were a secret nucleus within the larger party. The Cincinnati were under strong suspicion from the beginning and were denounced and mocked as aristocrats, even by such leaders of the Federalists as Franklin, the two Adamses, and John Jay. Their hereditary badges and other imitations of chivalry, their masquerade ceremony in the inauguration of members, too greatly offended the new sense of equality. But much more important, however, was the suspicion of their secret political action: "lowering over our Constitution eternally," Jefferson described them indignantly, "meeting together in all parts of the Union, periodically, with closed doors, accumulating a capital in their separate treasure, corresponding secretly and regularly."[50] In the year of the foundation of the Cincinnati, the half-pay pensions which were supposed to be paid to the officers and soldiers of the Revolution for the rest of their lives were converted into a single, one-time payment of five years' full pay; it was a measure which was condemned by the people as a

[50] Jefferson to Madison, December 28, 1794, *Writings*, ed. P. L. Ford, vol. VI, p. 516; cf. Jefferson's *Anas, Memoirs, etc.* (ed. 1829), vol. IV, p. 454.

deliberate creation of a moneyed aristocracy.[51] The fact was that it enabled the officers to take a part in the land speculation which began several years later. This explains why officers from the army of the Revolution were among the foremost founders of the Ohio Company, and there is a remarkable bit of economic history in the fact that General St. Clair, one of the leading shareholders, renamed a city on the Ohio Cincinnati in 1790, after his beloved order. At the same time it is clear why the Cincinnati were named among the most zealous supporters of the Constitution and the strongest supporters of the Federalist administration.

At the same time there rose up against the Cincinnati another quasi-political society which is better known today in its present form (the Cincinnati also are still in existence). By 1772 there existed in Philadelphia a society called the Sons of Tammany, after a more or less legendary chieftain of the Delaware Indian tribe in the days of William Penn. It was a society whose purposes were amusement and charity and which took pleasure in a quasi-Indian ritual of wigwams, peace pipes, tribes, and sachems. Out of this Philadelphia society came the Improved Order of Red Men, a secret charitable fraternity which now extends over the whole country and numbered 450,000 members in 1927.[52] The president bears the fancy title of Great Incohonee. Meanwhile Tammany brotherhoods were formed in other cities. A man named Mooney founded a Society of Saint Tammany in New York in 1786, which was also called the Columbian Order; in form it was related to the society in Philadelphia but in reality it was a continuation of the

---

[51] MacMaster, *History of the People of the United States*, vol. I, p. 177.

[52] *Handbook of American Indians*, ed. F. W. Hodge, vol. II, pp. 364, 683.

former Sons of Liberty. Its aims, in addition to charity, were the maintenance of independence, the freedom of the people, and the federal union of the country against the suspected monarchist designs of Hamilton and his friends. A poet of the society sang these verses to its eponym in 1794:

> Immortal Tamany, of Indian Race,
> Great in the field, foremost in the chace!
> . . . To public views he added private ends,
> And lov'd his country most, and next his friends.[53]

But there is a question whether or not from the beginning friends did not in fact come before country. The notorious organization of Tammany Hall grew up around this society as its core, and it claims to be the official representative of the Democratic party in New York City. Its notorious corruption under Boss Tweed, Boss Kelley, and Boss Croker drew the amazed attention of the world.

Tammany provides the most striking example of the "fraternal order" character of American party organization and the very early roots of this system, but there are other examples. The transition from the secret society to the political party is also illustrated by the Know Nothings in the middle of the nineteenth century. An American nationalism with an anti-Catholic coloration and opposed to the increase of immigration, especially of the Irish, was first embodied in secret societies—the Order of United Americans, the Order of the Star Spangled Banner, the Sons of America. All at once they developed into a political party with a secret society active at its core. The party was given the name of Know Nothings because of the secrecy in which the members cloaked the purpose of the organization. The Know Nothings were respon-

---

[53] Hart, *American History Told by Contemporaries,* vol. III, p. 295.

sible for riots against Catholics and for weakening the Whig party; with their slogan "Americans must rule America," they increased so rapidly within a few years that they had seven states, including New York and Massachusetts, in their hands by 1855. But their success suddenly collapsed during the presidential election of 1856 and they vanished as rapidly as they had arisen.

Later organizations remained below the level of a political party without differing in character, origin, or aim from the Cincinnati, Tammany, or the Know Nothings. A large number represent what we can call the Freemasonry type—the society whose activity is restricted to fraternal gatherings and mutual assistance. Since these pages first saw light, *Babbitt* has shown us the "Elks" in flower, with their 900,000 members; they are only one among many. A very special and novel form of this kind of association has even found its way from America to Europe—the Rotary clubs. The future will show whether this form of the old principle will have great importance in the creation of social harmony.

As soon as a specific policy or social aspiration of passionate character led to spontaneous and special organizations, the term *Fehmgericht* type applies with its full force. They arose under the spur of the most varied grievances. There is no reason for surprise that a question so strongly affecting the emotions as slavery, which was fought over with such bloody violence even before the outbreak of the Civil War, called organizations of this kind into existence. Levi Coffin, a Quaker from Cincinnati, was the head of the great secret organization called the Underground Railroad, which rescued escaped slaves from the Fugitive Slave Law. The seeds of the organization can be found as early as 1786, but its greatest activity comes after 1840. An extensive net of smugglers' roads along which the Negroes were brought to safety covered a largc part of the Union.[54] Mrs. Beecher Stowe borrowed the material for her novel from her active service in this organization and her association with its members.

The violent character of such a secret league against slavery appears even more clearly in the League of Gileadites for the rescue of fugitive Negroes, which was established by John Brown, the bloody fighter and martyr for Abolition. "Stand by one another and by your friends while a drop of blood remains; and be hanged if you must, but tell no tales out of school," ran their rule.

Nor did the advocates of slavery fail to have their own organizations of the same kind. They were called Vigilance Committees, Committees of Correspondence, Self-Defensive Associations, and so on. In the state of Indiana, where a considerable part of the population unwillingly suffered the policies of the Northerners, an extensive secret organization arose during the Civil War which adorned itself with the old name of "Sons of Liberty" or else "Knights of the Golden Circle." Their methods were violent: resistance to military draft, rebellion, an attack on the life of the governor. But their words were those of the old freedom-loving democracy, colored by the fanatical passion which was in the habit of painting a victory of the North as a danger for life and property and the honor of their wives and daughters. "This organization is bound to oppose all usurpations of power . . . Lincoln's government is a usurpation . . . , I will not agree to remain passive under usurped authority affecting my rights and liberties."[55]

After the war, the old habits of violence and seeking jus-

[54] See W. H. Siebert, "The Underground Railroad etc.," *Annual Report of the American Historical Association*, 1895, p. 395; id., "Light on the Underground Railroad," *American Historical Review*, I (1895–1896), p. 455.

[55] J. A. Woodburn, "Party Politics in Indiana during the Civil War," *Annual Report of the American Historical Association* (1902), vol. I, p. 250.

tice on one's own had more reasons for existence than ever in the devastated and exhausted South. A party government of the worst sort attempted to introduce the system of the conqueror from the North into the Southern states. Carpetbag politicians ruled their governments. The resistance of the Southerners who had been deprived of their rights and their property was embodied in secret organizations with fanciful names, The Knights of the White Camellia, The Pale Faces, the Constitutional Union Guards, the White Brotherhood, and the best known of all, the Ku Klux Klan.

What is noteworthy about the Ku Klux Klan is that it was founded in May 1866 by a group of youths in a Tennessee village only for amusement and kept the character of a joke for two years before it became a powerful and dangerous political instrument. Its members rode by moonlight in long costumes, with white masks and high round cardboard hats, with the horses' hooves in wraps; they caused mortal terror among the Negroes, and now and then kidnaped a white politician or schoolteacher. Meanwhile the organization spread from district to district and then from state to state, and at the same time took on a serious political character. Its slogan became protection of the people of the South against injustice and defense of the Constitution of the Union; its name became The Invisible Empire of the South and its work was often murder and violence, until gradually the government got the better of it after 1870.[56] The remarkable reincarnation of the Ku Klux Klan in the last ten years proves how powerfully the force of suggestion of such an example continues to work upon the American mind.

At the same time it was not at all necessary for the estab-

[56] Woodrow Wilson, *History of the American People,* vol. V, p. 59 ff. The name "Ku Klux Klan" according to some is a corruption of "Kyklos" [the Greek word for ring or circle], and according to others is an onomatopoeic phrase with the meaning of the Dutch children's phrase "Pief paf poef" ["bang bang," that is, the sound of a gun.]—J.H. [H.H.R.]

lishment of these organizations that the question involved be of such emotional character as slavery. Or would it be better to say that all political questions in the United States take on that same intensely perturbed character? In 1786 in Charleston, South Carolina, the advocates of paper money formed an organization which they called the Hint Club, which met regularly and designated a secret committee. The purpose of the club was to give secret "hints" to the advocates of hard money. If these did not help, then the club set a night-time rendezvous, which was indicated by lighting three signal rockets, and then it went as a body to the home of the enemy, "to hurl down," as they said, "public vengeance on the destroyers of the commonwealth."[57] We see something of importance in this case, the fact that the club considered itself to be a servant of the public interest and a purely political organization.

This character as a would-be political party is not absent even in the remarkable organization which forms the link between the societies of the *Fehmgericht* type and the modern labor unions—the Molly Maguires in the anthracite mines of Pennsylvania from 1854 to 1877.[58] Insofar as the Molly Maguires numbered only Irish Catholics among their members, it may be considered that they were not specifically American. The Irish, already accustomed to secret organizations and resistance to the government, had a full opportunity to develop these tendencies in American society, where similar customs prevailed. The Molly Maguires worked against the hated mine bosses by means of a well-organized system of warnings followed by murders; they were also able to raise themselves to the level of a political force, controlling the local govern-

[57] MacMaster, *History of the People of the United States*, vol. I, p. 287.

[58] J. F. Rhodes, "The Molly Maguires in the Anthracite Region of Pennsylvania," *American Historical Review*, XV (1909), p. 547.

ment, with a strength which others had to take into account. The eventual downfall of the society was the work of a spy for Allan Pinkerton's Detective Agency.

Already in their earliest forms American labor organizations betray a clear relationship with the *Fehmgericht* type. The Knights of Labor demonstrated this not only in their romantic name, but also in their highly secretive character and the religious fanaticism and prophetic expectancy with which they advocated the eight-hour day. Their part in the bloody strikes of the period 1870–1885 and their final collapse into the corrupt favoritism of their leaders puts them on the same level as so many other American societies in which secrecy, violence, and corruption went together. For its part the national government naturally saw the rising labor movement in the light of secret organizations, with which the people were familiar. The name "Labor conspiracy," which for a long time every movement for higher wages ran the risk of receiving, indicates this attitude perfectly.

How much secret societies were conceived as an element in the political life of America can be seen from the fact that a few states adopted specific clauses against them in their constitutions. Considered as a general phenomenon, what we have reported can probably be summarized as follows. In American history an important function belongs to the politically persuaded forces which organize themselves spontaneously, are usually directed more toward resistance and violence than to constructive ideas, and in which concern for the public interest is largely overshadowed by private interests. Every group interest that can be presented as a political principle possesses an immediate means of achieving its aims in the people's readiness for spontaneous organization, as well as in the great freedom of action which the government leaves to citizens. This strong sense of organization provides a rich source of social energy and drive but it is often also a direct cause of extensive corruption. A strong individualism continues to be characteristic of these forms of organization, even though the individual unreservedly puts himself at the service of the declared purpose; we might call it individualistic organization, or even better organized individualism.

It was none other than the great individualist Thomas Jefferson who put his compatriots' sense of organization at the service of national politics.[59] His opponents, the Federalists, were a powerful group with the prestige of wealth, political experience, and patrician status. They considered themselves the founders of the country's freedom, the creators and defenders of the state; they had their symbol in George Washington and their strength in Alexander Hamilton. How, then, are we to explain that a party of such strength had to give up the government in 1801, after only twelve years of rule, making way for opponents, the Federal Republicans, who seemed to be the weaker side in every respect? It is true that the [Federal] Republicans counted founders of freedom in their ranks, in the persons of Jefferson and Madison, but it is very probable that they would not have succeeded so quickly against the Federalists if Jefferson had not grasped the secret of strong political organization. In 1794 Democratic societies were founded in a number of cities; they were quasi-Jacobin in character and directed against the administration, which was accused of aristocratic tendencies. Jefferson saw that these societies could be the nucleus of a widespread political organization, and he was able to forge them into a large, superbly organized political party, under highly concealed leadership. The [Federal] Republicans were therefore ahead of the Federalists in organi-

[59] Literally "grand policy," *groote politiek* (equivalent to the German *grosse Politik*).–H.H.R.

zation, and their victory of 1800 endured. The Federalists might amuse themselves making fun of "self-created societies," which began their work after dinner, bolted doors, and voted in secrecy. They announced their contempt for the system of party conventions which their opponents developed, but they imitated it, although secretly and when it was too late.[60] Their party was marked for death; it wore out, slowly but completely, disappearing with the generation which had supported it. A period of weak party antagonism followed; "the era of good feelings," as the Americans call it, lasted until about 1824. Not until much later did the old economic conflicts again create a strong partisan division between the Democrats and the Republicans; the former were in many respects the direct descendants of Jefferson's [Federal] Republicans, but the latter were not the continuation of Hamilton's Federalists, although they had traits in common with them.

We will discuss in a later essay how the enormous and complicated organization of these two big parties developed and then degenerated. What we are concerned with for the time being is the fact that American party life has always preserved, despite its enormous size, the traits and moods of the spontaneous and emotional organizations from which it originated. There has been a constant tendency in America for direct political activity to take on at once the form of new, often very localized, parties, usually strongly moralistic and enthusiastic, and sometimes of very short duration. But even the two big parties continue to possess certain primitive traits.

Strict party discipline and unrestricted party loyalty, if they did not have their roots in the sense of fraternal "order" which already permeated the Sons of Liberty and Cincinnati,

---

[60] S. E. Morison, "The First National Nominating Convention 1808," *American Historical Review*, XVII (1912), p. 744.

would be difficult to reconcile with the individualist character of the American people. During the very period from 1865 to 1880 when the organization of both parties was brought to its highest perfection, so that their complicated machinery penetrated every fiber of civic life, the real political conflict which separated them was growing steadily less. There was no longer, if there had ever been, one great Republican system of principles opposed to a single Democratic set. There still remained some honored slogans, some variations in general attitude, for instance whether or not the government should intervene in various matters, but the organization down to its smallest parts was firmly bound to special interests, and the interests overlapped. The result was that the political organization preserved its own internal reasons for existence; it had become *sui generis*, a power too big and too beloved to be removed from society and from men's feelings. It was no longer political principles which held the members together but tradition and loyalty of a quasi-religious character. "The truth," says an American historian, "is that the political party is to many of its participants an order, existing for its own pomp and grandeur, and having in their minds no direct connection with public service."[61] Naturally this was even truer for specific organizations such as Tammany. The attitude of the "better sort" of supporters of Tammany is described by an American in this way.

> He considers that Tammany is, on the whole, a good body, that it gives New York a good government, that it stands for what is manly and patriotic. It troubles him somewhat that a few of the leaders are said to be acquiring ill-gotten gains; and if the scandal increases he will overthrow those leaders and appoint others in their stead. Meanwhile Tammany is his party, his church, his club,

[61] A. B. Hart, *National Ideals*, p. 178.

his totem. To be loyal to something is almost a necessity
of all incorrupt natures.[62]

This is the attitude which was given terse expression in the
remark of the Republican boss of the period 1860–1870, Thaddeus Stevens, when he was told that the candidate for a certain
office was a "damned rascal": "All I want to know is, whether
he is *our* damned rascal."

It is not only the old sense of "order" which testifies to
the continuing relationship of the American political parties
with the primitive forms of association. We should view in the
same light what may be called the sporting attitude in American party life, which is revealed especially during presidential
elections. Boutmy has expressed this strikingly: "American
democracy arose out of a society of adventurers and businessmen, that is, of speculators and gamblers, and a temperament
corresponding to this origin has been displayed in political
life. It is permeated by and receives its coloration and physiog-
nomy from its character as a hard-fought, large-scale, noisy,
crude and optimistic sport, without animosity or rancor, of
very low social standing and very good humor."[63] In truth,
politics in the United States has often had to fulfill the addi-
tional function of popular entertainment because of the
scarcity of other available forms of amusement. The element
of play, which is expressed in the most important aspects of
civilization among advanced as well as primitive peoples, is
strongly developed in the United States. This is evidenced by
the large part played by doggerel, slogans, effigy-burning and
so on ever since the days of the Revolution, as well as by the
mass meetings and parades with the display of flags, cockades,
and symbols, which have become a necessary part of presi-

[62] H. C. Merwin, *Atlantic Monthly,* 1894, cited by Bryce, *The
American Commonwealth,* vol. II, p. 402.
[63] Boutmy, *Eléments,* p. 143.

dential election campaigns since 1840. That was a year of particularly sharp struggle. The Whigs (as the Democrats' opponents had been called since Jackson's harsh administration) ran the popular old general Harrison, a famous Indian fighter and a victim of Jackson's vengeance, against the incumbent[64] Democrat, Martin Van Buren. Harrison was a strong candidate and the circumstances were favorable: the previous years had aroused much resentment. But the Whigs did not have a true program, a platform. Then a Democratic newspaper gave them something better—a symbol. Harrison, it railed, was such a poor man that he would be more at home in a log cabin than in the White House. At once the log cabin became the Whig party symbol. A log cabin was built on a field in every city and village in the North and was greeted with as much enthusiasm as even the Liberty Trees had ever received. Sometimes a log cabin was carried on a wagon from town to town. All one could hear or see was the log cabin, and the enthusiasm and numbers of the crowds was indescribable. The Whigs won, and the style of subsequent presidential campaigns was created—immense noise and an excited people at play.

The play element in presidential elections is still striking in the campaign clubs and in the ranking of candidates as "favorites," "dark horses," and "favorite sons," according to their chances of election, as if they were running a race.[65]

Local politics is also followed by the masses with the interest of a true sport fan. Take the case where a debater was getting the worst of it, and suddenly a voice came from the back of the hall: "Tom, call him a liar, and make it a fight."

Just as the sense of forming an "order" is increased rather

[64] Huizinga uses the term *aftredenden*, "retiring" or "resigning," which does not correspond to the position of a candidate running for reelection.—H.H.R.

[65] For the meaning of these terms, see Bryce, *The American Commonwealth*, vol. II, chap. 70.—J.H.

than diminished precisely by the powerful extension of organization, so the sporting sense in party politics is further increased by the opportunity since the expansion of the railway system to bring together astounding numbers of party members in huge meetings. At a national party convention for the nomination of a presidential candidate, with 1,000 delegates, 1,000 alternates and 14,000 spectators present, the very number of people generates excitement, just as it makes debate and judgment impossible in practice. That is why there has been a return to practices such as are supposed to have been followed in Sparta under the laws of Lycurgus—voting by acclamation.[66] The first party convention where the nomination was actually carried by such an outburst of enthusiasm was that at which the Republicans nominated Lincoln in Chicago in 1860. In addition to the spectators inside, there were thousands on the roof following the proceedings. "The Sewardites marched as usual from their headquarters at the Richmond House after their magnificent band, which was brilliantly uniformed—epaulets shining on their shoulder and white and scarlet feathers waving from their caps—marched under the orders of recognized leaders, in a style that would have done credit to many volunteer military companies. They were about a thousand strong, and protracting their march a little too far, were not all able to get into the wigwam [that is what the building is called in which a convention meets[67]]. This was their first misfortune. They were not where they could scream with the best effect in responding to the mention of the name of William H. Seward." The proceedings began in breathless quiet. As soon, however, as Seward's name was spoken enthusiastic applause broke out. "When Mr. Judd named Lincoln,

[66] Huizinga's term is *overschreeuwen*, "to shout down" or "outshout."—H.H.R.

[67] The bracketed definition is by Huizinga!—H.H.R.

the response was prodigious, rising and raging far beyond the Seward shriek." Seward's adherents did not give up and emitted an even louder shout. "The effect was startling. Hundreds of persons stopped their ears in pain. The shouting was absolutely frantic, shrill and wild." So another effort had to made for Lincoln. "I thought the Seward yell could not be surpassed, but instead the Lincoln boys . . . took deep breaths all round, and gave a concentrated shriek that was positively awful, and accompanied it with stamping that made every plank and pillar in the building quiver." The voting took place in the midst of this tension; the necessary majority went to Lincoln under the direct physical impact of the shouting. The politicians staggered home like drunkards.[68]

This practice of shouting still exists but has lost its spontaneity. The applause is organized and maintained by artificial means. When the supporters of one candidate begin shouting, the others must follow. In the Democratic convention of 1912 the name of candidate Underwood was cheered first for 20 minutes, then Clark's for an hour and 5 minutes, and finally Wilson's for an hour and 15 minutes.

Such traits are very suitable for putting the emotional character of American political organization in a clear light. The American sees this emotional character very plainly, at least in his political adversary. When Roosevelt broke with Taft and the split in the Republican party was complete, so that the Democrats gained the day in 1912 with Wilson, Taft taunted the new Progressives as "political emotionalists or neurotics." The Progressive convention in Chicago was marked by a spirit of pious fervency, to which the fact that women were granted a major place in it no doubt contributed. Roosevelt's declaration of principles was a confession of faith, and

[68] M. Halstead, "Caucuses of 1860," in Hart, *American History Told by Contemporaries,* vol. IV, p. 155.

even the hostile press had to admit that no party convention since the foundation of the Republican party in 1856 had matched the Progressives' in enthusiasm and devotion.[69] Nonetheless, by the time of the next Presidential election in 1916, the new Progressive party had as good as vanished, for it had dissolved and partly returned to the bosom of the old, solid Republican organization. Nothing more was heard afterwards of the Progressives as a party.

However strongly the American sense for joining and forming groups and for collaboration has been influenced by emotionality, there is one important field of organization in which this emotional quality is wholly lacking—economic organization. It requires no special proof that in studying the foundations of American civilization, economic organization does not come last. We do not go even half way when we define only the individual traits which characterize the feeling of the American people for political organization. Now the big questions rise for the first time: What is the relationship of individualism and organization in the history of America's economic development? Is there a conflict between these two concepts, or does the same interplay exist between them which binds individualism and organization so closely together in political history? In answering this question, however, a strictly historical approach falls short; it requires consideration by the methods of political science and sociology and is best left to those more competent than I. I wish to pilot the subject out of the historical harbor into the broad sea of society with only a single observation.

The capitalist business company was the first-born son of the American Revolution. Previously only large monopoly

[69] C. A. Beard, *Contemporary American History 1877–1913*, pp. 357, 370.

companies ruled by the interests of the mother country had
been known, and they were not popular with the majority of
colonial traders. The concept of privilege was connected with
the idea of a corporation, and fear of new monopolies retarded
the rise of business companies.[70] It was the Revolution which
first removed both the psychological and the political difficulties in their way. It called into existence all kinds of new
relations between businessmen and made possible the large
combinations of American capital.[71] The only thing that was
necessary for consolidating public trust in business corporations was the security of the new government and its institutions. Such security did not come until 1789, when the
Constitution went into effect. The rise of the corporations
began immediately afterward. If we find only 6 recognized
companies in the entire period before 1774 and 21 between the
years 1774 and 1789, there were 200 in the first eleven years
under the Constitution; one, the National Bank, received its
charter from the Congress.

Now it is worth noting that the corporation in its origins
was connected not only with the old, big companies but equally
with the private associations of nonmercantile or at least not
exclusively mercantile character. There continued to exist into
the nineteenth century in both England and America some

[70] The Dutch term used by Huizinga, *handelsvennootschap*, literally,
"trading (or business) company," does not correspond directly with any
American institution. The phenomenon described here by him is the rise
of the limited liability company, or business corporation, indicated in
Dutch by the term *naamloze vennootschap*, "anonymous society"
(= French, *société anonyme*). I have therefore translated *handelsvennootschap* both by "business company" (since their "trading" came more
and more to include industrial as well as strictly mercantile activities)
and "corporation."—H.H.R.

[71] S. E. Baldwin, "American Business Corporations before 1789,"
Annual Report of the American Historical Association (1902), vol. I,
p. 253; J. S. Davis, *Essays in the Earlier History of American Corporations* (Harvard Economic Studies, vol. XVI, 1917).

resistance among the public against corporations which worked only for their private advantage.[72] It was felt to be desirable that the very idea of a business company should involve some conception of cooperation for a public interest. We can observe in a number of points this transition from the beneficial association to the business company. This is where we find the tie between the spontaneous organizations discussed earlier and the economic associations. The first fire insurance company in Philadelphia began as a club which met monthly and fined absentees. The oldest life insurance company in Pennsylvania had the name in 1759 of "The Corporation for the Relief of Poor and Distressed Presbyterian Ministers, and of the poor and distressed widows and children of Presbyterian ministers." The oldest bank, Robert Morris's, developed out of a patriotic enterprise set up during the war to support the shaky credit of the United States. The first business corporation in New Jersey was carefully named the "Society for Establishing Useful Manufactures." The freedom to form corporations was still limited to societies with religious, charitable, and literary purposes. The state of North Carolina was the first to establish general freedom to form corporations in 1795.

Economic and political organization therefore had common roots in the native feeling for associations on behalf of purposes which were ethical as well as profitable. But while the political organization kept its spontaneity and emotionality, in brief its human character, economic organization under the pressure of capital did without such feelings from the beginning. Only in its more recent anticapitalist form of trade unions has economic organization again shared in the emotional elements of the primitive sense of association. But even in this form economic organization was much more strongly tied into the large process of mechanization of civilization than political

[72] Baldwin, "American Business Corporations," p. 267.

organization. To organize came to mean to mechanize. This was the fatal moment in the development of modern civilization. Thenceforth the term "sense of community" is much less applicable as the motive for political organization, and for the economic organization too. It was just there where the economic organization attained its most gigantic dimensions, in the American trust, that the feeling which pervaded it again became purely individualist. The great rulers of industry considered themselves as new pioneers, continuing the old work of the development of the natural treasures of the nation under changed circumstances. They demanded freedom for the unrestricted operation of the activities of big capitalism in the name of the old individualism which had made America great. We shall soon put the question whether this new individualism of big industry is anything more than an illusion and a delusion.

Even this hasty sketch of the problems which the history of economic association brings with it can only strengthen the conclusion which seems to flow from what has gone before—the twin concepts of Individualism and Association are felt as a contradiction in American history much less than one would expect on the basis of European history.

Chapter II

THE MECHANIZATION
OF COMMUNITY LIFE

When Tocqueville was about to finish his study of democracy in America, he brought together into a forecast of the future the results of his sober observations of the American community. As if musing with half-closed eyes, he saw what the processes he had observed would have to lead to. The picture he drew holds good not only for America; it is the future of democracy itself, considered in its greatest and newest representative. The characteristic element of that picture is leveling—the grinding away and obliteration of all individuality by mutual equality, with economic and intellectual differences vanishing along with political differences. "The wealthy . . . are few and powerless; they have no privileges that attract public observation. . . . Great wealth tends to disappear; the number of small fortunes to increase . . . ; extraordinary prosperity and irremediable penury are alike unknown. . . . There is little energy of character, but customs are mild. . . . The ties of race, of rank, and of country are relaxed. . . ."[1]

[1] *De la démocratie en Amérique*, vol. III, pp. 411, 542. [*Democracy in America*, vol. II, pp. 266, 349–350.]

When we read these words today, we must ask how it was possible that so clear a thinker as Tocqueville, with his sharp eye for real relationships, could have so mistaken the direction of the great stream flowing before him. The rich scattered and powerless! Minds without vigor! Relaxation of the ties of race, class, and country! Everything seems to have come out exactly opposite.

Could it be that Tocqueville was too exclusively a political thinker, that he was too much the product of the school of Montesquieu? Was he, despite himself, still too burdened with the rational explanation of Athenian political life, without enough understanding of economic factors? Or are we judging too quickly? Is the realization of Tocqueville's vision reserved for a future still to come, and for a more complete American democracy?

The men who in America itself had the task of guiding the great and growing democracy with all its shortcomings and contradictions saw the matter quite differently. When Andrew Jackson, at the end of his administration in 1837, looked into the future, he saw ahead a struggle of the moneyed aristocracy of the few against the democracy of the many; the prosperous people would make honest workmen into hewers of wood and drawers of water by use of the system of credit and commercial paper.[2] The individualist West (the West then still meant Kentucky and Tennessee) had long before grasped the danger which threatened it from the organizing power of big capital. A quarter of a century later Abraham Lincoln, who was also a Westerner (from Illinois) like Jackson, repeated the same concern and expressed it more urgently. In his presidential message to the Congress on December 3, 1861, he de-

---

[2] F. J. Turner, "Social Forces in American History," *American Historical Review*, XVI (1910–1911), p. 226. "Hewers of wood and drawers of water" is borrowed from Joshua 9:21, 23, 27.

clared himself bound to raise a voice of warning against the approach of a renewed despotism, the despotism of capital.

> It is not needed nor fitting here that a general argument should be made in favor of popular institutions; but there is one point . . . to which I ask a brief attention. It is the effort to place capital on an equal footing with, if not above, labor, in the structure of government. It is assumed that labor is available only in connection with capital; that nobody labors unless somebody else, owning capital, somehow by the use of it induces him to labor. . . . But these assumptions are false . . . labor is prior to, and independent of capital. Capital is only the fruit of labor, and could never have existed if labor had not first existed. Labor is the superior of capital, and deserves much the higher consideration. . . . No men living are more worthy to be trusted than those who toil up from poverty; none less inclined to take or touch aught which they have not honestly earned. Let them beware of surrendering a political power which they already possess, and which, if surrendered, will surely be used to close the door of advancement against such as they and to fix new disabilities and burden upon them, till all of liberty shall be lost.[3]

Lincoln's outlook on this great question was no more socialist than Jackson's. He saw it as the problem of protecting individual independence in economic competition, and obviously he still considered it to be a problem that could be solved by purely political efforts and by political means. After this, he was not obliged to devote his great and serious mind to this task. When he had finished the task of saving the country, his life's work was completed. And immediately after his death, the forces whose activity he had feared began to develop at a completely unprecedented rate. The two factors in the great process which brought about the concentration of capital

[3] *American History Leaflets,* ed. by A. B. Hart and E. Channing, no. 26, "Extracts from Lincoln's State Papers," p. 9.

—the mechanization of industrial operations and the corporate organization of business—increased enormously after the Civil War.

America has played an important part in the mechanization of production and transportation. The need for increasing the productivity of labor by improvements in technology was more urgent in America than elsewhere because of the great size of the country and the strong pressure to clear the land and put it to use. Solution of the problems of making raw materials into goods and the conquest of distance had been sought, impatiently and with devotion, since the days of the War of Independence. There was a host of would-be inventors; Fulton was one who succeeded. For a considerable time before England provided a practical means of steam transport on land, there were many plans considered in America for railroads, with or without steam.[4] When the planters of Georgia heard that the private tutor in General Nathanael Greene's house was an inventive person, they went to Greene's estate near Savannah to implore the young Eli Whitney to construct a machine which could remove the cotton seed from the fiber. Whitney, who had never seen a cotton plant in seed, set to work with borrowed money. Although he had to draw his own iron wire and prepare his own tools, it was not long before he had designed a cotton gin (gin = engine). Whitney then met opposition, deceit, and endless disappointments which so many other inventors also experienced. The model which he had built with so much difficulty was stolen from him when it was only half-completed. When he succeeded in building another machine, it was quickly imitated, and two states, in a most shameful act of injustice, revoked his patent.

In the meantime his discovery transformed the entire eco-

[4] See MacMaster, *History of the People of the United States*, vol. V, p. 138 ff.

nomic and social structure of the South. Cotton-growing, now that it was able to supply great quantities of an easily used product, came to dominate the whole region completely. As a result of the requirements of large-scale cotton-growing, slavery, which back in 1776 many in the South had thought was destined to disappear, became the indispensable foundation of the economic system. It was consolidated and became the pivot of all Southern politics. The work of one man's reason put thousands into bonds.

The invention of the harvesting machine was just as important for the new lands of what was then the Northwest, but more of a blessing in every way. Cyrus McCormick had grown up with the problem of inventing a machine which could do the work of harvesting on a large scale. His father Robert had designed such a machine in 1816, but it was not until 1831 that the younger McCormick was able to make a successful reaper. Then the development of the rich grain states south of the Great Lakes became possible. It was estimated about 1860 that the McCormick reaper had increased the annual income of the country by at least $55,000,000, and Secretary of State Seward declared that thanks to this invention the line of cultivation moved west by thirty miles every year.

It is obvious that the mechanization of agriculture could only be profitable in connection with the development of transportation, but application of steam power to transport had been transforming the entire character of the economic geography of North America since the second decade of the nineteenth century.

Before the development of steam transport, the lines of travel in the United States ran principally from north to south. This is the direction in which almost all the rivers that run into the Atlantic Ocean flow. Hence the somewhat ladder-like form in which the borders of the old Atlantic States meet each other.[5] The new lands in the west also had as their only artery of communication the waterway to the south, the Mississippi River. This was the only direction in which the mighty stream could be used; the flatbottomed boats on which goods were shipped downstream were sold and broken up when they reached New Orleans; the crew returned home overland in a long and difficult journey. The appearance of the steamboat changed the situation completely; it became possible to travel up the Mississippi. The result, however, was that the West would now probably seek to sell and buy its goods in the South even more than before. The Eastern states wished to supply and dominate the West themselves and there-fore sought with extreme vigor to have canals built from east to west. The debate over "internal improvements," the question of how far the Constitution permitted the federal government to promote the building of communication routes in the interest of individual states, became one of the points of contention in political life.

Nor did much time pass before the railways came and took over from inland steamships most of the task of the expan-sion of transport. The importance of the railways for America's growth can scarcely be overestimated. The natural line of com-munication from north to south was literally cancelled out by the construction of railroads. East-west now became the pre-

---

[5] It is not certain just what Huizinga means here. The Connecticut, Hudson, Delaware, and Susquehanna Rivers do all follow a north-to-south course, but only the Delaware separates two states, New Jersey and Pennsylvania. The principal southern rivers predominantly follow a west-to-east course, but of these only the Potomac and Savannah Rivers form the boundaries between states. In any event, significant traffic between north and south was by coasting vessels, not by river or road. Of course, that large-scale interstate trade followed a north–south direc-tion is beyond dispute and hardly surprising, since the original states, with the exception of New Hampshire, Vermont, and Pennsylvania were all situated on the coast.—H.H.R.

dominant direction of the entire economic development of the country. Once, while discussing the possibilities of military transport with a government official with a railway map before them, President Lincoln voiced surprise that all the railroads ran in the east-west direction: "Mr. President," the other man remarked, "if the railroad lines had run north and south, there would have been no war."

As early as 1844 Emerson considered the great political promise of the railroad to be that it would firmly hold the Union together. Otherwise, he felt, its days were numbered because it would become impossible to move representatives, judges, and officials over such great distances.[6]

In fact, however, the railways meant far more than just the speeding and extension of transport by machine power. It served not only to facilitate existing communications but also to make possible travel and even settlement in new regions. But in its function as an instrument by which civilization was brought into being, the railroad remained subordinated to the power of big capital. It was not the interests of the pioneers in the new frontier districts which dominated the construction of railroads, not the natural requirements of travel and the exploitation of the soil, but the financial interests of the great moneyed powers. The circumstances in which the old struggle of the individualist West against the organized capital of the East was continued were changed by the railway strongly to the advantage of capitalist power. In the railway the East now had at its disposal a superb means for dominating the West economically. Thus, in the first period, it was not unheard of for inhabitants of Western cities to resist the joining up of railway lines with pitchforks and sledgehammers.[7] But

[6] Emerson, "The Young American," *Works*, ed. Routledge, p. 626.
[7] B. H. Meyers, *Annual Report of the American Historical Association* (1907), vol. I, p. 119.

the West still became even more than before the field for large-scale speculation.

The railway became in turn the point of departure and the model for new forms of business organization. The earlier forms of economic association involved principally banking, steam and other means of transport, insurance, and to a limited extent industry. These were all organizations of small scope, with operations confined to a modest region. The railway, however, immediately imposed such high construction costs and expenses of operation that it made necessary the formation of large companies. These companies soon were so numerous that they fought each other with every means at their disposal. Between 1865 and 1884 the number of miles of railroad increased from 34,000 to 121,000. In one period of five years (1879–1884), it increased almost by half, or four times as much as the growth of population. Due to this unprecedented competition, the strictly economic function of the railway slipped into the background. A railway line was often built not with an eye to future development of transport but purely out of considerations of financial strategy, in order to thwart an opponent. Or it might be to support a tottering organization by attracting new capital, as in the example of the West Shore in 1882, which served only to keep the New York Central above water.[8] Weak lines sought freight shipments at any price. As a result of the excessive issue of shares, the railways ceased to represent real values based upon natural wealth. The promoters and entrepreneurs in the great financial centers of the East no longer looked for their profits in the first place to the freight shipper out in the country but instead to the speculative investor.

[8] It may be observed that Huizinga in this instance chose an unfortunate image, for he was apparently unaware that both the West Shore and New York Central lines run along the banks of the Hudson River.—H.H.R.

In consequence, a mechanistic element entered into the whole operation of the railways which constituted a danger to civilization in every respect. The force of capital, working automatically, had made itself master of the great new instrument, and it no longer simply served the immediate purpose for which it had been conceived. The government was not in a position to undo the damage that resulted—the railway companies had become the masters of the state legislatures and the courts by means of corruption. The preferential tariffs continued to favor large merchants over the small ones, increasing the importance of capital strength over the individual entrepreneur's ability, and concentrating trade in the great centers. It was once again the West and the South which pressed constantly for intervention of the federal government in railway policy.

In 1887 the Interstate Commerce Commission was established. In the long run it would be the means by which the government would exert its authority over the railways, but in its first years it did not have much power. Least of all was it able to halt the continuing concentration of railway companies, which developed automatically out of unbridled competition. The only result of regulations prohibiting "pools" and "rebates" was that secret arrangements took the place of public agreements. The period of great consolidations, which replaced the loose, temporary "pools," began about 1890. Five years later half of all American rail lines were united under the management of about forty companies. The great financial forces, directed by such individual leaders as Harriman, effected a harmony of interests among the big groups of railway companies which had already joined together. The rate wars halted and long-haul transportation benefited, but not as much as did the power of concentrated capitalist organization.

What is notable about technological progress is that at one and the same time it provides means making possible new and tighter forms of organization and creates the object on which this organization works as it takes shape. Without the means of fast travel which the railway provided, concentrated leadership of business was not possible; at the same time it was the railways themselves which were the first and most important object of this concentration.

Like the railways, but in somewhat different conditions, the telegraph and the telephone were both a way to intensify business organization and the objects of such organization. The operations of Jay Gould with the great telegraph companies can illustrate how this invention too provided food for big business and developed its methods. Of greater importance, to be sure, was the operation of the telegraph as a technical device which made new forms of business possible and brought them into being. In this respect it might be said that the telegraph and the telephone were even more essential than the railway, although their influence cannot be demonstrated as easily as the railroad's in figures of miles and times. The savings in labor which the telegraph and telephone provide are hardly to be expressed in numbers. Their effect is much more diffuse, but at the same time it is much more direct because it is a psychological effect. It made a reality of the old picture of society as a human organism. Only a year after the introduction of Morse's invention, the postmaster-general forecast the influence of the telegraph on the concentration of capital: In the hands of individuals it would become the most powerful instrument that the world had ever known to bring about great speculations, and in so doing to rob the many for the profit of the few.[9] It is obvious that the importance of the telephone in civilization in this respect is even greater than that of the telegraph, for the telephone abolishes distance even more by direct conversation.

[9] "Report of the Postmaster-General, 1845," in McMaster, *History of the People of the United States,* vol. VII, p. 132.

However much it was prepared for by the railway and the telegraph, it was the telephone that first made possible the modern leadership of concentrated business.

Some of the other victories of machine technology come to our attention primarily as means which make possible new forms of business, others as the motive and the object of the new forms of concentration themselves. America began earlier and went further in the mechanization of home industry and hand work than any other country. The invention of the sewing machine by Howe in 1845 was the first of the series. Businesses such as shoe manufacture and clockmaking gave up handicraft labor in America early and were therefore adapted to the forms of big business. The configuration of the modern business center—a central city for business, a residential city outside—first became possible through the application of electrical power to city and suburban transport. The concentration of retail trade in big department stores and the massing and concentration of business activity in towering office buildings were a direct consequence of the electric elevator. Grain elevators and similar devices have made the complete process of collection, storage, and movement of raw materials such as grain completely mechanical, and thus the businesses involved are subject to concentration. Time-saving inventions like the signature machine, the stenographic machine, the telautograph, and so on, permit an ever wider use of machines and a steadily greater speed of operation in every business center.

Every technical invention is intended to release mental energy and unlock natural resources but it also binds human independence by means of the more fully mechanical and efficient social organizations it makes possible. Organization, equipped with all the mechanisms that reduce human labor to guidance and regulation, itself becomes a machine over which the person no longer has complete control. For when guidance and regulation, which apparently flow out of free human judgment, are distributed over a multitude, they become obedience to the machine whom everyone serves. To the extent that the entire economic system becomes more complex and technologically advanced, the importance of free individual reason in business activity decreases and the mechanical element increases. If we compare several examples of the personal histories of the founders of several large American fortunes, then it becomes apparent how the personal element becomes smaller with the progress of time.[10]

John Jacob Astor (1763–1848), a German emigrant, son of a butcher at Waldorf near Heidelberg, still wholly fitted the type of the old trading adventurer. He came to America in 1783 after a stay in London, where his brother had a business in pianos and other musical instruments (the later Broadwood), bringing with him a shipment of musical instruments for sale. But while aboard ship he had a conversation with a fur trader, and he flung himself into the creation of an energetic, precisely planned, and broadly conceived organization of the fur trade. Within ten years he was independent and in a position to leave it to subordinates to travel into the wilderness and to trade with the Indians. He carried on trade with London and China in his own ships. After he had incorporated his business as the American Fur Company, he conceived in 1810 the great plan of establishing a complete monopoly of the fur trade by a continuous line of trading posts from Saint Louis to Astoria at the mouth of the Columbia River. This plan was upset by the war between the United States and England in 1812.

In the course of the years Astor's fur-trading interests become small in comparison with his speculation in building land at the edge of New York. He had begun to invest his

[10] Anna Youngman, *The Economic Causes of Great Fortunes* (1909; dissertation, University of Chicago).

profits in these lands as early as 1800. In 1834 he sold off his fur-trading business, reportedly because he observed that the style was shifting from beaver hats to silk hats, but probably also because the wilderness was no longer as productive as it had been. Thereafter the growth of the Astor fortune rested principally upon the expansion of the city of New York. In place of the adventurous fur trade, with all the personal characteristics which it required (even Astor no longer engaged in it personally), came automatic growth in the value of land bought early enough. The role of individual enterprise was reduced to a few far-seeing insights and taking advantage of the right moment. Although Astor's trading business was organized in the form of companies, it was at first still completely one man's; the companies were the arbitrary creations of Astor, who kept them completely in his own hand. The basis of his enrichment remained completely material and purely economic even when it shifted to speculation in land.

The picture of the business life of Jay Gould (d. 1892) is completely different. From beginning to end, his business was financial gambling, with railway companies (railways were still the only field in which there was a large number of companies) as the principal stake. Where we might say that Astor's fortune was his own free creation, Gould's arose out of a skillful utilization of the chances offered by the financial conditions of the railway companies. Gould got his profits not from the real economic earnings of the railroads but from speculating with their shares on the stock exchange. His speciality was bankruptcies; he gained his fortune not from strong but from weak companies. He himself had confidence in only three of the innumerable companies in which he was involved—the Missouri Pacific, the Western Union, and the Manhattan Elevated.[11] The growth of his wealth no longer signified the production of goods or a real increase in values. There was a

[11] Youngman, *The Economic Causes of Great Fortunes,* p. 99.

mechanical element in the process of his enrichment. None-theless there was something very personal and individual in his activities, to which Miss Youngman constantly draws atten-tion; for example, his effort to create a corner in the gold market, the "Black Friday" on the New York exchange of September 24, 1869, and the way in which he fought and subjugated the Western Union Telegraph Company.

Jay Gould represents the transition between the old period, with its simple economic relations, and the modern period of all-sided, hyperbolic, technologically and organiza-tionally perfected economic expansion. Although in the early period of this later stage the names of individuals still stand out—Rockefeller, Morgan, Carnegie, Harriman—their figures are more difficult to grasp as individuals and the history of their businesses is much more that of the great expansion of the enterprises as such. Great wealth was attracted to groups—the "Standard Oil men," the "Morgan men"—and not to individu-als. The Americans will not admit this; he wants, more than ever, to see in everything the person who is doing the job, and he will call attention to the figure of Henry Ford. But now the question arises whether it is not advertising which creates the phantom of a personality, where it is mechanical com-pulsion that really rules.

The concentration of industry in large corporations in-stead of the old individual enterprises began especially after the crisis of 1873. In the period from 1880 to 1890 the number of textile factories in the United States fell from 1,990 to 1,311, that of farm-instrument factories from 1,943 to 910, while the invested capital doubled; the number of iron works fell by one-third, while production increased by half. In ten years three-quarters of the leather factories disappeared, while pro-duction increased five times over. Concentration was first and most easily accomplished in the manufacture of articles of uniform character produced in large quantities; it was freight costs which contributed in large part to raising the price to consumers, as with petroleum, sugar, and salt. The Standard Oil Company set the example in the organization of trusts. In 1882 a small group of persons with holdings in the petroleum industry put all their shares in various companies in the hands of nine trustees, of whom John D. Rockefeller was the most prominent, so as to achieve unity of leadership at the cost of personal participation. The movement won ground in a short time in a number of large industries. In 1890 public opinion had become so aroused against the trusts, with their varieties of pools, corners, and syndicates, which threatened to result in monopolies, that the first federal law directed against the growing evil was enacted, the so-called Sherman Anti-Trust Act.

Belief remained unshaken in free competition as the foundation of a healthy economic life for a community. It was felt that infractions could be stigmatized as criminal and prosecuted under the penal law. Contracts in hindrance of trade and arrangements to avoid competition had already been treated under the law as violations of the public interest and therefore not binding. Now other steps were taken. The Sherman Act declared all such agreements under whatever name to be illegal, criminal, and punishable by fine or imprisonment; it was therefore a purely negative measure. The members of Congress who voted for it did not expect it to have very much effect, but public indignation against the threat of monopolies had to be appeased in view of their interest in the next election.[12]

The Sherman Act had in fact woefully little success. It

---

[12] A. T. Hadley, *Undercurrents in American Politics* (New Haven: Yale University Press, 1915), p. 74.

was applied only a few times in the first twelve years of its existence. Afterwards there was indeed a series of prosecutions and sentences against the trusts, reaching a high point in 1911, but the evil was not visibly diminished. Each trust was a kind of Hydra or Antaeus, as is demonstrated by the history of the meat-export industry. As early as 1888 a committee of the Senate began an investigation into the practices of the big packing firms, Armour & Co., Swift & Co., etc., which were harmful to free competition. The report published in 1890 was unfavorable to them, and it was one of the reasons for the passage of the Sherman Act. Nonetheless the very combination it had denounced was back in full operation by 1893, under various disguises. In 1903 it was struck down by a permanent injunction of the Supreme Court. Meanwhile the big firms continued to buy up their competitors at an unprecedented rate, leading to the formation of the National Packing Company, which was completely controlled by the big three packers, Armour, Swift, and Morris. Several of the big packers were tried on criminal charges in 1911–1912 but were acquitted; however, the threat of a civil suit in 1912 brought about the disbanding of the National Packing Company, and the Attorney General warned that the participants would be kept under scrutiny. These measures also did not have the slightest effect in shaking the packers' position of power. In the beginning of 1917, the President entrusted to the Federal Trade Commission, which had been established in the meantime, an investigation of the conditions in the food industries in general, but with the meat packers obviously intended as the first target. The report the commission issued in 1918 showed that the trust in the meat-packing industry was more immense and enjoying more prosperity than ever.

Such experience in fighting the trusts had to result in a realization that the causes of the process lay deeper than had been recognized at first.

During the first years it was still generally thought by outsiders that trusts were artificial machinations of sly, evil despoilers of the country, and they demanded their immediate and unconditional dissolution. The necessity[13] underlying the rise of this event was not yet glimpsed. Little by little, however, the new formations were revealed as the natural outcome of the drive toward simplification and savings in the process of production, subject as it was to the capitalist system. The trust signified an advance in economic organization: Production costs were reduced, by-products could be easily utilized, wastage of costs and energy in mutual competition was prevented, and advertising became superfluous; the process of selling was simplified by the elimination of the intermediary; there was an unlimited force of resistance to setbacks, a permanent availability of comprehensive experience and the most capable leadership, and an unhindered unity in management.

As a result, the period of absolute opposition to trusts had to be followed by a constructive antitrust policy. The remedy did not consist in punitive laws or in a vain effort to reestablish free competition but in permanent supervision by the government and the public. For this reason the Federal Reserve Act of 1913 took over the restrictions and penalties provided by the Sherman Act but at the same time permitted exemptions with the approval of the Federal Reserve Board and under its supervision. The Federal Trade Commission, which would continue in the path that the Interstate Commerce Commission had already trod for many years—supervision and assistance but not opposition to concentrated business—was established

---

13 The Dutch word *wettelijkheid*, literally "legality" or "lawfulness," is here used to mean "in correspondence with the laws of nature"; hence my translation as "necessity." It is significant that Huizinga, in general a harsh critic of materialism, here follows the neologistic meaning of the German word *Gesetzmässigkeit* (of which *wettelijkheid* is the Dutch parallel) given the word by German positivists, not least by their Marxist variants.—H.H.R.

in 1914. The Webb-Pomerene Act of 1918 relieved industrial combinations from the provisions of the antitrust laws
in certain cases, under the supervision of the Federal Trade
Commission, for the sake of export. In recent years the entire
problem has been completely transformed. The old definitions
of trust and monopoly, the judgment as to what is permis-
sible and impermissible in the system of price determination—
all this has become uncertain. There is an impression that both
the action of the big combines as well as the intervention of
the government have become, much more than before, a matter
of practical application of economic science, an economics,
however, that must reorient itself daily because of the rapid
expansion of business life itself. The ideal that is kept in view
is clear enough—to improve the economic apparatus, but at
the same time to permit its excellence to serve only the welfare
of the whole community. It was as such, as a memorable sign
of new prudence, that the decision of the Supreme Court in
1925 acquitting the flooring and the cement associations of
illegal restraint of trade was viewed.

When the concentration of industry was immediately
followed by a more far-reaching integration, it became even
more obvious that the whole process of the amalgamation of
business activity was inevitable.[14] After the loose temporary
combinations of enterprises in the same industry were merged
firmly into ordinary corporations, a need was felt for a new
kind of unification. Even a concentrated industry saw its
opportunity to purchase raw materials threatened because other
powerful combinations had taken over its supplies; these in
their turn faced as purchasers not a compliant crowd of small
customers but a few great organizations. So long as a complete

[14] W. F. Willoughby, "The Integration of Industry in the U.S.,"
The Quarterly Journal of Economics, XVI (1902), p. 94.

monopoly had not been achieved, each combination as it developed was driven to attempt to dominate the other: Either the manufacturers had to control the mines and transportation, or vice versa. The finished product of one became the raw material of the other, and one combination bought half or more of the entire production of the other. The enormous congestion of capital which had already developed from the single business firm made it possible for it to extend to every side over related and interdependent branches of business. If industrial combine *A* made itself the master of the mines and railways, then it prevented the competition of *B* in a still more fundamental way. Now it was not only the merchant between the producer and the consumer who became unnecessary but also the intermediary between the producer of the raw materials and the manufacturer who put them to use.

In this way the chain was forged which linked together mining, railway transport, steel mills, and finally iron and steel fabricators in all their forms under one ownership and leadership. The period when various industries battled for ownership of the ore beds and to penetrate each other's business was followed by one of large-scale consolidations.

By this time the railways in Pennsylvania had already brought completely under their control the anthracite producers who furnished them freight; at a later time the Pennsylvania Railroad was to build facilities for construction of warships. Steamboat lines were bought up by the railways. Standard Oil, which had already devoured the linseed oil industry, forced its way into lead mining. Department stores began to produce for themselves the goods they sold, at the same time that the big shoe factories opened their own stores everywhere.

The process did not stop at integration. The extension of businesses through conglomeration followed the stages of concentration, integration, and consolidation. The trusts became masters over the markets for many articles which had no relation whatever to their original products as a result merely of their financial power and their superior technique. This can be seen in the history of the meat-packing industry. According to the report of the Federal Trade Commission in 1918, the five large meat-exporting firms, Swift, Armour, Morris, Cudahy, and Wilson, formed a combine, the "Big Five," which by a loose arrangement among themselves maintained an appearance of serious competition in order to outwit the public and the government. In association they exercised almost total domination over meat exports not only from the United States but also from almost all other meat-exporting countries in the world, thanks to their participation in the business of Argentina, Brazil, Uruguay, Australia, and other countries. They were able to monopolize production and sale of the by-products—hides, wool, bristles, horns, and all other materials of animal origin—even more completely than the main product, since the small packers, although they were able to continue slaughtering and preserving, were not set up to produce such a variety of by-products. Now the octopus extended its grasp, as owners the Big Five disposed of all or a majority of the means of storage, canning, and transport. They had in their possession the cattle cars, the meat cars (which did not belong to the railways), the storage-houses for cattle, as well as 90 percent of all refrigerator cars and cold-storage houses, which were useful for a number of food products besides meat. Their sales organization throughout the country is so efficient and so extensive (Armour reached 24,681 cities with its own sales facilities in 1918) that they can easily penetrate the market for any article of general consumption they want to sell. In a single year, 1917, Armour jumped to the position of the largest rice dealer in the world. When the report appeared, the meat packers were busy assuring themselves of supremacy in canned fruits, vegetables, sugar, potatoes, beans, coffee, eggs, cheese, vegetable oils, and fish. Armour in particular moved into the field of grain, breakfast foods (oatmeal, etc.), cattle fodder, chicken feed, artificial fertilizer, coal, barbed wire and fence posts, sheet iron, twine, lumber, cement, limestone, sand, gravel, and roofing. The packing concerns furnished business capital for the establishment of all kinds of factories, which were therefore dependent on them. They established banks for cattle ranchers. They obtained an immense property in land, not to speak of their bank shares. The total sales of the Big Five in 1917 were estimated at $2,127,245,000.

How dangerous such an industrial position is for a country, not to speak of the world, is probably seen most clearly if we realize that the packers, by their control of the fertilizer supply, have food production within their power, and that, by their storage facilities and their financial strength, they can control the market independently of supply and demand. Thus it happened in 1917, when there was an unprecedented demand for leather, that some of the packers stored up hides in such quantities that they had to be kept in cellars and under the open sky.[15]

In August 1919, Attorney General Palmer (the head of the Department of Justice), declaring that he was convinced by the evidence of the Federal Trade Commission, announced that the packers would be brought to trial. At the same time a bill was introduced in Congress to limit their power (the Kenyon-Anderson Bill). But nothing more happened than an agreement reached in 1920 between the Department of Justice and the Big Five in which, among other things, they accepted an

[15] All of this is based on the *Summary of the Report of the Federal Trade Commission on the Meat-Packing Industry*, Washington, Government Printing Office, 1918.

obligation to give up their connection with all so-called un-related lines within two years. The consent decree which embodied the agreement listed about a hundred of these articles in which the meat industry was involved.

Five years later the Federal Trade Commission had to report that Armour & Co. was still the owner of five companies producing canned fruits and vegetables and had a stock of goods in unrelated lines with a value of more than $1,000,000, while Swift & Co. completely dominated the great canning company of Libby, among others. Meanwhile a court action had already been instituted in 1912 by the California Coopera-tive Canneries, who were business friends of Armour, seeking abolition of the ban against the packers' trading in unrelated lines. Soon Swift and Armour in their own names demanded withdrawal of the decree. Since the end of 1924 the case has dragged from one court to another while the packers continue, undisturbed, their immense business in poultry, eggs, butter, and so on. The impotence of the statute book against the pres-sure of economic organization is demonstrated *ad oculus* [to the eye] in this affair. This, and only this, could happen be-cause of the simple fact that excess space remains in the refrigerator cars under the hanging meat carcasses which needs to be used, and the packers have at their disposal the most efficient system of distribution in existence.[16]

The steel industry provides the major example of industrial integration. Carnegie for his part had long before introduced such integration by bringing into his own hands, under the supreme control of the Carnegie Company, all the branches of business—extraction, transport, and production—connected with the steel industry. He worked through a number of

[16] I am grateful for the details of the course of this affair since 1920 to the friendly information given me by Dr. Heinrich Pollak, from whose hand a study on industry in the United States is expected.—J.H.

separate organizations but took care to own at least 50 percent of the stock in each of them. In the meantime began the unification of the different enterprises engaged in steel production into great combinations, such as the Federal Steel Company, the National Tube Company, the American Steel and Wire Company, the Tin Plate, Steel Hoop and Sheet Steel Companies. They all sought to win control of the ore deposits and of the production of crude iron. Competition continued until about 1898, with intervals of pools and accords, but then Carnegie linked up with the Rockefeller interests. Now he was in complete control of the situation. In 1900 he began a struggle against the Federal Steel and American Steel Hoop Companies. At this point a depression in the iron and steel industry as the result of overproduction played into his hands. The Carnegie Company announced that it would produce bar iron, plates, wire, nails, and tubes on an unprecedented scale. The danger that threatened all the other steel interests brought Morgan into the field. In February 1901, his syndicate organized the United States Steel Corporation, with a capital of $1,400,000,000, a sum which did not in fact reflect at all the real worth of its assets. The shares of many of the companies were already "overstretched" by the time of the merger. Soon after the formation of the company, a sudden fall of the stock occurred, ruining many outsiders.

The great combines no longer represented the pure and natural process of concentration of industry because of the factors of transportation and technology. On the contrary, the immediate cause of their formation lay in the concentration of financial power, which in turn did not arise out of normal economic development but was rather the result of morbid symptoms. In any case, it was always great financial crises or catastrophes which provided an opportunity to bring about new concentrations of financial power. Astor had long before made use of the panic caused by the war with England in 1812, and then again the crisis of 1837, for his land purchases. The upsurge of Morgan's immense power dates from the railway bankruptcies of 1893. Gould's fortune was also founded on bankruptcies, as were Harriman's big operations in 1898. A depression also created the conditions for establishing the petroleum and the steel trusts.

The trusts merely constituted the units from which were built the great financial powers which dominate the business life of the United States. The trusts all coalesced around two interest groups, Standard Oil and Morgan's. The railway king, Harriman, and the bankers, Kuhn and Loeb, formed only a component of the Standard Oil group, which entered into alliance with Carnegie and brought Widener and the older Vanderbilt and Gould interests into its sphere. Standard Oil soon just meant the petroleum industry extended even more widely. The transformation from a petroleum trust to a financial power under the same name happened as follows. It soon became a problem for the stockholders of the Standard Oil Company to invest their profits outside of the petroleum industry, and Rockefeller obtained their agreement to solve it in the same way, not individually but in combination. He organized a system of common investments which set the Standard Oil group, an investment company, over the Standard Oil Trust, the industrial enterprise. The group was no longer in rivalry with competitors in an industry but with similar groups of financiers. The dissolution of the Trust in 1892 and of the Company in 1911 had little real meaning; the Standard Oil group remained the master of the constituent elements into which the company was divided.

The financial magnate appears to present a personality of strongly individualist character. He is a despot in whose hands is placed the total governance of immense operations. Harriman declared that the great entrepreneurs were inspired by the old individualism of the pioneers—the spirit of enthusiasm, the force of imagination and the bold calculations which had made America great. If these qualities were curtailed by legislation limiting complete freedom of enterprise, then it would be all over with America's development, he declared.[17]

But if we look instead at the way in which, in general, the concentration of capital was actually prepared, then we do not find that much of the old personal element persisted. What dominated the activity of the persons involved in the great process was just the opportunity presented for a constant extension of organization, which they could not resist. The impulse which drives an industrial monarch who already owns more wealth than he can enjoy to keep on inventing new ways of accumulating profits and power, even in sickness and old age, is nothing more than machinelike obedience to a power that lies in the very system of organization. In a purely automatic way the profits from the principal business seek new investment by monopolization of related articles. There is no spark of true freedom in the operation of a trust or the management of a huge fortune. It remains doubtful whether Morgan intervened voluntarily or was really a dupe in the formation of the Steel Trust.[18]

The great combinations have become independent forces. They make the individual man a slave, threaten the community, and strive to dominate or supplant the state. Just as in the early Middle Ages society ossified into the manorial and the feudal system, so it threatens to do the same now in the corporate organization of industrial capital. American developments display a certain similarity to feudalism in various points. It was

[17] Turner, "Social Forces in American History," *American Historical Review*, XVI (1910–1911), p. 222.
[18] Youngman, *The Economic Causes of Great Fortunes*, p. 133.

the specific trait of the feudal system that private economic forces and relations of personal dependence took the place of the state; the state was eaten away by relationships of economic power, and political functions were tightly attached to possession of a source of income.

The danger of a similar development was very great in America because until quite recently the state never exercised any very vigorous activity. From the very first the state (and this means primarily the individual states) gave free play to the expansion of economic forces. Emerson used the word "feudalism" in this respect long before the rise of the trusts. Trade, he said in 1844,[19] has broken the old feudalism but restores it in a different form. "Feudalism is not ended yet. Our governments still partake largely of that element. Trade goes to make the governments insignificant, and to bring every kind of faculty of every individual that can in any manner serve any person, *on sale*." He even went on to predict that the private telegraph system (which had just been invented) and express companies would displace the national mails, and even feared that the mint would fall completely into private hands.

Although developments followed different lines than Emerson expected, feudal elements are still present. Great fortunes are invested in such ways, with such protective measures against the threat of dissolution, that they have become permanent forces in every respect. The founder of the Astor family, on his death in 1848, established his eldest son as his heir, as is done in a kingdom. The Goulds did the same thing. Wealth thus became institutionalized. Precisely as in a primitive land ruled by conquerors, pride in the amazing extent of power operated as an irresistible motive not just to hold this power together but to expand it steadily. True dynastic feeling

[19] Emerson, "The Young American," *Works*, ed. Routledge, pp. 626–680.

rules great fortunes in the most complete form. The great families of the money magnates are closely joined by marriages in the same way that the trusts are mutually bound by cross-investments and overlapping managements. Just as the vassals formed ranks at a prince's side, the smaller groups of capitalists took their place at the side of the two mammoth groups which formed the heart of American business activity: the Morgan interests and the Rockefeller interests. What can have a more feudal sound than the way the American speaks of "Morgan men," "Armour people," "a Morgan road"? In the private correspondence of related concerns "our people" becomes the ordinary way they speak of themselves.

The conditions of early medieval large-scale landed property recurred here and there in the great businesses. Immense estates were created which extended over entire counties; the managers who operated them for an absentee millionaire landlord were absolute masters over a populace of farm workers who labored under the worst of conditions. In mining, lumbering, and even in the textile and steel industries, the situation was such that the owner was ruler over the whole social and political life of the community of workers, either because the industrial enterprise had wholly absorbed local government or because the political officials were at their beck and call. The rights of free speech and assembly, the use of the public highway, the secrecy of the mails were violated without compunction. In the closed camps where the operator was the owner of an entire district, not only did he control the local government on the basis of his ownership of private property, but he also arbitrarily denied entry to whomever he pleased.[20]

It is possible to resist and wipe out these newest versions

---

[20] *Final Report of the Commission on Industrial Relations, Senate Documents no. 415, 64th Congress*, Washington, Government Printing Office, 1916, p. 78.

of feudalism in their concrete form, but hardly the large-scale feudalism of huge fortunes and groups of capitalists. The report of the commission on industrial relations, from which this data was taken, says of the forces of great wealth: "In fact, such scattered invisible industrial principalities are a greater menace to the welfare of the nation than would be equal power consolidated into numerous petty kingdoms in different parts of the country. They might then be visualized and guarded against; now their influence invisibly permeates and controls every phase of life and industry."[21]

Some writers have already described as a new form of serfdom the dependence of the consumer on the big department stores caused by installment buying.[22]

The most serious thing about these modern forms of feudalism is that they lack the two elements which formed the core of feudal idealism—the loyalty of the man to his lord, and the solicitude of the lord for his man. It was precisely these which formed that human element in the old system of vassalage which was probably sorely neglected most of the time but which nevertheless permeated and inspired it. What is the source of the difference? It is not the evil intentions of persons that is responsible for the absence of this ethical element, but the impersonal force of organization itself preventing humanity from developing within the conditions of economic life. "We are all caught in a great economic system which is heartless."[23] No longer is the businessman an individual: he has become "a material piece of society." The worker knows the manager of the business as little as the manager knows him. But if there

[21] Ibid., p. 34.
[22] Installment buying, considered as a purely economic process, represents a wholly new development of credit of the greatest importance. See Edwin R. A. Seligman, *The Economics of Instalment Selling* (2 vols.; New York: Harper, 1927).
[23] Wilson, *The New Freedom*, p. 9.

is no possibility of a humane management of business based on a charity which knows the man it helps and shares his suffering, yet an abstract sense of justice or even considerations of utility would still prescribe concern and gentleness. But there is no adequate expression of such motives, for the whole operation of the great system of production is purely automatic. Everything human has been squeezed out of it. The major leaders bluntly deny their responsibility. John D. Rockefeller, Jr., testified before a congressional investigating committee: "Those of us who are in charge there elect the ablest and most upright and competent men whom we can find, in so far as our interests give us the opportunity to select, to have the responsibility for the conduct of the business in which we are interested as investors. We cannot pretend to follow the business ourselves." And J. Pierpont Morgan answered the question: "In your opinion, to what extent are the directors of corporations responsible for the labor conditions existing in the industries in which they are the directing power? —Mr. Morgan: Not at all, I should say."[24] From the very first the trusts in their machinations took advantage of the circumstance that it was not possible to locate responsibility in a given place: The individual companies declared that they had no knowledge of the intentions of the leaders of the trusts, and vice versa.

The first aim of the management of the big corporation is no longer the sound development of the branches of production on which it is based but only the financial interests of the enterprise. The directors know nothing and care nothing about the quality of the product or the condition and the treatment of the workers. Their leadership of the business really consists only in the dismissal and replacement of firm managers who do not produce profits as anticipated.

[24] *Final Report*, p. 34; what follows is also drawn from the conclusions of this report.

The managers themselves are leaders only in appearance. Production is increased or limited by their order, a factory put into operation or closed down, wages raised or lowered. Yet they too have hardly any direct contact with the working people and act upon inspectors' reports. Their data in turn are based on the complete statistics of the business, which report every piece of material that goes out or comes in, every penny spent or received, but knows nothing about the men and women whose work makes the whole mechanism go, just as if they did not even exist.[25] The officers may be quite humane persons who are convinced that the workers' welfare is the principal prerequisite for a well-run business, but their activity is guided not by their personal intentions but by the inexorable requirements of production and dividends. It is not left up to them to improve their factory as much as possible in every direction. "The constant demand is for high production at low cost, not through improvements and good conditions which might give them next year, but this very month. In the high pressure of business every superintendent knows that if his plant is at the bottom of the comparative scale for two months his position topples, and if for three months it is virtually gone. He cannot afford to experiment with changes that will not give immediate results. If he were his own master he might take a chance, knowing that the loss of this year would be compensated by gains under better conditions next year; but the monthly cost sheet does not wait for next year; it demands results now."[26]

This organization with its great power therefore no longer serves an economic interest which was real even if purely material. It is not a healthy outgrowth of the combination of technology and transportation; it was shaped by the principle

[25] Ibid., p. 27.
[26] Ibid., p. 28.

of financial manipulation, so that it lost its strictly economic purpose. This is illustrated in a glaring way, once again, by the report of the Federal Trade Commission of 1918 on the meat industry. The failure of meat production in the United States to keep pace with the growth of population was ascribed in this report to market conditions deliberately created and maintained by the Big Five. Thousands of cattlemen began, not without reason, to consider that the large cattle markets were a hazardous gamble in which the packers really controlled the game. The cattleman's business was a difficult one, demanding months of hard, careful labor and a large investment of capital, just to bring a single load of cattle to the market. It was put in constant peril by the unnatural price fluctuations created by the purely financial calculations of the trust leaders. In discouragement the cattlemen abandoned their businesses or restricted them. Nor was this all. The system by which the packers concentrated marketing and storage facilities in a few major central points meant that the farmers and the small ranchers near small cities could no longer raise cattle with profit, for they no longer found a market for their cattle nearby. In certain districts, where for one or another reason the packers did not wish to own slaughterhouses and canning plants, and specifically in New England, they deliberately eradicated the raising of cattle.

With the nationwide decline of small-scale cattle raising, the fertilizer industry suffered and the opportunity to use damaged or superfluous crops as fodder was lost. What has already happened to cattle raising now threatens dairy production and poultry raising in the near future.[27] Yet the developments of the last few years appear to have given the lie to these melancholy prognostications. From 1920 to 1924 the use of butter and cheese rose from 15 to 17.25 pounds per capita for

[27] *Summary* . . . , pp. 42, 43.

butter and from 3.5 to 4.2 pounds for cheese. The establishment of cooperatives and the improvement of methods have
enabled the food industries to expand production and sales
steadily.

Although the enormous number of shares issued by the
great corporations such as the Steel Trust or the Central Pacific
may in general still continue to fulfill a function as a means
of investment in the productive process, the real tie between
the shares and the businesses whose names they bear has long
since disappeared. The stockholder has no interest in strengthening the firm or having it make sound products. He buys stock
as a speculation or an investment; if its price falls he will make
no effort to strengthen the company but will sell his shares,
sending them into the maelstrom of the financial market.

As time goes on, there has remained less and less of the
old American individualism, the self-help of the man who personally built, directed, and improved his business. "America,"
said Wilson in 1912, "is not a place of which it can be said,
as it used to be, that a man may choose his own calling and
pursue it just so far as his abilities enable him to pursue it."[28]
The man of ability no longer escapes the necessity to place
himself at the service of the big interests, who do not value
his inventiveness as he expects. Just as before it was handicraft
labor that resisted the machine, now it is the old machine which
resists the new. When so much money is invested in an earlier
process or in advertising yesterday's product, a new invention is unwelcome, and the corporations buy up inventions in
order to stifle them. A monopoly such as the Pullman Car Company has long remained indifferent to improvement of its
service. Only financial decline opens the eyes of businessmen
to the necessity for new improvements of technology. It has
been observed in mining and iron manufacture that the years of

[28] *The New Freedom*, p. 12.

great prosperity are usually unfavorable for technical progress.[29]

It is matter's terrible revenge over mind, which thought that it had taken matter under its sway. The mind has entered the machine and there it sits, locked up as if in a bottle under Solomon's seal.

Improvement of the economic-technological process by every means has become an evolution which cannot be reversed. The ideological aspect, that is, the conviction that in the end a constant striving to reduce the need for labor and make it more efficient will lead to a liberation of intellectual forces, has fallen into the background. The improvement of the machine is followed, logically and inescapably, by the adaptation of man to the machine. This step was taken by the Taylor system, as it is usually called in Holland, although Americans speak of "scientific management."

It is the keystone of the edifice of the division of labor in the modern factory, a structure erected with such effort. When Eli Whitney designed his cotton gin, he had to make his tools and draw his iron wire himself. But later, when he turned to the manufacture of firearms, he was the first to introduce an efficient division of labor; each workman had only to perform a few manual operations, but the thousands of parts of the weapon which they prepared simultaneously always fitted together. Whitney, who had also created the conditions for the perpetuation of slavery in the cotton states, is therefore an excellent example of how one man's free inventiveness binds countless others who come after him. The scope that the division of labor long ago attained in the modern factory through repetitive, mass work is generally known, but it is only when a stage of high development has been reached that scientific management comes in. Already during the years 1880–1890,

[29] *The American Year Book, 1916*, pp. 486, 489.

various speed-up systems were applied in American factories but without a deliberately elaborated scientific basis.

Frederick W. Taylor, a superintendent for the Midvale Steel Company, wrote his *Shop Management* in 1903 when given instructions to oppose the ca'canny (slow-down) system. His fundamental idea was that no matter how steadily a machine works on its own and no matter how much time and labor it saves, its operator always has considerable leeway to waste time and labor, depending on his zeal and skill. It must be possible to calculate these differences and to restrict wastage by a scientific study of all the physical and mental operations involved. "He considers," says a describer of Taylorism, "a manufacturing establishment just as one would an intricate machine. He analyzes each process into its ultimate, simple elements and compares each of these simplest steps or processes with an ideal or perfect condition. He then makes all due allowances for rational and practical conditions and establishes an attainable commercial standard for every step. The next process is that of attaining continuously this standard, involving both quality and quantity, and the interlocking or assembling of all these prime elements into a well-arranged, well-built, smooth-running machine."[30]

In other words, it is now man himself who has become utterly mechanized. The divisions of this method of investigation are called "time study" and "motion study." All modern science is brought to bear—the psychology of fatigue and attention, the physiology of muscular work, etc. The motions are recorded in motion pictures or still photographs by attaching a small electric light to the worker's finger, which then

[30] Quoted by A. W. Sanders, *Het Taylorstelsel, de Arbeiders en de komende Vrede* (Leiden, 1917), p. 10. Out of the already very extensive literature on this subject, one may refer to Dr. J. van Ginneken, S.J., "Zielkunde en Taylorsysteem," *Zielkundige Verwikkelingen*, I, i (1918).

describes the required path. Once an optimally efficient pattern of work and hence a permanent maximum of productivity are calculated in this way, then standard conditions for the performance of daily tasks are fixed and a system either of bonuses for success and fines for falling behind or of piece work according to a strongly differentiated scale is introduced. If possible, tasks are even more rigorously divided than had been true before in the ordinary modern factory. A special group of officials is given the duty of preparing the statistics which report in scientific form the qualities and shortcomings of each workman.

The success of the Taylor system in eliminating superfluous motions, in saving time and hence in increasing production, rapidly drew wide attention. It was pointed out that in the laborious operation of moving crude iron the Taylor system increased each man's daily performance from 12.5 to 59 tons. But soon sounds of disappointment were heard from America, where it was first possible to assimilate a considerable body of experience in the field of scientific management.

In the first place, practice did not always match the much praised theory. Often little remained of the objective science with which the system was supposed to operate in determining wages and duties, which was probably fortunate. Much more turned out to be involved than just the adoption of a few new, quite carelessly applied routine practices. Furthermore, the movement for scientific management is pervaded with quackery. It asserts that the system handles each worker as an independent personality, but in practice this means that it allows those who are weaker to fall hopelessly behind and makes those who are older feel painfully the decline of their forces, and that it favors the skillful and the strong-nerved, while providing no built-in precautions against overwork and exhaustion. With all its psychological pretensions, it makes the major psychological mistake of failing to recognize the importance of rhythm for work. The older machines still worked rhythmically but the new technology attempted to replace rhythmic by circular movements, at the cost of the relaxation created by the satisfactions of rhythmic movement.[31]

The Taylor system can be used as a means of oppression by strict application of the definitions of tasks and wages. It limits the skill of the worker even more than the modern industrial factory had already done. It usurps technical competence for management and increases the number of the unskilled and semiskilled workers. It weakens community feeling and economic democracy. It is hard to believe that this will be the way the liberation of the mind from the machine will be reached.

The mechanization both of labor and of the forms of economic life is immediately visible as a primary, elemental process, but it is only a part of the general mechanization of the life of society which keeps pace with the development of modern civilization. A mechanization of political life and intellectual life is also under way in close connection with that of economic life, but it is not as close to the surface or as easy to define.

The American has already recognized the degeneration of politics by mechanization in a phrase of common speech: He calls the effective apparatus which keeps party life going "the boss and the machine." Such an application of terms taken from the factory to functions of democracy holds a deep meaning for the history of civilization. It defines what we attempt to demonstrate in the following observations.

In order to understand the mechanization of party life, we must survey rapidly the development of the political parties themselves. Party differences in the United States arose out of economic conditions. We briefly set out above (pp. 21 ff.)

[31] Van Ginneken, "Zielkunde en Taylorsysteem," p. 29.

how two opposite tendencies found expression in the struggle over the adoption of the Constitution between 1787 and 1789— the interests of big capital required a strong governmental system, more centralization, a vigorous federal power; the agrarian interests feared in a strong governmental authority the superior power of capital and desired continuation of the independence of the states even in the smallest things. In this way an antagonism arose which continued to dominate politics even after the Constitution was adopted. The parties received the names of Federalists and Federal Republicans.[32] It was an antagonism to which very important ideological attitudes were connected. In any case, the difference of conceptions was presented in theory as the conflict between order and freedom. In the mind of the advocates of the Constitution, the wealthy merchant circles of the coastal towns, prosperity was paramount; to serve it the first necessity seemed to be the maintenance of order by a sturdy government. The opponents, the groups which saw peril in the superior power of trade and finance which threatened them, on the contrary placed first the maintenance of the rights and freedom of individuals and feared the Constitution.[33] There was therefore an antagonism between government and

[32] We may remind the reader again that it was these early Republicans who were the actual predecessors of the modern Democrats, while the Republican party which was consolidated in 1856, although it did not arise directly out of the former Federalists because that party had already long since disappeared, nonetheless represented important principles of the old Federalism, among other things the strong unity of the country, in opposition to the Democrats. In this connection, we may call attention to a peculiar difference in the meaning of the term "Federalism" in American and French or Dutch history. In the French and Batavian revolutions, the point of departure was the doctrine of strong unity of the state. Hence the term Federalism meant for them the goal of confederation, and abandonment of the doctrine of the unity of the state, and therefore a centrifugal tendency. But in America, where the point of departure was the doctrine of the complete independence of the states, Federalism meant just the opposite—the goal of close unity, and hence a centripetal tendency—J.H.

[33] See Bryce, *The American Commonwealth,* vol. II, pp. 5–18.

individualism. Some wished to place emphasis on the executive principle, the active force in government, and others on the legislative principle, which protects and conserves. But there rested in this latter conception, which belonged to Jefferson and his friends, a stronger ideological component than in the conceptions of the Federalists. The Federalists were those who shared the conviction of Adams and Hamilton that only material interests ruled and could rule the country. "Your people, Sir," exclaimed Hamilton after an enthusiastic toast at a dinner, "your people . . . is a great beast." The Federalists were "the able, the well-born and the rich"; the real, positive force, which had to find practical expression, was in their hands. How much more honorable it sounded to believe in freedom and human virtue with Jefferson, and that was what the Federal Republicans professed. Under their pressure the old, cherished principles of freedom were incorporated into the first ten amendments to the Constitution, and hence a certain balance between the two principles was achieved.

To a certain extent, therefore, the first party conflict in the United States, which came into existence with the Constitution in 1789, may be conceived as a distinction between political realists and political idealists.

But it did not stay that way. The original conflict was transformed by a general rule in the history of human societies, which operated here too. Each group of the politically dissatisfied can garb its goals, honestly and naturally, in the luster of idealism. We can with impunity see what we do not possess in the semblance of the perfectly good and the perfectly pure. But as soon as a group obtains political power for itself, the possession of power compels it to become realistic and hence inevitably to desert principle. In few statesmen can this be shown as clearly as in Jefferson. In 1794, when his enemies, the Federalists, were still at the helm, the young commonwealth saw placed before it the thorny question of choosing between gratitude and a spiritual connection with revolutionary France, on the one hand, and on the other the commercial interests which enjoined a good understanding with England. For the Federalists this was not too difficult a decision; the great capital interests, who were their driving force, compelled them to choose advantage before fidelity; friendship for the French ally during the struggle for freedom was abandoned and an advantageous commercial treaty concluded with England, the so-called Jay treaty. Now for the first time the opposing party had reason to contrast such unfaithful egoism with the idealism of its own principles; the [Federal] Republicans raged furiously against the violation of the most holy duties. But when the [Federal] Republicans themselves won the presidency with Jefferson in 1800, then the burden of the state power and the state interest at once put upon them the burden of realism in politics. When in 1803 Napoleon suddenly offered to sell Louisiana, that is, the entire region on the right bank of the Mississippi, to the Union, it was none other than Jefferson, the great opponent of executive authority acting on its own, who, under the compulsion of the superior necessity of the affair, took the most important of all decisions for the future of the Union, *without Congress,* and concluded the purchase.

During the long period of the uninterrupted authority of Jefferson's party (1801–1825), the old opposing party disappeared. The Federalists were worn out and behind the times, and there was no more talk of the Federalists, just as in the Netherlands the Conservatives have now vanished as an official party. But the tendencies which the Federalists had represented—support of a strong government and the interests of big business—did not at all disappear. They made their way into the heart of the [Federal] Republican party itself. By 1820 this party, then in undisputed control of government, was no longer the spokesman of agrarian individualism. Out of Jefferson's own school there came a Monroe who gave strong expression to the unity and activity of the Union in foreign relations.

The country had become ripe for a new party division following economic lines and the differing conceptions of the task of government. The years of placidity, "the era of good feeling," came to an end in 1824. Then, as in 1878, the great economic conflict between the various parts of the country made itself felt. A young West (Kentucky, Tennessee, etc.) poor in capital but rich in energy, full of the old individualist ideal of freedom and fearing the domination of the capitalists on the coast, again resisted the rich East of commerce, finance, and industry. This fear of Eastern capitalism also determined the attitude of the South, but it represented, however, a different, agrarian form of capitalism, thanks to the development of cotton growing. This meant that there were three geographical-economic groups facing each other. Although it was already obvious in 1824 that a majority of the people wanted the Westerner, Andrew Jackson, the administration remained for another four years in the hands of the East with President John Quincy Adams. Then the younger forces triumphed, and Jackson came on the scene as president in 1829.

Jackson's election seemed to mean that the time had come for a new form of individualist democracy carried through to the extreme. But once again it also became apparent how powerful the principle of the unity of the country had become even though a centrifugal theory of the state had been dominant for years. The nation, by its weight, by its tradition of just forty years, by its very mass, as it were, had become a driving force and a great ideal. It is a striking fact that it was Andrew Jackson who had to save the Union from the danger that threatened it.

The South had long been resisting the tariff policy of the

commercial and industrial states. Out of a fear of becoming the victim of a protectionism that did not correspond to the cotton interests, the South held as firmly as possible to the doctrine of the independence of the states, so that, if things came to the worst, it would be able to throw off the will of the majority. The fiery John Calhoun, whose point of view was undoubtedly correct historically and in political theory, preached the right of a state to declare invalid federal laws which it considered harmful to its existence. This was the principle of nullification. From whom could more sympathy for this doctrine have been expected than the new democrats of the West, who had just put their hero Andrew Jackson, the wild pioneer, the man of freedom, at the helm of state? Fully confident, South Carolina went ahead with its preparations to put nullification into effect.

But the first words that Jackson spoke were: "Our Federal Union, it must be preserved." And he vigorously resisted the effort to withdraw a state from the federal authority, which would inevitably end in secession. The inherent, compelling force of the principle of the unity of the nation had already become so strong that it operated in practice even when theory seemed to testify against it.

A coarsening of political life began when Jackson's Western democrats came to power. "Jacksonian democracy" became a harsh and arbitrary party regime which inaugurated the spoils system and introduced a vulgarity into political manners which would be hard to drive out again. Its opponents felt it to be a bitter tyranny, and they set against it their own ideal of respect for law and honest administration. As the representative of these ideals, Henry Clay, Daniel Webster, and their collaborators took the historically honorable name of Whigs. Thus the sense that their political rights had been violated gave the opposition a look of idealism.

The Democrats (this name had now completely driven

out that of Federal Republicans) for their part appealed with
equal force to a strict maintenance of the Constitution and a
series of economic ideals. In 1842 Calhoun, full of hope, announced: "The great popular party is already rallied almost en
masse around the banner. . . . On that banner is inscribed:
free trade, low duties, no debt, separation from banks, economy, retrenchment and strict adherence to the Constitution."
These were therefore all principles of true freedom. But there
was one which was not present, however—freedom for Negroes.

It would be easy to imagine that the question of slavery
was the primary point which had divided the parties for
decades, but such was not at all the case. The question of
slavery, however much it entered into every question of
domestic politics, remained incidental for a long time. The real
Abolitionists were at first also held in abhorrence in the North.
The political struggle concerned not the abolition of slavery
but its limitation to those parts of the Union where it had been
long established. The advocates of this limitation, the Free-
Soilers, were to be found among the Democrats as well as
among the Whigs. It was only when the Civil War began to
draw close and the Democrats became over-reckless in the use
of their long supremacy that a new major political party was
formed in 1854. It called itself the Republican party (the same
name that its opponents, the Democrats, had originally used),
and it brought together Whigs, Free-Soilers, Abolitionists, and
before long the former Know-Nothings as well. The struggle
against slavery became the major factor uniting the new
party, more by the course of events than by deliberate purpose.

When the Civil War broke out and the Republicans became supreme in the North, they represented at one and the
same time the most exalted ideals and the greatest power—
unity of the nation and freedom for all, but also big capitalism

and intensive exploitation of the country. Their superior strength made it inevitable that the Republicans would win, and they did, although the struggle was harder than they had expected at first. But once they had achieved victory, abolished slavery, and assured national unity, that is, once they had realized their ideal goals, the administration of the Republicans became a worse party tyranny than had ever existed before, because the defeat of the opposition party made it invulnerable for many years.

Actually there no longer existed any positive political goal for which the Republican party had to remain united. And the same held true for the Democrats. They could not attempt to obtain restoration of the old conditions; for in fact the Democrats had never been uniformly in favor of slavery. For a time repression gave to the defeated party a certain idealist tone in its turn, but it had no connection with any specific ideas. Thus American political party life after the Civil War fell into a paralysis which gave free play to the process of degeneration of the parties from organizations to machines.

A strong and careful organization of the parties was more indispensable in America than elsewhere; constant activity was demanded of the parties in connection with the many elections to which the citizens were repeatedly called.[34] There were elections for a vast number of local and state offices. Only permanent specialists could handle the preparatory work, the nomination of candidates. A network of permanent committees directed activity down to the last detail. In the years after 1865 organization itself has become more and more skillful, but in the end the true political purpose went by the board. The system of nominations and elections was so complicated that

[34] For all of this, see Bryce, *The American Commonwealth*, vol. II, part 3: *The Party System;* and J. T. Young, *The New American Government and Its Work*, 1915.

it destroyed the freedom of the citizen instead of safeguarding it, as had been its intention. The party conventions left no room for real discussion; the programs were drafted by a few men and the approval of the many was expressed by "machine-made applause." Congress is not a Parliament. Most political questions, because of their special character, are not fitted for solution by a genuine body of popular representatives. An individual member of Congress is powerless unless he belongs to the narrow organization of the leaders. In every political arena, large or small, it is the machine which rules. "A machine is that part of a political organization which has been taken out of the hands of the rank and file of the party, captured by half a dozen men."[35] It was therefore the old caucus, carefully organized and stabilized. The man who steers the machine is the boss.

The machinery of democracy has absorbed democracy itself. The essential moving force of the whole party is the national party committee. It is composed of one member from each state, chosen by the state's delegates in the national party convention, who themselves are chosen by the people of the state. In form, therefore, everything is purely democratic, but in reality the national committee is an oligarchy with complete power.[36]

It is a few persons who really count. "We might have expected," says Bryce,[37] "that in the more democratic country [more democratic than England], more would turn upon principles, less upon men. It is just the reverse." In appearance this importance of men means the opposite of mechanization, but in fact there is thoroughgoing mechanization, for the active people are not real political leaders but party officials and

[35] Wilson, *The New Freedom*, p. 216.
[36] Young, *The New American Government*, p. 550.
[37] Bryce, *The American Commonwealth*, vol. II, p. 225.

business leaders. What counts is not their human talents and their free political intuition but their usefulness as parts of the machinery when a candidate is nominated; the question is not who the best man is but who has the best chance, given the composition of the party. The nomination for the vice-president ordinarily occurs according to the strict principles of party strategy, either in order to attract the doubtful states or to appease the disappointed faction of the party itself.[38] In the party convention political wisdom and knowledge are not needed, only intrigue and rhetoric. The party platforms are "nets to catch votes," or, like the platform of a train, "something to get in on, not to stand on." Before the presidential election the national committee drafts a textbook for speakers and workers, which includes, besides the party program and the speeches of their candidates, a cut-and-dried supply of statistical and other data, designed to show that the party has always acted for the interest of the people, and that the opposing party has always committed mistakes. The boss has his wardheelers and party workers, mere henchmen without political thoughts of their own. The struggle is waged at least as much among the factions within a party as against the opposing party.

At the same time that organization achieves perfection, real political differences are eroded. Some general slogans remain which are treated with sacred respect. A Republican believes with Lincoln in "government of the people, by the people and for the people." A Democrat believes with Jefferson that "governments are republican only in proportion as they embody the will of the people and execute it." There are certain social traditions in the older parts of the country: In the North the "best people" are Republicans, in the South Democrats. Now and again the Democrats repeat their old dogmas—opposition

[38] Young, *The New American Government,* p. 559.

to government intervention, a tendency in favor of free trade, an antipathy to imperialist policies—but in practice these no longer determine their actions. How little unity of ideas the Democratic party possesses can be seen from the following example. In 1916 the Republican party leadership lengthily discussed what they would use as a "paramount issue" against Wilson in the presidential election. There were seven proposals for such a slogan.[39]

Since about 1870 the two big parties have not been able to adapt themselves to the new problems. The important questions of the day are only exceptionally party questions on which Republicans and Democrats divide. There exists no sharply delineated Republican or Democratic standpoint concerning protection of trade, railway policy, or the struggle against the trusts. As a result, special small parties are repeatedly formed for the achievement of new interests, while the platforms of the big parties must remain vague and rhetorical just because they are compelled to respect all the sorts of heterogeneous principles and interests they include. The result is also that the victory of one or the other party of itself says nothing about the course legislation will take. "In our country," says an American, "we fool the people with some pretended differences between one party called the Republican and another called the Democratic." "We vote," said Woodrow Wilson in 1912, "we are offered the platform we want; we elect the men who stand on that platform and we get absolutely nothing. What is the use of voting? We know that the machines of both parties are subsidized by the same persons, and therefore it is useless to turn in either direction."[40]

This is the basic evil. The commercialization of the parties has gone hand in hand with the mechanization of the political

[39] *American Year Book, 1916,* p. 25.
[40] Wilson, *The New Freedom,* p. 24.

function, because the party organisms have become operative forces *sui generis*. They have become communities of interest with immensely wide ramifications. Each of them holds firm to the "special interests" on numberless points and these forbid the party . . . to act like a real party and take sides.[41]

The darkest period in the political life of the United States was the time from about 1865 to 1884, when the perfecting of party machines coincided with the first phase of unprecedented economic expansion and the new economic forces were still left completely on their own. The spoils system ruled then without shame or reticence, and public office was conceived purely as the property of the party forces. Between 1872 and 1878 a series of scandals broke which even included Cabinet members and members of Congress; a Secretary of War and a Speaker of the House of Representatives were revealed to have taken bribes. The incredible practices of the Philadelphia Gas Ring and of Tammany Hall under Boss Tweed in New York fall in this period. Since then corruption in a sense has been normalized, like an illness which loses its harmful character in the long run. The party machine has been more and more subordinated to the big corporations. The boss who plunders the public treasury for himself and his pals has become a rarity; his place has been taken by the boss who is the agent of the trusts. The system of letting trade bodies which have something to fear or hope from the administration in power pay for the costs of election campaigns, notably the gas, water, and transportation companies, was devised before the Civil War; the honor of its invention is attributed to the journalist and political promoter Thurlow Weed. In this way the large com-

---

[41] Huizinga here has used an untranslatable pun, *verbieden de partij . . . om partij te kiezen,* literally "forbid the party . . . to choose sides," reflecting the continued meaning of the Dutch *partij* as "a side" and "a party" in the political sense; the former usage has been lost in English. —H.H.R.

panies fell into the habit of paying tribute to both parties. At first the companies were still more or less helpless victims of a system of blackmail, but as they continued their immense growth, their position changed steadily from that of passive object to that of the active agent, and it was the party boss who became their obedient servant. The trust leaders were assiduous in political activity. They contributed to election campaign funds; although a law of 1907 forbade the acceptance of contributions from corporations in election campaigns, no one is under the illusion that this has restricted their influence. The corporations maintain so-called lobbies with the Congress, agencies which seek to influence legislation in their special interest in whatever way offers itself. Each major trade association has its legislative committee and legislative agents, who have the task of opposing bills considered harmful to their interests.[42] An investigation of the year 1913 found that such lobbies were maintained by the National Association of Manufacturers, the National Council for Industrial Defence, among other business associations.

The big business groups make no distinction of parties. During an investigation in the year 1893, the Sugar Trust admitted that it was "a Democrat in a democratic State and a Republican in a republican State." In a state where the parties are able to stay in approximate balance, the corporations support both of them. This means that the boss loses his party character too. "A boss is not so much a politician as the business agent in the politics of the special interests. The boss is not a partisan, he is quite above politics! He has an understanding with the boss of the other party. . . . The two receive contributions from the same sources and they spend those contributions for the same purposes."[43] In 1915 former President Roosevelt accused bosses Barnes and Murphy of

[42] Young, *The New American Government*, pp. 576, 583.
[43] Young, *The New American Government*, pp. 576, 583.

corruption and asserted that there existed a close connection between the Democratic and Republican machines in New York state. According to the sentence, a corrupt "ring," composed of members of both parties, had indeed dominated the government of the state from 1898 to 1910. In this lawsuit, Barnes in his defense set out the theory of "boss rule." It was, he testified, the only form of administration that could exist under the party system. The principle of the two-party system was that it was the party organization which had to direct the legislative process; but if the business interests providing money for the organization were not protected, then they would not contribute and party organization would be impossible![44]

Can one think of a better example of a *circulus vitiosus* than this? The circle, besides, is one from which the people are excluded.

Thus in the end the commercialization of the parties actually wholly takes away conflict between them. Big business has engulfed political life. A question such as the protective tariff, which in any case has never had the character of pure principle in America, has been completely dissolved into one of the special interests of the various products of industry. Each industry, each "special interest" (the clear American name for them), is a power which exerts itself in politics independently. The national government, said Wilson in 1912, has been in fact under the control of the trusts for sixteen years.[45] Whole states have fallen into the grip of a powerful industrial combination. For a quarter of a century, said a former governor of Illinois about 1900, there has been no one named to the federal courts unless he was a corporation lawyer or was known for opinions which made him acceptable to these interests.[46]

[44] *American Year Book, 1915,* p. 75.
[45] Wilson, *The New Freedom,* p. 189.
[46] R. W. Trine, *In the Fire of the Heart,* p. 106.

For this reason free political thought and pure political principle are driven out of the machinery of political life, commercialized as it is. Matter rules and the spirit is doomed to superficiality.

The old picture of society as a human organism, which was expressed in a number of mythical conceptions as the foundation of ancient and medieval political theory and is still hidden underneath the most recent sociological thought, has become a more and more striking comparison ever since production and trade have made the functioning of society resemble a system of nerves and nutrition. But to the very extent that society becomes more human in form, the function of man within society has itself become degraded to that of a tool.

And yet he feels himself to be freer than ever before, a greater master over matter. Is this self-deception? Or has the process of mechanization not attacked the pure life of the mind as yet? It is not easy to expect it, for intellectual life is dependent on the forms of business life in so many respects. In modern, highly developed society, how could intellectual life escape the degradation, the leveling, and the mechanization which are indissolubly bound up with the commercialization of society?

The production of food for the mind is just as subject to industrialized concentration and mechanization as the production of the material necessities of life. A traveler from the Old World was astounded that he found so little choice in models of hats and collars[47] in America. Each season one model was in fashion, for industry made everything on a large scale. A hat or a collar is not food for the mind, but nonetheless the choice

[47] The reader should remember here that in the Twenties the attached collar had not yet come into general use, and men bought separate collars attached to their shirts by collar-buttons.—H.H.R.

of one is a cultural activity of a modest kind. When we read "furniture" instead of "hat" or "collar," it becomes obvious at once that mass production and machine industry mean cultural impoverishment. The stamp of distinction cannot be attained through mediocrity.

The intellectual food of modern times is first and foremost the newspaper. Its remarkable many-sidedness, combined with its obligation to be ready and up to date every day, already introduces an inevitable element of routine and mechanical work into the collecting, selecting, and writing of the news: The absolute necessity that the newspaper come out again after a few hours means that the innumerable minds in its employ are compelled to produce without any delay. If this by itself brings about a certain degree of mechanization, the way in which the newspaper achieves its results adds to it. The repetitiveness of its daily appearance and the shallowness of attention that it demands operate upon the mind like a mechanical stimulus which is received unresistingly. The more widely it is distributed and the more comprehensive its content, the more the mechanical way it is read contributes to a homogenizing and leveling effect. The poor, hurried reader, without much time or mental preparation, can no longer protect himself against his newspaper; it overwhelms him with a cut-and-dried wisdom about life and relieves him of the duty to think for himself. The newspaper constantly erodes individual opinions in the very broadest circles; it makes minds as interchangeable, we might say, as the articles produced by big factories.

In order to achieve an impact despite the weak attentiveness of its readers, the newspaper must resort to exaggeration. This appears first of all in the section which wholly serves the business interest—the advertisements. But the newspaper itself is also a business and therefore has to engage in vigorous competition. Its news dispatches must also compel attention with noisy or catchy headlines. The American newspaper has already wholly adopted advertising style for its real content. Where a Dutch newspaper would still use the heading "Sarah Bernhardt Operated Upon," in America each phase of such an event is announced by snappy headlines: "Dr. So and So wields the knife with five physicians in attendance!"

But advertising style, which is used as a way of overcoming low attention, is a remedy that is worse than the illness. Like every other stimulus it becomes dulled with use. It assumes superficial reading and that what is read is only half-believed. For what would ever happen to the poor citizen who took every advertisement and every political article *au sérieux?*[48] But familiarity with this style in turn results in the reader's wholly disbelieving or only half believing what he reads, for he knows that it is advertising. The mind becomes accustomed to taking its food carelessly: it chews it badly and therefore digests it badly. A dangerous volatilization of intelligence and superficiality of intellectual life is the result.

Furthermore, intellectual nourishment has become a by-product. Newspapers and magazines live from advertising. The news content has to be catchy only because it makes the newspaper a desirable place to advertise. Intellectual content has ceased to have any commercial value.

Just as the newspaper devours literature, so the cinema devours both art and literature. It was estimated as early as 1915 that the film industry had become the fourth largest industry in America.[49] It would be hard to overlook its importance as a cultural factor. The film shifts to the surface of the mind the feeling that one knows or experiences something. It gives rise to the delusion that one can learn something merely

---

[48] French for "seriously."—H.H.R.
[49] *American Year Book, 1915,* p. 745.

by mechanical visual observation. We are all familiar with the assurances that so much technical learning can be gotten from films by observing industrial enterprises and processes. As if watching only a few manual grips and operations, without thinking about the process of which they represent a visible part, has any value as knowledge.

The film is an extraordinarily democratic component of culture. Even more than the newspaper, it gives rise to a solidarity of emotions and interests in the broadest circles. In America where the egalitarianism of intellectual life already exercises such a strong leveling effect, this solidarity is doubly effective. The newspaper is rich and many-sided and it can include a pearl of world literature every day in its columns.[50] But the film remains impoverished and monotonous despite all the inventiveness, imagination, and heavy expenditures invested in its production. Its technique keeps it bound to a very limited stock of elements of form and requires that these be reproduced in a conventional style without richness. The film provides the people with a standard of beauty in the romantic forms they covet. It creates a necessarily limited and crude code of expression and imagination, and it does so in accordance with a purely commercial attitude. It develops from the already existing low taste a catchy, crudely romantic, sensational, gruesome, and low-comedy taste, and then mechanically delivers such as excess of satisfactions in this taste that it raises it to a cultural norm of the very greatest weight, which is enforced every day in a thousand places. When we accept the art of the cinema as the daily spiritual bread of our time, we acknowledge the enslavement by the machine into which we have fallen.

[50] Huizinga here seems to be drawing conclusions about the American press from the European, where the *feuilleton*, either a short story or an instalment of a novel, has a long and honorable journalistic tradition.—H.H.R.

Still another form of mechanization is the penetration of the methods of the business world into intellectual activity. Systems of commercial classification are praised as useful for scholarly purposes. What is sought is a sort of Taylorism of the mind. But every thinker who accepts the compulsions of his pigeonholes abandons an element of intellectual freedom. It is as if he chooses for his instrument not the violin with its unlimited possibilities of tone production, but the piano, with its limited machinery. A mechanical element enters the arrangement of his ideas; no doubt it permits him to comprehend many more things and to produce more quickly, but it threatens to make his personal intuition superficial.

A clear example of this limiting effect is provided by the so-called decimal system of scholarly, and in particular of bibliographical, classification, invented in 1873 by the American librarian Melvil Dewey. It divides the whole of knowledge into ten categories. The encyclopedia, etc., has number 0, philosophy 1, theology and religion 2, social and political science 3, philology 4, natural science 5, technology 6, art 7, literature 8, history and geography 9. In reality these are decimals: 0.0, 0.1 and so forth, but for convenience' sake the 0 may be left out. Thus we have 0.5 natural science, 0.51 mathematics, 0.52 astronomy, 0.53 physics, 0.54 chemistry, etc. The divisions of physics are optics 0.535, physiological optics 0.5357, the function of the retina in vision 0.53575, etc., *ad infinitum*.[51]

The system has great advantages for the purposes of libraries, to be sure, although it requires an extraordinarily discriminating judgment to determine the categories. Everywhere it requires decisions with rigorous consequences. In the example given above, mathematics is proclaimed to be a natural science. An impure definition of the category creates incal-

[51] Melvil Dewey, *Decimal Classification and Relative Index*, 7th ed., 1911.

culable harm and there is no end to its continuing spread, while at the same time living connections must be broken for the sake of the classification. As soon as an individual scholar applies the system to his own literary materials, he is threatened by enslavement. In defining the categories he performs massive and unproductive intellectual work; he puts his mind in the grip of the decimal system and faces the inevitable consequences of the pressure of the system. These perils of intellectual mechanization are hidden in every overly ingenious and technically perfect system of classification.

One of the preeminent elements of modern civilization is sport, in which intellectual and physical culture meet. In it too mechanization seems to attain the opposite of its purposes. Gregarious modern man tries to save his individualism, as it were, in sport. But sport is not just the strictly physical development of skills and strength; it is also the giving of form, the stylizing of the very feeling of youth, strength, and life, a spiritual value of enormous weight. Play is culture. Play can pass over into art and rite, as in the dance and in sacred stage presentations. Play is rhythm and struggle. The competitive ideal itself is a cultural value of high importance. Play also means organization. But now, as a result of the modern capacity for very far-reaching organization and the possibilities created by modern transportation, an element of mechanization enters sport. In the immense sport organizations like those of football[52] and baseball,[53] we see free youthful forces

[52] *Voetbal*, Huizinga's word, is the Dutch for what Americans call "soccer" and Europeans, including the English, "football." It is not clear whether he means the European national soccer leagues and the international competitions of soccer, or the intercollegiate football leagues of the United States (professional football had not yet attained importance when Huizinga wrote).—H.H.R.

[53] Huizinga uses the English word "baseball," not the Dutch *honkbal*, as the game, which is played now in the Netherlands, is called there. —H.H.R.

and courage reduced to normality and uniformity in the service
of the machinery of rules of play and the competitive system.
If we compare the tense athlete in his competitive harness with
the pioneer hunter and the Indian fighter, then the loss of true
free personality is obvious.

Personality is the cry. But what is heralded as the cultivation of free individuality sometimes displays a strongly mechanistic element on closer examination. Energy courses, with
their techniques for developing systematically force of will,
memory, intellectual stamina, and working ability, have come
to us from America. Apparently at the service of a conscious
individualism, a concept of personality, they actually reek instead of the application of mechanical ideas—training and
fixing spiritual activities.

America is also the country where eugenics is taken
seriously. The states continue to pass laws for the sterilization
not only of criminals but also of the feeble-minded. The
sciences of criminology and mental health are not always
convinced of the social efficacy of these methods, but the step
has been taken. Is it the first step in the great road to the
future, toward actual control of who is born, for the welfare
of society? Then it will indeed mean the beginning of another
far-reaching stage in the mechanization of civilization. The
country, says the American eugenist Davenport, has the right
to dispose of the germ plasm of its citizens. To regulate human
reproduction in a judicious way is quite an old idea. It was
adopted by Utopians like More and Campenella. One of the
many communistic societies established in America, the Per-
fectionists of Oneida in New York State, which existed from
1848 to 1881, added to multiple marriage the practice of
"stirpiculture or scientific propagation."[54] It was a result of the

---

[54] F. A. Bushee, "Communistic Societies in the U.S.," *Political Science Quarterly*, XX (1905), p. 646.

anti-individualism which inspired the society, and the most extreme application of the organizational principle. If the regulation of marriages by government on the basis of the studies of heredity should become general practice, then the mechanization of human society would be as complete as if the homunculus had been discovered.

Man, as he searches for the strength and the means to live a free life, at the same time subjugates himself. In every act of mechanization of the life of the community, a quantity of human freedom is tied fast. As soon as the bow is invented, it is not only the man who uses the bow but also the bow which compels the man to use it. As soon as a governmental function is established, it produces a surplus of effect beyond the immediate goal which it must serve. Every tool and every organization is burdened with its own activity, which compels man to work with the tool and make the organization operate. Without this mechanization, there is no civilization, for the indispensable precondition for man's becoming conscious of his human value is that he organize his strength. The process of improving civilization is indivisible from the process of mechanization. Man hopes to live in new and greater freedom as a result of each improvement of his tools and every energy-saving combination of the will and the knowledge of the many. But each better tool and each improved organization binds him again to the blind force which he has invested in them at a usurious rate of interest. Every school, every doctrine, every form of government and business, puts man into a harness and limits his activities.

There are periods when the power to bind which is inherent in the machinery of civilization seems to be greater than the power to liberate. For example, in the late Middle Ages life was in danger of petrifying in the perfection and completeness of the all-inclusive structure of the Church. Or the age in which we are living, when mankind seems to be becoming the helpless slave of its own perfected means of material and social technology.

No image permeates considerations upon the history of civilization more frequently than that of Goethe's sorcerer's apprentice. The much cited phrase, *"die ich rief, die Geister, werd ich nun nicht los,"*[55] remains the text par excellence of all great movements of civilization. And the picture of the dumb broom that always comes back with the water, the water, is more striking today than ever. Poor mankind remains still the sorcerer's apprentice, and it is rare in history that the Master comes home.

---

[55] "I cannot get rid of the spirits which I have called up."—H.H.R.

Chapter III

THE SENSE OF THE STATE
AND THE BUSINESS SPIRIT

The American uses the name of his country in the singular: "The United States is fabulously rich." If we go back some sixty years, we are likely to find the verb still in the plural, at least in the language of diplomacy. Implied in the shift of language feeling is one of the most important developments of American history. The country has become a unity for the American; he no longer feels the United States to be a plural; in his ideas the Union has risen above the states.

In this change thought has only followed reality. In fact, since the middle of the nineteenth century, the states have slipped all the way into the background in American history.

Yet those who knew America best had made very different predictions. Tocqueville wrote, on the basis of what he had observed in the years from 1831 to 1833: "I am strangely mistaken if the Federal government of the United States is not constantly losing strength, retiring gradually from public affairs, and narrowing its circle of action. . . . Unless some extraordinary event occurs, the government of the Union will grow weaker and weaker every day." "The Union is an accident, which will last only as long as circumstances favor it."[1] A quarter of a century later Tocqueville's prediction seemed about to come true: the Union was breaking up. When the Civil War began, most observers in Europe, including such men as Gladstone, were probably of the opinion that the Union was done for. But the extraordinary circumstances which Tocqueville considered necessary for its preservation, but which he scarcely expected and he could not foresee, actually occurred.

During the Civil War, economic relations, which had already undergone substantial change since Tocqueville wrote, began to exert their influence in favor of the preservation of the Union. In the period after the Civil War the mighty expansion of the economy worked with ever greater force toward strengthening the federal authority against that of the states, and toward commensurate growth of national consciousness and respect for government as such.

From the beginning, business in America has exerted pressure upon government. For a long time, government remained a secondary factor in American society. Not only the Union but all government as such enjoyed little authority. In America there was found no trace of the reverence for the state as the body which took care of things in every kind of way, and which was given childish love and obedience, such as existed in most European countries. The government was either feared as a burdensome supervisor over private economic interests, or it was used in order to serve and promote those interests. The idea that dominated conceptions of government power remained Jefferson's view that the rights of the whole could not be more than the sum of the rights of the individuals.

[1] Tocqueville, *De la démocratie en Amérique,* vol. II, pp. 379–399. [*Democracy in America,* vol. I, pp. 432–433.]

The weakness of political feeling is explained by the whole history of the formation of the United States. While colonies of England, they were located far from the heart of the English state; they did not undergo the influence of its luster and its glory, nor did they have daily experience of its protection. For the most part the government in England left them alone. When the governors acted on behalf of the king, it was generally by prohibitions and compulsions which thwarted and disturbed the free development of economic interests. The colonists, already often dissatisfied with the mother country which restricted their religious freedom, learned to know government much more as undesirable interference than as needed protection.

The colonists' revolt against England was intended much more to shake off the authority of government than to establish a government of their own, but this is what happened because the war required concentration of all forces and unity of leadership. The form of government chosen, however, was that which bound them as little as was conceivable—a loose alliance of thirteen independent states. The terms of this alliance recall those of the Union of Utrecht[2]: the Confederation of 1776 was intended to be "a firm league of friendship for their common defence, the security of their liberties, and their mutual and general welfare." Each state was to be sovereign and each had a vote in Congress; such important powers as the right to declare war and peace, the mint, post office, and general finances were given to Congress, but not the power to compel the members of the alliance to act. Congress had no

[2] The Union of Utrecht of 1579 was more or less the constitution of the Dutch Republic; it was more an alliance for continuing the rebellion against Spain than a formal fundamental law defining the institutions of government. It attempted to combine central government for waging the war with total internal sovereignty for the provinces.—H.H.R.

right to raise taxes, it could only request contributions. A majority of nine states was required for important decisions.

Because of the fear of a strong central government, the Union was granted pretty much those rights to which it had been desired to limit the English crown. Such narrow powers as were granted Congress in 1776 withered away completely afterward; no state was willing to take a subordinate position; each looked out for itself and was jealous of the others. In part it was the war itself which drove them to act individually: In the face of dispersed attacks over an immense territory, the states could not entrust their own defense to a sluggish and powerless body like Congress; each had to act on its own behalf to keep from going under. When independence was attained in 1783, the young Union had apparently performed its task.

It was the unsatisfactory economic situation which at once compelled the country to strengthen its central authority. After the peace of 1783 the new states found themselves in an almost hopeless position. They had large debts and their paper currency was both varied and worthless. The Articles of Confederation were violated without compunction, as when New York and Rhode Island taxed the products of their neighbors. Means of redress were frustrated by the recalcitrance of the states and the requirement for unanimity. In 1784 a committee proposed as the conclusion of an unfavorable report on trade that the regulation of commerce be entrusted to Congress for a period of fifteen years. Once again the necessary unanimity was not obtained. Two years later, Virginia called all the states to a meeting to discuss a uniform regulation of commerce. It was a failure; only five states sent representatives. Still the Trade Convention at Annapolis in 1786 resulted in a call by Congress the next year for a Convention with a much broader purpose, a review of the Articles of Confederation as a whole. It was at this Convention that the Constitution came into existence. It was conceived and achieved primarily by the great commercial interests and the spirit of unfettered capitalist expansion.[3] Government now became a useful instrument.

It was a useful instrument, but as yet that was all. The Constitution was an attempt to apply strictly the political theory of the eighteenth century. The separation of the three powers was considered to be the source of all political wisdom. The executive, legislative, and judicial powers would work independently alongside each other; whenever one threatened to become dominant over the others, it would be held in check by an artificial system of mutual "checks and balances." None of the three powers was conceived as a driving force. Least of all was the executive branch intended to be a force of leadership; rather it was to be the servant of the legislative power. The whole political system was intended to operate negatively much more than positively. Why would a strong and active government be needed except in times of danger from abroad? It was believed that the foundation upon which the welfare of the community rested safely had been established for good. As long as government by the people and equality under the law were assured, nothing would be lacking for sound political and social conditions. A strong government could only be aristocratic, and hence it would be more of a threat to freedom and equality than their protector. Jefferson's observation seemed to hold true: "It is error alone which needs the support of government. Truth can stand by itself."

The slight value that an American was ready to accord government still applied not to the Union as such but to the individual state of his birth. He felt himself to be primarily a Virginian or a citizen of Massachusetts. It was the states which continued to provide for almost all public interests. The

[3] See above, pp. 20–21.

administration of justice and legislation, education, and taxation were almost wholly the business of state governments. In their ordinary experience, men had almost no contact with the national government. To be sure, ever since the War of Independence, there had been strong national pride in America's freedom, prosperity, rich promise and energy, but it was a sentiment kept for holidays or display toward foreign countries; it had little effect on the attitude toward government in daily life. And it was more pride than love. One loved Virginia, "the Old Dominion," or the soil that had been made sacred by the Pilgrim Fathers and their trials.

All in all, it was a love of a very familiar kind. Government was called upon when it was needed and bent to one's will if possible. First and last, business continued to dominate the activity of government. The economic interests, large and small, those which encompass the world and those which are just local, have permeated the organism of American government in all its fibers.

It is most remarkable how, on the one side, one of the most important political principles of the United States was born out of an agreement of covetous speculators, while, on the other side, legislation intended to be purely political in character was transformed by the force of circumstances into protective measures for the free reign of capital. Even before the Constitution was adopted, the Ordinance of the North West Territory was passed in 1787. It established the great political principle providing for future formation of new states and their admission into the Union, prepared by wise and effective methods. Nonetheless the origin of the Ordinance lay wholly in the land speculations of the Ohio Company and its intrigues with the financiers of New York.[4]

The Constitution provided that no governmental agency

[4] Max Ferrand, *The Development of the United States from Colonies to a World Power* (Boston and New York, 1918), p. 63.

could take possession of any private property without a special judicial enquiry to determine that such a measure was needed for the public good. Another provision forbade states from making any law limiting the binding force of contracts. These articles were conceived purely in political terms, in the spirit of the eighteenth century, as precautionary measures against governmental tyranny or arbitrariness. It could not be foreseen that they would become two sheet-anchors for the railroad companies and the industrial trusts, safeguarding their freedom of action. A court decision of 1816 on behalf of a college in New Hampshire[5] whose charter was threatened by that state became the basis for the inviolability which industrial corporations could later enjoy for their own charters. The fourteenth amendment to the Constitution was adopted in 1868, after the Civil War, with the aim of protecting the Negro by forbidding all legislation giving special treatment to different persons; it was later invoked, and successfully, by the industrial corporations, to protect themselves against being taxed on a different base than individual citizens.[6] It seems, doesn't it, that the god Plutus has always watched over America and the wisdom of its legislators with a smile?

For much of the nineteenth century, economic processes seemed to have destructive effect on government. Business literally devoured government, which led a weak, sickly, and often ignoble existence. The degradation of the American political organism caused by intrusion of economic interests can be pointed out in many details. These interests strengthened in many respects the negative tendency already characteristic of government, as the Constitution had originally intended.

One of the fundamental shortcomings of public adminis-

[5] Dartmouth College. It is curious to note that Huizinga calls it a *academisch college*, since in Dutch *college* means either a "board," a "university lecture," or a "university course."–H.H.R.

[6] A. T. Hadley, *Undercurrents in American Politics,* pp. 41, 55.

tration in America has always been the lack of continuity and cooperation of the various organs of government. As a result of rotation in office, that is, replacement of officeholders after a short time, which was held to be one of the sacred methods of democracy, there was no bureaucracy, and hence many evils were avoided, but at the same time there was no permanent and binding force in the public administration. Nor is there an administrative hierarchy; there is coordination among government bodies but no subordination especially in the administration of the states. "The government of the States," says Boutmy, "having no bureaucracy and no administrative hierarchy, is like a mute and one-armed master who cannot be of help to himself, to whom two clumsy and self-conscious assistants give help at their own convenience. One of them is the legislature, which gives all commands in broad terms but does not watch over their execution; the other is the judiciary, which perpetually exhausts its forces on individual cases."[7]

A state governor is not represented in local administration by any official dependent on him. It is not the administration which holds officials to their duty; the injured party must bring charges against them. Each branch of government forms a small specialized and autonomous organization. The whole system of administration is an extension of the principle of local self-government. In city governments there also exists the pernicious system of "boards" which have no relationship to each other.

As a result, private business interests have been able to intrude unhindered into city and state government. The entire system of private understandings, mutual favoritism, concession and job hunting, and intrigues, can arise because government, having been deliberately created with weak powers, can offer no resistance to the penetration of private interests. Once

[7] Boutmy, *Eléments*, p. 216.

people become accustomed to seeing the public authority working frequently in the interest of individuals, the resistance to energetic activity of government can only increase. Out of fear of abuse of power, the power of government has been shackled wherever possible. In the state constitutions, which are very long and frequently amended, the most specialized matters are introduced in an effort to remove them from the influence of the state legislatures, in which the professional politicians have become the masters. The people long ago lost their respect for the representative bodies in the states.

Because of the limited extent of government activity, private organizations with public functions have been developed. The government gave little police protection, so that citizens got into the habit of protecting themselves. Private bodyguards, under European notions of public law, belong to the Middle Ages; in America, they have developed as a form of modern business. The Scotsman Allan Pinkerton established his National Detective Agency in 1852 in Chicago. He did great things, thwarting an attack on Lincoln, catching big railway thieves, and organizing an espionage service in the South during the Civil War; later, he successfully defeated the dangerous Irish brotherhood of the Molly Maguires in the coal mines of Pennsylvania.[8] In later years some of these detective services developed into strikebreaking agencies. They called themselves "labor adjusters," but "Pinkerton's men" was the workers' name for them. According to American law they could be clothed with police authority as deputy sheriffs and thereby obtain a dangerously irresponsible power. One detective company declared that it could provide 10,000 armed men in three days. In such cases business shoved government right out of the way.

Yet the direct influence of economic interests on the

[8] See above, pp. 48–49.

American political system has not been only destructive. At
the same time that it enervated government, it prepared the way
for its later strengthening by developing organs which now
more than ever seemed called upon to play the leading role in
public administration.

The national government took the lead from the states as
the direct result of the vigorous economic development after
the Civil War. The federal system had been planned for a situation in which each business looked after itself and as a rule
could not extend its sphere beyond the boundaries of the state
in which it was established. At first each state had, to some
extent, formed a closed economic circle and it was a rare event
for the national government to be directly involved in problems created by economic life.

But the federal system had become inappropriate to
modern conditions of production and exchange; from an industrial and economic point of view, the United States had
become a single country and none of the individual states
possessed natural independence any more. The economic life
of the country can be arranged in four or five large geographic
divisions (sections, as the American says): the old East with
its industry and banks; the South, which is no longer exclusively
a cotton-growing region as it used to be but has a promising
agriculture and mining industry; the grain-growing district of
the North Central region, or "Middle West"; and finally the
West, with its cattle raising, lumbering, mining, fruit orchards,
and other branches of production. All these great regions are
interdependent. Massachusetts manufactures almost half of all
shoes, Pennsylvania more than half of all iron products. The
capital of the Eastern cities is invested in the mines of the West
and the young industries of the South, and everywhere in railways and mortgages. The railroad systems cross right over
state boundaries.

In such conditions, mutual competition among the states became an obsolete absurdity. Where it continued to exist, it had only an obstructive effect. Thus, for example, the laws on insurance are still a chaos as a result of the early independence of the states in the legislative field. Corporation law too is not yet uniform. Some states advertise easy conditions for establishing business companies. If one state enacts a sound corporation law, the shaky companies move to another state. Businesses which are strong and broad in their interests demand that the national government be given authority in all these matters, or at least that state legislation be made uniform. A very important movement for uniform state laws has been repeatedly successful since 1878, overwhelmingly in the field of commercial law.[9]

Here we have a striking example of the beneficial side of the federal principle. The American, who is accustomed to be left alone in his business, would find it hard to accept direct intervention of the national government. Furthermore, all sections of the country are not ripe for the same laws at the same time. Uniform state law meets the needs of this situation perfectly. A state which is not ready to join can wait, and when it changes its mind it will be received joyfully.

Yet there are areas in economic life where only the central government can maintain law and order, or create the conditions for unhampered development. The national government has had to conquer its authority foot by foot over the recalcitrant forces in these fields. Its original basis was the clause of the Constitution[10] granting to Congress the right to regulate commerce with foreign countries, among the states, and with the Indian tribes. But it was the arbitrary power of the railroad

[9] See *American Year Book, 1917*, p. 248; *1918*, p. 286; *1919*, p. 273; McLaughlin and Hart, *Cyclopedia of American Government*, 1914, *s.v.* Uniform State Legislation.

[10] Art. 1, section 8, par. 3.

companies which compelled the national government to become directly involved in economic life by the establishment of the Interstate Commerce Commission [the I.C.C.] in 1887. In a long struggle against the railway magnates and the conservatism of the courts, the I.C.C. was able to increase its power until it was an organ of permanent supervision over everything involving transportation, including the telegraph and the telephone from 1910. The fixing of freight tariffs, an extensive right of investigation, and the establishment of uniform accounting rules, are the principal methods by which the I.C.C. works. Experience with the Interstate Commerce Commission encouraged the establishment of the Federal Trade Commission with similar powers but a much broader range of activity in 1914.

While, on the one hand, the national government thus creates organisms to keep the arbitrary and private concentration of economic power within limits, on the other it promotes its concentration by direct government action or under government supervision. The Federal Reserve System of 1913 gave to the United States a grandly conceived central banking organization, which avoided the excessive concentration that brought hatred upon the National Bank in the first days of the Union and finally caused its downfall. The Federal Farm Loan System, organized on the same principles, followed in 1916.

Where a federal law on child labor had still been generally considered an absurdity 15 years before, such a law was adopted in 1916. Nonetheless the conservative principle of the independent authority of the states was victorious for a while, for the Supreme Court declared the Federal Child Labor Act unconstitutional in 1918.[11] Six years later the Congress sent to the states for their approval an amendment to the Constitution providing for federal regulation of child labor. Only

[11] *American Year Book, 1918,* pp. 434, 457, 465.

four States approved it, four took no action, and 40 rejected it.

In 1918, when the newspapers brought almost daily the most astonishing proof that the war legislation had made the national government supreme over economic production, when one enterprise after another—railways, telegraph and telephone, mining, iron production, food supply—had been put under government administration, it was quite possible to think that the government was victorious over business once and for all. But to do so would have been to underestimate the spirit of American business. In general, government operation was very unpopular. The telegraph and the telephone systems were returned precipitously to private ownership in 1919. Among the various plans proposed in that year for settlement of the railroad question, only one sought to make them government property, the so-called Plumb Plan from the radical side; all the others wanted supervision and uniformity, to be sure, but not direct government operation.[12]

The obliteration or at least blurring of state boundaries which is occurring in the economic field is also being experienced in the strictly political area. Party cohesion as something shared nationally was only felt after the railway made it possible to travel throughout the country effectively on behalf of a political cause. Then, for the first time, the unity of the country began to take precedence over the multiplicity of states in the minds of the people. And above all it was as always the new West where a strong upsurge of national feeling was experienced. The residents of the Atlantic states remained strongly attached to their old states, where they had been born and brought up, except if they moved away. But those who went West and mingled with newcomers from other regions lost this more narrow patriotism. So long as the region where

[12] *American Year Book, 1918,* pp. 6 ff., 365, 566; *1919,* pp. 31–43.

they settled had not yet been admitted to the Union as a state
but continued to be administered from Washington as a territory, they had much more direct contact than the inhabitants
of the older states with the national administration. When in
time the territories were recognized as states, the new units,
because of the very rapidity of their population growth,
never obtained that special individual character resting on old
tradition which in the East distinguished Georgia from the
Carolinas and Rhode Island from Connecticut.

From the beginning the national government had one
very strong positive role—it had the task of conducting relations with foreign countries. When the Constitution was made,
it was imagined that foreign relations would be mainly of a
negative kind and that America would be able to devote itself
undisturbed to its own development. Events took a different
course, however. The period of the French Revolution and
Napoleon repeatedly compelled the American Republic to
choose a position in very thorny foreign questions. From that
time, therefore, the executive became much more important
than the drafters of the Constitution had desired. After 1815
a long period at last seemed to have come in which the United
States did not need to involve itself with the Old World any
more than it wished to, all the more because it had lost its
importance as a maritime power during the Napoleonic period.
The Monroe Doctrine of 1823 put the seal upon this negative,
defensive attitude: America wanted to be left alone.

For a long time interest in questions of the expansion of
power remained small. There were indeed the old yearnings
for Canada and the West Indies, but these remained utopian.
The war with Mexico in 1846 and 1847, which added Upper
Mexico and Upper California to the Union and confirmed the
annexation of Texas, was of significance nationally because of
its connection with the slavery question. The invaluable pur-

chase of Alaska in 1867 was not only so unpopular in the United States that the treaty with Russia had to be pushed hastily through ratification, but there were even those who wondered whether the principal advocate of the plan, Secretary of State Seward, did not have in mind all sorts of political considerations much more than a grasp of the future importance of the new territory.[13]

Meanwhile the enormous economic expansion was under way which soon raised the United States to an exporting country. It began to produce for the world. Thereafter the large economic interests needed an active world policy; American imperialism was in the cards, and the importance of the national government, which had to conduct this policy, was therefore strengthened to the utmost.

A coaling station was established on the Samoan Islands in 1878 and on Hawaii in 1884. Samoa was divided between Germany and America in 1899, while Hawaii was annexed in 1898, the same year in which the United States garnered the Philippines, Puerto Rico, and Guam as the spoils of the war with Spain. In 1900 America took part in the expedition in China,[14] and in 1905 it mediated peace between Japan and Russia. The world policy of the United States maintained a certain aspect of idealism because it continued zealously to emphasize the calling of the great commonwealth to promote peace, law, and prosperity. Cuba was allowed to remain politically independent, whatever such independence might mean in practice. The Democrats continued to press for the abandonment of the Philippines, but when they came to power they found themselves unable to carry out this demand. Indissolubly linked to American imperialism is the promotion of arbitration.

[13] F. A. Golder, "The Purchase of Alaska," *American Historical Review*, XXV (1920), p. 424.
[14] The punitive expedition against the Boxer rebels.—H.H.R.

Pan-Americanism, with its great promise for the future, is as much a part of this imperialism as the digging of the canal through the Isthmus of Panama, one of the old ideals of the United States which has now been accomplished. All this world policy, accepted because it was forced on the nation and was crowned with such great success, has caused a steady increase in the unity of the country and in the strength and prestige of the national government. But this whole process of political growth has been accomplished under the direct influence of economic forces.

The economic factor in America's politics means on the one hand the definition of the direction and the goals of policy by business interests, and on the other hand, the intrusion of business habits, the business spirit, and business forms into the operation of the political apparatus.

At the time when the constitutions of the states and the Union were adopted, a time of still unshaken rationalism, the operation of the powers and institutions of government was conceived as a simple play of forces, easy to calculate according to the laws of nature and human reason. But of the laws of nature only those were known which governed the external relationship of bodies; nothing whatever was known about social psychology. The political conceptions of the eighteenth century stood wholly and completely under the influence of Newtonian theory. Gravity was the only image in which it was possible to think of political activity. If one designed and constructed a government properly, then it would necessarily follow that all things would come out right.

Yet John Adams and Samuel Chase knew better: "We shall be governed by our interests, and ought to be."[15] And interests knew no Newtonian theory but brought into the operations of

[15] See above, pp. 10–11.

the governmental machinery the forces of human society, sociological forces. It was precisely in a society like the American, in which there was so much energy and it in turn enjoyed so much freedom, that the practical leadership of the state from the beginning put these questions before all others: Who can do the job? How can it be managed? It was a question of immensely greater importance than whether or not the laws were well-constructed and balanced in theory. In the end, it came down to a man who knew what to do and was able to do it. Because economic interests now stood directly behind all political questions, persons who served these interests came to the fore in all activities, which was just the opposite of what the drafters of the Constitution had intended. The American felt instinctively that the drafting of laws must not be entrusted to a few government departments with much too widely defined fields but to closed committees of specialists, the committees of Congress. This principle may be considered an expression of the practical business idea of entrusting all matters to persons who know what they are doing. In 1919 the Senate had 74 committees and the House of Representatives 62. The task of these committees varied from the removal of waste paper in government offices to problems of incalculable importance such as irrigation and the reclamation of the arid regions.

As a result of this tendency to concentrate everything in the hands of a man who could do the job, there also developed a number of less desirable forms of power. The Speaker of the House of Representatives became a figure who more resembled the manager of a business firm than the president of a chamber of deputies. As chairman of the rules committee, the majority of whose members he himself chose, he was able to designate the other committees and their chairmen, and thereby to concentrate all legislative work in the hands of a few men. He was

able to limit debate, to deny the right to speak, and to determine the agenda. No member could get the floor to present a
bill unless he had first "seen" the Speaker. The older members
had a monopoly of the important committees. This principle
has great advantages; work is done in a practical way and by
men who know what they are about. But it was democracy
which suffered by its application. In 1910 an end was made to
the alarming power of the Speaker, at the time the Republican
Joseph G. Cannon, but "Cannonism" remained a danger that
would come up for discussion again.

If therefore it was people who came to the fore in governmental bodies, this was even more the case in party organizations. All party life, although apparently constructed upon
the very purest of democratic foundations, was subject to
personalist influences, even where "bossdom" had not triumphed in its most brutal form. It was personal work from
the bottom up which kept the party on the go; the wardheeler[16] was the low man on the party ladder, but he could go
far. The national party committee, which has the supreme
leadership for four years,[17] was in name chosen by the national
party convention, but in fact it was designated by the leader,
who often named himself to the first place. In the same way,
the chairman of the state party committee is the man who gets
the job done while the committee itself seldom meets.

Thus American politics has always been especially effective in bringing to the front the man of daring, insight, strong
nerves, and broad conscience, but who is in fact not primarily
a servant of the public interest but rather of the party interests
and behind them of business interests. An outstanding rep-

[16] Huizinga uses the Dutch word *kroegbaas*, literally "tavern-
keeper," but clearly the American wardheeler, who has no real equivalent in European party politics, is intended.—H.H.R.

[17] Between presidential nominating conventions.—H.H.R.

resentative of this sort of powerful personality was Thaddeus Stevens, the leader of the Republicans in the House of Representatives in the years during and after the Civil War. Personally respectable,[18] he put all his energy into the service of the hardest and most unscrupulous party policy: to continue to rule and exploit the defeated South as a conquered province. In this case, however, his motive was more than personal interest, however narrow and unjust it was as a political tendency. The system continues to operate as it must: Courage and combativeness, strong will and skill do not usually benefit the public welfare.

It is one of the most important turns in recent American history that this principle of private arrangements and personal ascendancy which so long worked to the country's harm now seems to be working to its good. The American was never blind to the great failings of his government; public opinion has always raised its voice in loud, sometimes even exaggerated, accusations against it. "We have come," said Wilson in 1917, "to be one of the worst ruled, one of the most completely controlled and dominated governments in the civilized world—no longer a government of free opinion, no longer a government by conviction and the vote of the majority, but a government by the opinion and the duress of small groups of dominant men."[19] For twenty or thirty years now there has been wide recognition throughout the nation that an immense task of purification and reform confronts it.

It would be expected, then, that these endeavors have resulted in removal of the deep-rooted system of personal ascendancy and machinations. But the opposite is the case. American government must pass through sickness on its way to health. It is public opinion itself which in all things calls

[18] *American Historical Review*, XII (1906), p. 567.
[19] Wilson, *The New Freedom*, p. 195.

precisely for a man with the ability and the boldness to undertake the job and to get it done; it wants to give its confidence
to him, so that it will no longer be the interest of party or
business which will be served but the welfare of the community. Being a businessman himself, the American sees that
the machinery of government is much too complicated to
operate if left to itself. He wants a businesslike management,
a businesslike directness of method. "Our national government," says James T. Young, "is passing through an era of
sweeping and important changes. The one central fact that
stands out clearly in all these changes is the concentration of
power." "The keynote of this newer American government is
Efficiency." "Executive leadership to-day is the outstanding
feature of our institutions."

To the extent that the state governments have more and
more forfeited their authority in the eyes of the people, the
need has arisen to entrust the leadership of a state to a strong
personality. The great business interests prefer to have a strong
man who will act against strikes; the people want a strong man
who will act against the big business interests. Thus the position
of state governor is invested with more power on every side.
Wilson won the confidence of the people, which brought him
the presidency in 1912, by undertaking a struggle against the
trusts as governor of New Jersey and by snatching the state
from the grip of the Pennsylvania Railroad Company and the
Public Service Corporation.

In city government there was already a tendency under
way to increase the power of the mayor at the cost of the
council, in which the people had lost confidence, when this
development was in turn overtaken by administrative forms of
much more radical novelty.

The immediate occasion for the rise of this remarkable
development was a natural catastrophe. In the year 1900 the

city of Galveston, Texas, was ravaged by a tidal wave, and as a result all the iniquities of an evil and corrupt city administration were destroyed and washed away. Under the necessity of rebuilding the city at once, the people understood that they could not do it by simply restoring the old organs of government with all their shortcomings. The field would be too open to favoritism, deceit, and plunder. On the initiative of several businessmen, a commission of five trusted men was chosen to whom the entire work of reconstruction was assigned. It fulfilled its task so well that it was reelected to govern the city, and in this way commission government came into being. Other cities immediately imitated what Galveston had begun; in a short time commission government became a tested remedy for the eradication of old sores in the city governments. The commission combined in itself the functions of mayor, cabinet, aldermen, council, and treasurers. It is obvious that efficiency, which is what the American wants more than anything else, was achieved.

But commission government was just the first step. The next was the election by the commission of a city manager to whom the entire direct administration of the city was entrusted, while the commission guided him and passed ordinances. He may be compared with the *podestà* in medieval Italian cities, the man called in from outside in order to hold power temporarily and govern a city confused by civil strife. Or should we instead call him by the humbler and less romantic name of hired agent or contractor? This would be more accurate; but in any case it is clear that with the introduction of these organs city government took on completely the form of a business. The commission seeks its manager by advertisement, and when he is not satisfactory, he is fired.[20] The business

[20] Huizinga uses the characteristically Dutch phrase, *aan de dijk zetten*, literally "to put up on the dike."—H.H.R.

principle has here wholly permeated government, which has passed through the phase of illness.

In practice, the system has until now brought to light only a single case of failure through fraud. But there has been no lack of attacks on it and some cities gave up commission government after a short trial. But in general it is a growing element in American government, especially the institution of the city manager. In the years from 1916 to 1920, the number of cities with commission government rose each year by 24, 21, 26, and 9 respectively, but against this must be balanced a number of abandonments. The number of cities with a city manager was one in 1908 and 357 in 1928; the largest increase occurred in the year 1921. The system has already also found acceptance in Canada and New Zealand. A county manager plan is in constant discussion in various states. Of 128 city managers about 1918, 48 percent were engineers and 45 percent businessmen; 77 percent had previously been in public service; 31 percent had university degrees or training in a "bureau of municipal research"; 35 percent were called from outside the city which gave them their assignment.[21]

But just what is a city manager but a purified boss? He is the boss cleansed of the blemishes of party and corruption, "made a public servant again,"[22] and now, by virtue of the public will, put in charge of public business as the man who can undertake the job and gets it done. There are real indications of a transition from the boss type to the city manager.

[21] *American Year Book, 1916*, p. 209; *1917*, p. 190; *1918*, p. 248; *1919*, p. 237.

[22] Huizinga here uses an invented word, *geré-publiciseerd*, which he calls "a very fine phrase." It means, of course, "made public again," but such a straight translation would utterly lose both meaning and force. In view of Huizinga's general distaste for such neologisms, it may be taken for granted that he is having fun with the kind of jargon used in political science.—H.H.R.

"Of late years," it was written as early as 1907, before the manager plan arose, "the boss has sometimes been a courageous man who by the force of his character, backed up by public confidence, accepts a popular mandate to carry on the government. The causes which produce the corrupt boss are turned into the support of an honest boss."[23]

As for the public services, for a long time they remained in a backward state because they had little importance and because private enterprise was predominant. But then a time came when a deliberate effort was made to reorganize them on a businesslike footing, to make them practical, rapid, and accurate. In a number of states, commissions for "State efficiency and economy" are at work in an attempt to improve the administrative methods by bringing them into line with the forms of business organization. Multifarious bureaus and agencies are merged; a practical system for estimating expenditures and investment of public funds, and responsibility according to the requirements of modern accountancy, are introduced. But such introduction of business methods is limited to the public administration as such. American society has no intention of bringing business enterprises of public utility, like transportation, electric lighting, and water supply, under public operation. What does exist everywhere is consolidation of public administration. In 1919 Philadelphia replaced its bicameral town council of 144 persons by a council of 21 members; Detroit put 9 paid councilmen in place of 42 aldermen. In Oregon the consolidation commission recommended placing a single superintendent over all branches of government. Idaho in 1919 organized the entire state government into nine departments. At the head of each is a single commissioner, appointed by the governor and dismissible at his pleasure,

[23] A. R. Hart, *National Ideals Historically Traced* (*The American Nation: A History*, vol. XXVI) (1907), p. 176.

with authority to issue regulations not in conflict with the law. "Idaho sets its house in order," it is triumphantly proclaimed. But how Jefferson would have shaken his head over such a displacement of democracy![24]

All these governmental reforms form a part of what in America is called the Short Ballot Movement. The principle long prevailed in America that it was a guarantee of truer democracy to fill as many offices as possible by election, with short terms and frequent elections to preserve rotation in office. Thus, for example, the state geologist and the state statistician were chosen by election in Indiana until 1919. As a result of this system, the ballot became so long and covered so many offices and persons that the voter was not in a position to cast his vote with personal knowledge of the issues. The management of elections therefore fell into the hands of the boss and the machine, and all the evils of the system of personal arrangements made their entry. There are two ways of removing them. One is to get rid of the boss and the machine and to enable the people to exercise their electoral powers independently of the party hacks. But this does not solve the difficulty that the people cannot pass judgment on so many offices and so many candidates. The advocates of the short ballot, who propose another way, admit that the democratic ideal of governing as much as possible by elections was itself an error. Let us limit election, they say, to those offices which are so important that they have general interest and that the ability of the candidates can be judged by the general public. Let the political role of the people be limited to election of a very small number of officials; give into their hands the complete power of administration and let them fill the innumerable lower offices by appointment. "When you want representation,

[24] *American Year Book, 1916*, p. 211; *1917*, p. 277; *1918*, p. 234, 247, 329; *1919*, p. 224 ff., 237; for the new organization in New York state, compare ibid., *1925*, p. 167.

elect; when you want administration, appoint." What the states of the old world possessed as an inheritance from a previous absolutism—trained, permanent administrative boards and bureaus—must be achieved with difficulty by America, at the price of abandoning cherished ideals of democracy. What is involved now is not just working with defined rights and principles, but with men and forces.

Shouldn't we see in this realization that in the end reliance has to be given to a person who must be allowed to act for the general good according to his own understanding, a new expression of the old American individualism?

The other way to improve the operations of public administration, which is to reform democratic institutions themselves, is being followed with equal assiduousness. The watchword of direct legislation is heard together with that of the short ballot. The tendency inherent in direct legislation is in fact the very opposite of that of the short ballot. We may call the short ballot an economic and direct legislation a political solution of the problem.

On every side there is a feeling of being shackled by the party machine. Public opinion has long since outgrown the parties, which it knows no longer have vital importance. Yet in their great majority the citizens still run in harness as Republicans and Democrats. True, the idea of nonpartisanship is constantly gaining ground.[25] Once upon a time those who threw off party discipline were railed at as kickers and bolters. The first independents who strove vigorously to make their influence felt, the Mugwumps of around 1880, were assailed and reviled. But in later years the number of independent voters has grown steadily and it happens repeatedly that a state votes for a Republican as president and immediately afterward for a Democratic governor.

All the same, the old major party organizations are so

[25] *American Year Book, 1914,* p. 65; *1917,* p. 32; *1918,* p. 30.

strong, they have become so interwoven with the whole of public life, that it seems more effective to seek reform through them than outside them. A movement has therefore arisen to reform and control the activity of the parties through the agency of government. In order to prevent the machinations and intrigue indissolubly connected with the system of local, district, and state party conventions composed of delegates who are manipulated by bosses and their henchmen, almost all states, at first in the West and then in the East, have gradually intervened in the activity of political parties by direct primary acts. These establish legal regulations for the fundamental assemblies of the party members, so as really to restore to them the nomination of candidates, and election officials therefore supervise the party meetings in a formal capacity. Some states immediately tried to negate the entire party system but not always with success. Massachusetts, for example, had to repeal by 1916 clauses of the primary law of 1914 providing that all voters without distinction of party could nominate their candidates in a single general convention without revealing their party adherence. Twice, in 1915 and 1916, the voters of California rejected a proposal to eliminate party distinctions from state politics.

Even when it has been possible to remove the worst evils of the party system, much remains to be done. The continuous direct influence of special interests on legislation, the shortcomings of state governments, the inadequacies of public administration, all continue to exist. A beginning has been made in resisting the interference of the large business corporations in the process of law-making, more by means of controls and restrictions than by an outright ban. An effort has been made to render the influence of the lobbies and legislative agents of the big industrial organizations over Congress and the state legislatures harmless by assurances of publicity.[26]

[26] Young, *The New American Government,* p. 583.

For almost twenty years now, the members of the United States Senate are in the great majority of states no longer chosen by the state legislatures, in which there is little public confidence, but by the people themselves. A contrary movement to abolish the state senates, which began in 1914 in Kansas and Nebraska and was tried by Arizona in 1916, has not yet had any other success.

A very important movement which began many years ago is the civil-service reform movement directed against the spoils system. The system of dismissing government employees every time there was a change of the party in power has ruled without limitation since about 1830, when Jackson fearlessly applied the rule that "to the victor [belong] the spoils." The system was closely bound up with the needs of the party organization itself; it was the indispensable means for paying services to the party. Each time the administration changed, the broom swept away every one from ambassador to village postmaster. In the introduction to Hawthorne's *The Scarlet Letter* we can read what may be called the individual psychology of the system. It is true that a law instituting examinations for civil servants, designed to keep out incompetent officials, and to introduce a measure of ability, was adopted in 1871 under the pressure of an agitated public opinion, but the politicians, seeing in it a danger for the spoils system, did what they could to oppose it. The law had still borne few results when President Garfield was assassinated in 1881, shortly after his inauguration, by a disappointed office-seeker, and the force of the civil-service reform movement increased in consequence. Shortly afterward the Democrats obtained a majority in the House of Representatives and achieved the establishment of a Federal Civil Service Commission in 1882. When Grover Cleveland, the first Democrat elected in many years, took office as president, for the first time there were no partisan dismissals. The desire of the nation for a sound administration had been the cause of Cleveland's victory. In this concern the nation was acting as much out of its feeling for business as out of a feeling for the state as such. "What civil service reform demands," said Carl Schurz, one of the most zealous advocates of the cause, "is simply that the business part of the government shall be carried on in a sound, businesslike manner."[27] From that time civil-service reform, amid many difficulties and adversities, has gained foot by foot and the spoils system has lost, in the national government as well as in the states and cities. By around 1915, 600,000 civil service positions, or about two-thirds of the entire number, had been removed from the direct influence of the political parties; the spoils system still keeps its strongest hold in the states.[28]

In view of all these changes, it becomes clear why Bryce, in revising his *The American Commonwealth* in 1914, had to note, in his somber depiction of the American government, that improvement had begun on every side.

Yet these were not the most important changes toward restoration of a truer democracy. These were the introduction of referendum, initiative, and recall.

When the German historian Friedrich von Raumer traveled through the United States in 1844, he recorded the anecdote of a parade of government officials who were having difficulty making their way through a crowd. One of them shouted: "Out of the way! We are the representatives of the people." The reply rang out: "Get out of the way yourself. We are the people!" This remark could be the motto for a history of American popular institutions since the beginning of the twentieth century. There is no longer a desire for repre-

[27] "Annual Meeting of the National Civil Service Reform League 1894," in Hart, *American History Told by Contemporaries*, vol. IV, p. 636.
[28] W. D. Foulke, *Fighting the Spoilsmen: Reminiscences of the Civil Service Reform Movement* (New York: Putnam, 1919).

sentative institutions but for direct government of the people.

The reforms we have in mind are not of original American manufacture. The Swiss example was deliberately followed: The big democracy learned the art by watching the little democracy. But quite typically American are the ways in which it has been carried into practice and the motives for its adoption. It is in fact the continuation of the struggle of Western democracy against the forces of capitalism, which I discussed above[29] in an earlier phase. And characteristically it was the extreme West, the states on the Pacific Ocean, which set the tone this time, that is, about 1900. Boutmy had remarked shortly before that the instability and thinness of the population in the West prevented the expression of a truly political feeling among the people. Individual interest, which saw itself as isolated, everywhere maintained its supremacy, says Boutmy. Politically the West remains a nullity, but that will change: "The rapid settlement of these regions will transform all of this before the first third of the twentieth century."[30]

But in fact the transformation came much earlier than he foresaw. For a number of years now the West has been politically of the first order: It is an innovating and inventive force in the country. The motive for the drive to achieve direct government of the people was the lack of confidence in the corrupt, partisan, and commercialized state legislatures and city councils. "Our governmental institutions to-day, not in theory perhaps, but as they actually exist, are neither democratic nor representative."[31] Give the power back to the people, who have entrusted it to incompetent and unworthy men.

The method is simple. It is known from its practice in Switzerland, where, although modern in form, it has its roots

[29] See above, p. 29 ff.
[30] Boutmy, *Eléments*, pp. 46, 56.
[31] R. W. Trine, *In the Fire of the Heart*, p. 236.

in the ancient principles of primitive democracy, which it actually reestablishes. The initiative means that a group of public-minded men who cannot persuade the legislature to do what they consider to be useful and necessary can draw up a bill themselves and if they obtain five to ten per cent of the voters to support its introduction it will be presented directly to the people for their approval. Or it may go instead to the legislature, which accepts or rejects it, or amends it, or puts something completely different in its place, or does nothing; but whatever it does, at the next election the people decide the matter themselves. The referendum, which is distinct from the initiative, can also apply to a measure of the legislature, or merely to a special question put before the people in order to obtain a truer and definite expression of public opinion.

The initiative and referendum were adopted in South Dakota in 1898 with the support of the Knights of Labor and the Farmers' Alliance, but a considerable time passed before they were applied in practice. The victory of the system began when Oregon adopted it in 1902, thanks to the action of Senator U'Ren, who used it successfully in that state "to put bosses out of business." There was incessant activity through the country on its behalf. "Direct Legislation [and Guarded Representation also] means control of your servants instead of letting your servants control you." In Missouri, where the condition of state government was intolerable, Governor Folk said: "Vote for the Initiative and Referendum, a system that will be the death blow to corruption, and the only true remedy for bribery. Why elect me unless I am given the proper tools?" One state after another followed: South Dakota in 1898, Utah in 1900, Oregon in 1902, Nevada in 1904, Montana in 1906, Oklahoma immediately after its acceptance as a state in 1907, Missouri in 1908. The old states of the East continued to hesitate and were generally hostile. Maine accepted initiative and referendum in 1908 with some limitations, Maryland only the referendum in 1915, and Massachusetts both in 1918. Of the major parties, which always followed warily the development of new principles, the Democrats were the first to accept it; now it is tolerated in Republican circles as well. In 1925 18 states had the initiative and referendum and two the referendum alone.

The logical complement to initiative and referendum is recall. Not only must the people be able to influence legislation directly, but they must also be able to remove unsatisfactory officeholders. Unsatisfactory in this case means chiefly that they put themselves at the service of corporate interests, so that recall is an open struggle against concentrated capital. In a state where recall has been introduced, a specific number of voters can present a petition for removal of an officeholder, and this proposal then must be submitted to a referendum. If it receives a majority, the official is recalled.

Recall is directed principally against judges. Because an American judge has the task always to test the constitutionality of laws and their enforcement, he is often a strongly restraining force, especially in matters of social justice. It is principally the most needed labor legislation which is nullified by judges as unconstitutional. Nor are workers adequately represented on juries. Recall can be used against all such practices. Not all of the states that have introduced recall have been so bold as to extend it to include judges. On the occasion of the acceptance of Arizona as a state in 1911, the question of the recall of judges came before Congress. President Taft vigorously opposed inclusion of this measure in the constitution of the new state, and Arizona was accepted with the provision that it would scrap this clause. Nonetheless, immediately after admission, Arizona amended its constitution to include the provision for recall. Since 1916 ten states have possessed the system of recall, but four do not apply it to judges.

Recall works principally by preventive means, and it does not have to be used very often. Officeholders feel the power of the people above their heads and take it as a warning; previously it was the threat of a change of the party in power which they had felt over their head. Should we not consider recall as the spoils system put to better use, just as we can call the city manager a boss serving a better cause? When the spoils system was first employed, it too was considered to be an application of true democratic principles, but it became a servant of faction and office-seekers. Now it has been made a servant of the public interest.

There can be no doubt that the enthusiasm for initiative, referendum, and recall, or Popular Government, as they are called together, has abated for some time.[32] After 1916 no other states introduced recall; the interest in initiative and referendum was greatly weakened in the war years. More benefit is expected from the other way to improve democracy: by efficiency and consolidation. The discovery that initiative and referendum in practice have a much more conservative than radical effect, which has been made in Europe too,[33] will not be the principal reason for the disappointment in America, for conservatism and democracy are not contradictory there. Much more it is the lack of visible results in practice. Criticism is directed principally at recall, and the direct primary does not satisfy in every respect either. It seems that a new force of compulsion will take the place of the party machine—the press.[34]

[32] Young, *The New American Government,* p. 612; *American Year Book, 1919,* p. 229.

[33] A. W. IJzerman, "Referendum en Volksinitiatief," *Socialistische Gids,* IV (1919), p. 890.

[34] Hadley, *Undercurrents,* pp. 148, 153–169.

The Far West was also in the forefront in the introduction of the woman's vote.[35] In 1916 it was in force in 12 of the 48 states, that is, in all the Pacific states, 7 of the 8 Mountain states, but only 2 elsewhere. In 1919 it had been adopted by 29 states, including the northeastern and northwestern Central states, and also New York from 1917. The opposition came principally from the South, where none of the coastal states and only 4 of the 8 southeastern and southwestern Central states took the step. But in the same year, 1919, Congress proposed the nineteenth amendment to the Constitution, which extended the women's vote to the whole country, and it came into force in 1920, after it had been ratified by the required three-quarters of the states.

The special importance of the West in the political development of America is the special theme of one of the best contemporary American historians, Frederick J. Turner, whom I have already cited a number of times. He connects the recent movements of political reform which conquer the country from the West with the disappearance of unoccupied territory west of the boundary of civilization. As long as the wilderness afforded an opportunity to gain new property and new prosperity, it formed a safeguard for democracy, the old individualist pioneer democracy of former times. But now the maritime frontier has been reached; there is no more free land. Since this time the West has had to wage its fight directly against its antagonist, which is capitalism, just as it was in the days of the Articles of Confederation and Andrew Jackson. But in this case it is not an industrial proletariat which rises up against capitalism in order to smash it, but an agrarian middle class, which is basically just as capitalist as the East in the sense

[35] It was introduced in Wyoming as early as 1869, when it was still a territory. At that time it was still so unprecedented that it was looked upon only as a joke.—J.H.

of devotion to private property; but as a debtor class it must defend itself against the financial power which is the creditor class. The Greenbackers after the Civil War struggled for the preservation of a means of payment of lower value, the strongly depreciated greenbacks, which they thought would make them independent of Wall Street. The Grangers of about 1870 resisted the arbitrary rate charges of the railway companies, which prevented them from garnering the profits from grain production in the Middle West for themselves.[36]

In both movements a very concrete economic interest in the West opposed the capitalist interests in the East. The same was true in the struggle of silver against gold. But at the same time the Western movements were the defenders of the principles of democracy against everything that threatened to suffocate them. The Granger movement was the first to attack the strength of a group of great wealth that wished the power of money developed exclusively to its own advantage. Bryan, the onetime fighter for silver, became at the same time the reformer of the Democratic Party. And in the long run the Western principles of reestablishment of true democracy and opposition to the overpowerful interests on every side penetrated the East. Much of what now stands in the programs of both major political parties as basic proposals originated in the demands of the once scorned Greenbackers and Grangers of an earlier day.

It may be an exaggeration when Turner brings together all the great demands of today—strengthening of the federal government, and most of all opposition to the trusts—as "the voice of the insurgent West." But he is certainly right so far as the movements for finding new safeguards for democracy by the regulation of party practices and the introduction of

[36] Hadley, *Undercurrents,* pp. 57, 65 ff.

initiative, referendum, and recall are concerned. They had to come, once the old, natural safeguard of democracy, the abundance of available land, ceased to exist.[37]

But Turner also names the growth of socialism as one of these movements. The European reader cannot but be amazed to see socialism given such an auxiliary or even secondary role. It certainly cannot have been Turner's intention to dismiss socialism as nothing more than a reaction phenomenon.[38] But there is some basis for the subordinate position in which he places it. Much more than in Europe, socialism in America has been until now one movement among many, for one thing because it has little strength, for another because a number of other political movements fulfill a much more active function in America than in the Old World.

Everything happens in America through a movement. Here the old principle of spontaneous organization for a concrete purpose of a political or social character, which I earlier indicated as a powerful factor in American history, comes once again to the fore.

Almost every question of principle and every demand for reform is introduced in America by a few public-spirited persons who form an association and begin a movement. This was the case with the movement against the death penalty shortly after 1840: there were committees, an excited discussion of the question in the press, and then action by various states. At the same time one woman, Miss Dorothea Lynde Dix, in eight

[37] Turner, "Social forces in American history," *American Historical Review*, XVI. A number of Turner's articles on the West will be found gathered in his collection *The Frontier in American History* (New York: Holt, 1920).

[38] *Reactieverschijnsel* has for Huizinga its physiological meaning of response to a stimulus, not the ordinary political meaning of "reaction."—H.H.R.

years of activity, persuaded almost all the states to improve their care of the insane.[39] Similarly, the reform of the civil service was entirely the achievement of the National Civil Service Reform League, which compelled an unwilling Congress to adopt the first legislative measures in this field. They were mocked as dreamers and "mugwumps," but patient activity in newspapers and magazines educated the public over a few years to an understanding of the evil and the means for reform. Now civil-service reform is one of the generally recognized points of constant concern in government. Similarly the movement for uniform state legislation owes its origins to an association of lawyers formed in 1878.

A National Child Labor Committee has the honor of obtaining legislation against child labor, although it has not yet been crowned by a federal child labor act. The movement for initiative and reform is in large part led by Eltweed Pomeroy, who made precise studies of the Swiss system and worked indefatigably for the idea in a number of states by praising it in meetings, in university and school conferences, and in town councils. The temperance movement, which was crowned by complete victory on January 16, 1919, has had a much more political character in America than among us Dutchmen; the Prohibitionists formed a party, and were in many respects the successors of the pre-Civil War Abolitionists. The Prohibitionists were accustomed to presenting their own candidates for president, without success of course, but with the result, for instance, that the Republicans were defeated in 1884.

In character, these associations still have much in common with the primitive organizations I spoke of earlier: an enthusiastic understanding of the immediate need for the concrete purpose which they advocate, a vigorous zeal, a strong

[39] McMaster, *History of the People of the United States*, vol. VII, p. 145.

humanitarian coloration, true sincerity and sacrifice. All they have abandoned is the pattern of Fehm courts; the element of secrecy and "order" seems to have passed away. Also, as time goes on, the action of these associations becomes more and more positive instead of negative, constructive instead of critical and oppositional. Citizen committees, such as the Committee of One Hundred, did powerful work of the negative kind by bringing about the downfall of the Tweed Ring in New York and the Philadelphia Gas Ring, which were notorious hotbeds of corruption around 1870. In recent times, according to Young, writing in 1915, the Civil and Good Government Clubs, which previously had usually not gone beyond pointing out faults in the government, have been turning more and more toward the original preparation and presentation of plans for public reform.[40] He gives a list of the causes which such private associations are now pressing on the national government, the state governments, and the city administrations.[41] They concern waterways, the civil service, limitation of immigration, regulation of foreign trade and trade among the states, treatment of the Indians, arbitration treaties, settlement of labor disputes, forestation, irrigation, as well as tax reform, public care for the poor, prisons, road improvement, measures against deforestation, school administration, health, child labor, temperance, supervision of food supply, the establishment of parks and playgrounds, manual training and nature study in the schools, public libraries, action against gambling and prostitution, and introduction of modern accountancy into public administration.

What is unique in this respect, however, is that it is not only strictly civic associations which show an interest in all these matters; commercial and industrial corporations, and spe-

[40] Young, *The New American Government*, p. 585.
[41] *Ibid.*, p. 586.

cifically the associations of employers and workers, also participate in this activity. They naturally fall under the suspicion of serving their special business interests in doing so. It is just a short step from the bona fide movement for a good cause to the lobbies and "legislative agents" (bureaus and officials with the task of influencing the legislatures) of the employers' associations. But the business associations have at their disposal an inestimable knowledge of affairs; they have experts in everything who can prepare plans, and in legislative matters the American wants above all the guidance of experts. They also have at their disposal large advertising facilities, large resources, and an obedient organization. Strictly political associations cannot help but compete with them: They avail themselves of ordinary commercial methods and advertise as much as they can.

All in all, the associations are at present the driving force in legislation.[42] The people, through spontaneous organizations of public opinion and the techniques of modern advertising and communication, are taking government into their own hands over the heads of their representatives. Initiative is nothing else than the incorporation of this principle directly into government: If the government or the legislature does not act, then three citizens put their hands together and the job gets done. Secrecy and oaths are out of date, but the Rütli principle is still at work.[43]

The emotional character of American politics now again finds expression. It is sustained, much more than is European politics, by a steady feeling of ethical humanitarianism. Such an assertion will probably elicit astonishment. And, in fact, it does not mean that material economic interests do not operate

---

[42] Young, *The New American Government*, p. 583.

[43] A reference to the legendary oath taken at the Swiss mountain meadow of this name in 1291, which initiated Swiss resistance to Habsburg rule.—H.H.R.

very strongly in American politics despite all the public's desire for honesty and improvement; yet this does not take away the fact that political feeling in America contains a high measure of moral enthusiasm. Important magazines have the special purpose of seeking action on all ethical political problems; the New York *Nation* celebrated its fiftieth anniversary with a special number, "Fifty years of idealism." The *Arena* places itself at the service of the battle "for civic righteousness and [note well] individual growth and development." An agitator like the Eltweed Pomeroy just named is described as follows: "He belongs to a group of thoughtful young Americans and to a band of thoughtful workers, who reflect the spirit of altruism, or co-operation and brotherhood, as opposed to the spirit of commercialism, greed and egoism that is struggling to establish an oligarchy or plutocracy under the mantle of republican institutions."[44]

This emotional basis of political life is one of the elements which explain the weak growth of socialism in America, but it is assuredly not the principal explanation. That is to be sought in the situation Tocqueville already called attention to when he explained his expectation that there was little chance for big revolutions: "I know of nothing more opposite to revolutionary attitudes than commercial ones."[45] This appears to me to be a profound piece of wisdom fully demonstrated by present-day America. Society in America is too strongly, too thoroughly commercialized, too many individuals are involved in keeping the machinery of production in operation, for a revolutionary doctrine to be able to get much of a grip there. The Socialist Party in the United States numbered only 74,519

[44] An unnamed person, quoted in Trine, *In the Fire of the Heart*, p. 252 note.
[45] Tocqueville, *De la démocratie en Amérique*, vol. III, p. 409. [*Democracy in America*, vol. II, p. 268.]

members in 1918, apart from the organization of the Industrial Workers of the World; in 1919, before it split, the number was 108,000. The only Socialist in Congress was refused a seat by a vote of 309 to 1. The number of Socialist votes for president is much larger, it is true: it rose from 420,000 in 1908 to 898,000 in 1912. But what is suggested by these votes is not so much a belief in the correctness of Socialist doctrine as a feeling of opposition to social inequality in general. Under the emotional impact of the war, the figure fell in 1916 from 898,000 to 590,000. In the presidential election of 1924, the Socialists joined with many trade unions to vote for Senator La Follette, although he was no Marxist at all; their hope was that in this way they would create a Labor party on the English model, but they did not succeed. The Congress now in session [1928] numbers among the 435 members of the House of Representatives two members of the Farmer-Labor Party and one Socialist. The Workers Party, which follows the lead of Moscow, numbered in 1925, according to its own statement, no more than 20,000 members, of whom 2,000 spoke English. The once intensely feared I.W.W. (Industrial Workers of the World) has slipped into insignificance in recent years.

In Europe until a few years ago the idea of democracy was linked to a certain extent with that of the revenge of the propertyless. This was never the case in America. When the rather patriarchal democracy of the first period was succeeded in America about 1830 by a truly democratic system, the change did not mean in the least a weakening of the rights of property. On the contrary, the groups which obtained power at that time, in a word the West, were as much interested as their predecessors in government in easy creation of capital and strong protection of personal property. Bourgeois democracy has an old and strong tradition in America. Democracy there is completely compatible with conservatism, and when

we see institutional processes such as initiative and referendum work in a conservative way, we have, from the American point of view, absolutely no right to call the result undemocratic for that reason.

Socialism in Europe for a long time had its greatest attraction for many in the fact that it seemed to be synonymous with the true ideal of democracy. It cannot make such an appeal in America; the democratic ideal was already achieved there in the government itself, however great its failings. Democracy in America is almost equivalent to patriotism. The result is the vigorous moral indignation with which the national campaign against radicalism was waged after the Great War [World War I]. The American feels an attack on private property much more passionately than the peoples of Europe. Furthermore, the presence among the revolutionary-minded of a very large majority of foreign-born was for the American another spur to hostility. Finally, something of the lynch instinct remains still inborn in him: The round-up of "alien Reds," the attacks on the homes of revolutionaries, the large-scale deportations, satisfied a very complicated but lively feeling of political sentimentality. "I am delighted," wrote a well-known American journalist, "with these irregular acts, these evidences of a new virility. They are pink with health."[46]

The dogma of the class struggle has very great weight in the public opinion of Europe, even among non-Socialists, but not in America. Basically American public opinion is uniformly capitalist and patriotic. It allows itself to be placed without resistance at the service of the giant organizations of Democrats and Republicans, which are able to arouse a mass enthusiasm from which the American is hardly able to escape. Even when a stimulating man and a stimulating slogan are present, it is still

[46] E. Price Bell, quoted in *The New Statesman*, January 31, 1920, p. 487.

always the two major party organizations which are best able to provide two vessels into which public opinion pours itself in almost identical mixtures, precisely because they have in fact ceased to have any political content of their own. In reality public opinion no longer finds direct expression in the parties, but it is the parties which adapt themselves as much as is necessary to public opinion. They give the indispensable dramatic structure of a great duel to political activity. In the ritual acts of earlier ages, the sacred idea was often expressed in the form of a symbolic struggle, and the same is true in American politics today. If there is no antagonist, why get excited? Fundamentally, the parties are on quite good terms with each other, but they need each other as enemies.

The successes of Roosevelt and Wilson in the first decades of this century should be considered in this light. What the people sought in them was a man who wanted to do the job and was able to do it. Roosevelt was elected in 1904 (after he had automatically succeeded President McKinley in 1901, being Vice-President) for his personality; it was not a victory of the Republican party, whose standpoint he represented less and less with the passage of time. He became the idol of the middle classes which were looking for social reform. He stimulated the imagination by traits so authentically American: He was a great sportsman and he led the Rough Riders in the war in Cuba. And he stimulated feelings of political righteousness by his long career of struggle against corruption and by his preachment of "honesty, sobriety, industry, self-restraint, brotherhood, social uplift." Were these just phrases? They were, on the contrary, the expression of what the nation wanted to hear, the words which would spur it to vigorous democratic action.

Roosevelt remained strongly handicapped, however, by the enormous capitalist interests which were the driving force in his party, the Republicans. In 1904, when reports appeared that Wall Street and the Trusts were opposed to him, this only greatly increased his popularity. But later it came out that the Life Insurance combination and Standard Oil had had an important part in the campaign in his favor. "It would appear that Mr. Roosevelt was unaware of the economic forces which carried him to victory."[47] Under the presidency of Taft (1909–1913), the great financial forces won still more strength despite the attacks on the trusts on the part of the government, which had been under way for many years. Taft inclined more and more toward capitalist conservatism, and finally Roosevelt broke with his old friend and the Republican party. He felt that public opinion, which was in a state of great enthusiasm, wanted other things; in order to remain its leader and spokesman, he established the new party of the Progressives and preached the New Nationalism: a vigorous maintenance and strengthening of the federal government against the continued excesses of the great financial powers. Liberated from the old party tradition, he could express through the Progressives the new spirit of reform in all its sacred enthusiasm; the Progressive campaign of 1912 was like a political revival.

But the split resulted in the victory of the Democrats with Wilson. At that time Wilson still seemed to have nothing to stimulate the imagination: He was a scholarly former professor of history at Princeton University who until then was reputed to be a conservative. But he had fought the trusts successfully as governor of New Jersey, and he was one of those conservatives who become more progressive with the years. Against Roosevelt's New Nationalism, he set the New Freedom, which was more Democratic in tone. Break government away from the forces of big business.—It has become "a foster-child of the special interests." Do not believe that this

[47] C. A. Beard, *Contemporary History,* p. 271.

can be done with well-intentioned supervision by the government and with warnings, as Roosevelt wanted; break the tie. "It is time that property, as compared with humanity, should take second place, not first place." (This recalls Lincoln's words of 3 December 1861.[48]) "Bring the government back to the people." "I feel nothing so much as the intensity of the common man." But at the same time there was this for the businessman every American is: "I am for big business and I am against the trusts."[49]

Four years later, in the presidential election of 1916, there was so much in Wilson that stimulated the political imagination that the stiff scholarly figure was able to win the same kind of success that the great hunter had done before him. Roosevelt did not run. "It would be a mistake to nominate me unless the country has in its mood something of the heroic," he had said. He bitterly disappointed his loyal Progressives by withdrawing at the last moment, and it was the deathblow to his own creation. But it was at the same time Wilson's victory. That public opinion which had found an expression in the Progressive party did not allow itself to be drawn back into the bosom of the Republican organization by an election maneuver. Wilson was reelected for what he was himself, not because there was a Democratic majority. The Progressive West had an important part in his victory.

"Without doubt," Young thought in 1915, "the immense majority of the electors have now definitely accepted a governmental leadership in the matters of administration and social questions which ten years ago it would have still considered as dangerous and subversive."[50] This refers principally to the recognition that it was desirable for the central government to be able to make itself felt vigorously in economic and social

48 See above, pp. 62–63.
49 Wilson, *The New Freedom*, 1912, pp. 55, 72, 101, 174, 196, 260.
50 Young, *The New American Government*, p. 527.

matters. The forces of big finance in the Republican party had to accept the government's intervention in business. The Democrats gave up their old hostility to state intervention. It was reserved for the Democrat Wilson to extend immensely during the war the authority of the federal government over the resources of the country: the railways, iron industry, slaughterhouses, the telegraph and telephone systems.

Of the two political minds that most strongly embodied the political tendencies of the American commonwealth in the first years of its existence—Hamilton and Jefferson—which has won out? In other words, which tendencies have triumphed, those which were directed toward a strong government with the broadest powers, toward unity over variety, toward subordination over self-determination, or those which wished to tolerate no infringement of sacred individual freedom, for no matter what reason? It seems, therefore, that the prize belongs unreservedly to the former, that is, to Hamilton. But if we look at the matter more closely, we shall see that such strong shifts have occurred in the situation that it is more than doubtful whether Hamilton has indeed won.

The unity of the United States has never been so strongly established as today. The executive power has never been as strong as it is now. Everywhere what matters is finding men who know what to do and can do it; important traditional principles of democracy are abandoned in order to achieve a smoothly working, sound administration, to make government efficient, operating with the driving power of a good business. Isn't this just what Hamilton and his friends had in mind?

There is one great difference, however. Hamilton wished to make government strong for the sake of capital, and for a long time this policy was so successful that capital came to dominate and overpower the state completely. But what is sought now is to make government strong against capital. Not that those who profess Hamilton's and Adams's doctrine that the state can only be governed by those who have the largest share in business died out at once. The "standpatters" believed with Marcus A. Hanna (d. 1903) that the principal task of government was to help business without enquiring into its ways and practices, and that businessmen were most fitted to be the heads of government. Wilson could still speak of "Mr. Taft's conception that the Presidency of the United States is the presidency of a board of directors."[51] But the rule of the standpatters is a thing of the past.

The better part of Hamilton's thought, which was the realization that in the end everything depended upon men, flourishes again in the short ballot movement. This is an attempt everywhere to clothe the competent person with great power, but in the service of the public cause.

On the other side, the movement for direct legislation represents Jefferson's old idea in a new form. Initiative, referendum, and recall all acknowledge the right to direct, personal democracy. In direct legislation the rights of the many are preserved in every way. The direct, spontaneous expression of the people's will, which Jefferson could not imagine except as resistance and revolt, has found a form which operates normally and is truly political.

While on the one hand the fading of state boundaries means a victory for the old principle of unity, at the same time the federal structure of the Union demonstrates its advantages more than ever. Consider how beneficial it is in just such reforms as the initiative that one state can undertake the experiment and the others follow its example with modifications. The legislation of the states in this area displays all kinds of small variations which make it as a whole a continuing experiment. While power becomes centralized and concentrated on the one hand, there exists simultaneously a tendency to transfer as

[51] Young, *The New American Government*, p. 190.

many powers as possible to small units. A kind of polarizing movement has been under way in the states during recent years. On the one side the supervision of state governments over local finances, education, water supply, health, transportation, and so on, is constantly expanding, so that there is talk of the centralization of state authority. But on the other side we find the drive for "municipal home rule." For some years there has been discussion of the secession of Chicago from the State of Illinois in order to seek admission to the Union as a separate state.[52]

The idea that "social units" are important as the natural nuclei of society and that their independence should be promoted has gained greater influence than ever.

Neither of the two old opposite forces in American history, individualism and organization, which have always stood in a relation of mutual influence with each other, has been abolished. Restoration of the rights of the individual, recognition of individual skill and energy as the effective means of political action, release from the compulsions of a rigidified and mechanized organism of government—these are principles which are still embodied in the American attitude toward the state. But the old, undisciplined, self-willed pioneer individualism has had its day. There is no more place in the country for Jefferson's ideal of personal freedom and independence. More than ever the vindication of personality will be attainable only in the form of association. Association and organization are more indispensable and convenient than ever, but they still retain much of the spontaneity which has been prominent in American history from the first.

The European is somewhat pharisaical when he talks about America. He hears the shouting of political ideals and the enthusiastic grand phrases. He recalls all the failings of American

[52] See *American Year Book, 1925,* pp. 173, 198.

government: the unprincipled bustle of the political parties, the corruption. Then he smiles and says, "the land of the dollar," and declares the rest to be just words. But with this cheap judgment he misses the essence of the American spirit. There is a great contrast between words and deeds in America, but probably no more than elsewhere. The words ring out so shrilly because all public life is conducted with much more noise and ado than among us. But words are not false just because they are loud. There is perpetual tension in America between a passionate idealism and an unrestrainable energy directed to material things. And because the popular mind in America is naïve and easily moved emotionally, it often does not observe the contradiction between what the country does and its resounding democratic ideals.

American patriotism, as a mass expression of the feeling of nationhood, does not notice when the country falls short of its ideals. The individual American, however, does not fail to see such contradictions. There is no abuse in American society which is not attacked first and most fiercely by Americans themselves, with self-denial even to the point of martyrdom. The national conscience has not been silent about such things as slavery and Indian policy in former times, and later corruption and labor conditions. To an outsider, a patriotic ideal therefore seems to be so hollow because it is necessarily so simplistic. It brings things together and denies the contradictions in them, it adds to its own colors, and above all it anticipates. It is a promissory note drawn against the future. Nowhere is this done as confidently as in America, where the concept of the future is so much stronger in all intellectual life than in the Old World.

One who does not know the future has no right to pass censure on America's ideal. It is with this understanding that we must look at the idealism of the Americans, quietly, and if we can, with appreciation.

Americans like all great peoples possess the idea of a mission. From the birth of their nation the feeling has lived in them that they are called upon to give the world the model of a wise, mighty, and prosperous democracy. This ideal is expounded from the political platform and the pulpit with visible sincerity.[53] It is closely related to the ideal of the mighty task of conquering the raw, rich continent by work. If we wish to express this notion in Marxist fashion and say that it is the ideological expression of the economic pressure which drove them to occupy the West and drive out the Indians, and to conquer California and New Mexico, all right! I cannot see that it makes much difference in the notion itself.

However conceived, there is in this ideal the feeling of strength and youth and the delight in work: there is the thrill of physical pride and courage which makes the young man eager for work or for the play of bodily strength. Here is another remark of Wilson's from 1912: "You know how it thrills our blood sometimes to think how all the nations of the earth wait to see what America is going to do with her power, her physical power, her enormous resources, her enormous wealth. The nations hold their breath to see what this young country will do with her young unspoiled strength; we cannot help but be proud that we are strong."

That was before the war. In 1917 America was faced by the task of fighting for its own cause and thereby intervening decisively in the fate of the world. No matter what hopes were placed on America and disappointed, one thing became quickly evident: War was not the element in which the American nation lived naturally. The country disarmed in 1918 as quickly and completely as it had in 1865, and returned to work and civilian life. Despite the present policy of naval construction, there exists no danger of a permanent militarism in America. The whole country rests upon a perspective of peace, safety,

[53] Bryce, *The American Commonwealth*, vol. II, p. 353.

and prosperity. As John Calhoun said in 1846: "Peace is pre-eminently our policy. Providence has given us an inheritance stretching across the entire continent from ocean to ocean. . . . Our great mission, as a people, is to occupy this vast domain; to replenish it with an intelligent, virtuous and industrious population, to convert the forests into cultivated fields; to drain the swamps and morasses, and cover them with rich harvests; to build up cities, towns and villages in every direction, and to unite the whole by the most rapid intercourse between all the parts."

A whole book could be written about the emotionalism of American patriotism, its tone, fantasy and tradition. The tradition is still primarily that of 1776, but not at all limited to it. Boutmy writing in 1902, could already declare[54] that the development of the Western states had watered down the heroic and historical patriotic tradition of 1776. The newer states had no part in 1776. A state like Minnesota has no memories older than 1860. Boutmy compared the Republic with a lady who after a noble marriage takes a bourgeois for a second husband and has both noble and bourgeois sons. But what he forgot was that the few years 1861–1865 count as a century. Patriotic fantasy and tradition are as strong for the Civil War as for the rebellion against England. Lincoln has largely displaced Washington as a national hero venerated by the people. Nowhere can the rise of this new national emo-tionalism be read more clearly than in Whitman's "Specimen Days" and his verses about the war and the president.

There is also an element of fantasy in American patriotism which is even stronger than that historical glorification of great deeds of struggle. This is nature, not the beauty of nature but its power, and not only nature in its untouched state but also

[54] Boutmy, *Eléments*, pp. 80 ff.

man's part in it: his incessant activity, the eternal roar of his labor. There is a picture of America that we all carry in ourselves, as there is our picture of Holland, and we all also feel to some extent what the picture of *"la France"* is for a Frenchman. We incorrigible dreamers and quiet anglers for beauty and quiet, when we see the picture of Holland in our mind's eye, think first of all of the open air. But in our picture of America there is the beating of hammers, the roar of thunder and of tumbling waterfalls and the rippling of prairie grass in the wind. Let Emerson and Whitman tell us what that picture is.

"America is beginning to assert itself to the senses and to the imagination of her children . . . I think we must regard the *land* as a commanding and increasing power on the citizen, the sanative and americanizing influence, which promises to disclose new virtues for ages to come. . . . Here shall laws and institutions exist on some scale of proportion to the majesty of nature."[55]

"Leaves of Grass" is the expression of that feeling of America's grandeur repeated a thousand times over. Let yourself experience the dithyrambic power of Whitman's insistent catalogues, which are always the same and always new, and which he bellows like innumerable demons out of a wild litany: the industries, the products, the trees and plants, the landscapes, the states, the rivers with their wild Indian names!

> Daughter of the lands did you wait for your poet!
> Did you wait for one with a flowing mouth and indicative
> hand? Toward the male of the States, and toward the
> female of the States, Exulting words, words to Democ-
> racy's lands.

[55] Emerson, "The Young Americans" (1844) [*Works,* Macmillan ed., vol. 1, p. 295.]

Interlink'd, food-yielding lands!
Land of coal and iron! land of gold! land of cotton, sugar,
    rice!
Land of wheat, beef, pork! land of wool and hemp! land
    of the apple and the grape!
Land of the pastoral plains, the grass-fields of the world!
    land of those sweet-air'd interminable plateaus!
Land of the herd, the garden, the healthy house of adobie!
Land where the north-west Columbia winds, and where
    the southwest Colorado winds!
Land of the eastern Chesapeake! land of the Delaware!
Land of Ontario, Erie, Huron, Michigan!
Land of the Old Thirteen! Massachussetts land! land of
    Vermont and Connecticut!
Land of the ocean shores! land of sierras and peaks!
Land of boatmen and sailors! fishermen's land! . . ."[56]

The feeling of might, greatness, and productivity surges
through all his glorification of America. There is no dividing
border between nature and democracy in his spirit. "I conceive
of no flourishing and heroic elements of democracy in the
United States—without the Nature element forming a main
part—to be its health-element and beauty-element—to really
underlie the whole politics, sanity, religion and art of the New
World."[57] Is there not a striking similarity to the words of
Emerson just quoted?

Democracy came to have a cosmic content for Whitman;
it was his bride, as Poverty was for St. Francis. Democracy
includes for him his flowing love for all men. "The idea of the
books is Democracy, that is carried far beyond Politics into
the regions of taste, the standards of Manners and Beauty and
even into Philosophy and Theology."[58]

[56] "Starting from Paumanok, 14," *Complete Writings*, vol. I, p. 27.
[57] Walt Whitman, *Specimen Days in America*, London ed., 1887
(*The Camelot Series*), p. 309.
[58] *Notes and fragments: Meaning and intention of "Leaves of Grass,"*
Complete Writings, vol. IX, p. 13.

And therefore Whitman was not pained when the imperfect democracies did not conform to his ideal. "He saw democracies die in democracy." His was the spirit of the prophet.

> "I see Freedom, completely arm'd and victorious, and very
>   haughty, with Law on one side and Peace on the other,
> A stupendous trio all issuing forth against the idea of caste;
> What historic denouements are these we so rapidly ap-
>   proach?
> I see men marching and countermarching by swift millions,
> I see the frontiers and boundaries of the old aristocracies
>   broken.
> I see the landmarks of European kings removed,
> I see this day the People beginning their landmarks, (all
>   others give way;). . . ."[59]

When he was dying, the imperialist tendencies which were then (1892) on the rise in his country were under discussion. Whitman said: "They are momentary. They leave the real work undone. The real America is not to establish empires but to destroy them. Any America that stopt with America would be a story half told."[60]

---

[59] *Years of the modern, Songs of Parting, Leaves of Grass, Complete Writings,* vol. II, p. 271.
[60] *Complete Writings,* vol. I, "Introduction," p. xc.

Chapter IV

TAME AND WILD AMERICA

Anyone who has traveled in America will tell you of the extraordinary herd spirit which prevails there. On a given day in autumn, straw hats disappear from every head; the foreigner who violates the ban is corrected and becomes a scandal for his host. The same furniture and the same opinions are to be found everywhere. The attachment to the *opinion reçue*,[1] the obedience to the given word, the pliant everyday conventionality which prevail in America, arouse the European's mild disdain. The American seems to him to be remarkably without independence in the content of life.

By 1837, Emerson was already complaining: "the spirit of the American freeman is already suspected to be timid, imitative, tame."[2] A feeling for conformity, a fear of deviating from the good model, controls behavior. "People like to be

[1] French for "accepted" or "traditional opinions."—H.H.R.
[2] "The American Scholar," *Works* (Macmillan ed., 1884), vol. I, p. 91.

amused just as their neighbors are, so that they buy the 'best-selling book of the year.' "[3] The annual surveys of literature keep an accurate count of these best-sellers: The idea of competition has crossed over from sports to literature. Americans would like to have a watchword for everything—politics, morality, esthetics—on which they can rely.

How is such a spirit of uniformity, such lack of independence, to be squared with the strong individualism which we have observed to be an essential characteristic of American civilization? At first glance, we can reconcile them only a little or not at all. Should we therefore limit individualist traits to economic and political life, while intellectual life bears wholly the stamp of conventionality and uniformity? Or would closer examination show here too that one element can exist next to and beneath the other?

In order to be ready for the possibility that the latter is true, we may in fact set forth an indirect argument. In England too, conventionality prevails in every area and among the best-educated people, to a much greater extent than is customary among us Dutchmen. And yet does anyone doubt the genuine individualism which is nonetheless characteristic of the English spirit? It holds true for the foundations of virtually every cultural process that it can only be understood by describing it in an equilibrium of constant contradiction. Where should this hold more true than in America, which it is a commonplace, isn't it, to call the country of contradictions?

The historical foundations of these characteristics of tameness in the American spirit could therefore be sought in Anglo-Saxon characteristics, to begin with. Nevertheless, to proclaim a phenomenon that impresses one in the history of a people as a racial or tribal peculiarity is as a rule nothing more than to

[3] Hart, *National Ideals*, p. 232.

offer a proof that is both irrefutable and meaningless.[4] When one passes such a judgment, there is nothing left to say. It cannot be proved; no living knowledge flows from it; it leads nowhere. If the explanation of American gregariousness is to be something more than such an empty clincher, then grounds of explanation must be sought on which one can get a better grip.

American civilization was a colonial civilization during the first two centuries of its existence. Every colonial civilization is, apart from climatic influences, bound by certain limiting conditions that cause it to differ from the civilization of the mother country, which is not simply taken over, transplanted, and developed further. In the first place, little or nothing is brought over of whatever is bound up with the history and legends of the mother country, the emotional implications of its ancient monuments, the romantic glory of its past. Once transplanted to the new land of his choice, the colonist ceases to have much contact with all the history which gives color to life in the mother country. At the most, that history becomes a far-off and strange glimmer for him—the graves of his ancestors, the clock of his church, respect for his squire. The elements of culture which are bound to the old, traditional atmosphere of the aristocratic society remain behind in the old country—not only feudal attitudes, but also refined literature. We need only think of the puritanical Pilgrim Fathers, to be sure, but the planters of Virginia also make us realize that they did not bring over much of the English Renaissance in their baggage. It was a while before Spenser and Shakespeare traveled over the ocean.

The hard pioneer's life in the wilderness, the isolation in

---

[4] Huizinga uses the colloquial Dutch word *dooddoener*, which carries an implication of false conclusiveness not present in the usual translations of "clincher" or "knock-down argument."—H.H.R.

the midst of constant dangers, were in themselves enough to limit all ideas to a concern for self-preservation, which with the return to very simple and primitive economic conditions, reduced the colonist from the level of culture in the mother land to a more primitive basis. Furthermore, the quest for material prosperity, which had to be won by the most vigorous exertions, absorbed everyone's energies completely.

Two elements of the civilization of the mother country which the colonists bring over with them retain their vigor undiminished, however—the attitude toward government, and religion. But the former ceases to be shaped and developed by the complicated political conditions of the old country; in the colony it is crystallized into a few terse notions about freedom and law. Religion, often in any case the cherished motive for emigration, becomes even stronger in the new surroundings where it has to fill the gap for intellectual culture. In the beginning the intellectual life of a colony is almost exclusively religious.

Calvinism and the bourgeois life-style define the civilization of seventeenth-century New England. Its traits were intolerance, formalism, veneration of the law, petty-bourgeois narrowness, and a ferocious sanctimoniousness directed especially against the sin of unchastity. The somber colors of this Puritan culture, tempered by the softness of Hawthorne's serene spirit, can be observed in his *The Scarlet Letter*. It is expressed with much more bleakness and gloom in the historical works of the contemporaries themselves: the journal of John Winthrop, the *Early History of New England* of Increase Mather. The best-known events of the history of New England testify to a hidebound passion for persecution and intolerance— the exile of Roger Williams and Mrs. Hutchinson, the witch trials of Salem. It is a hard and narrow spirit, somber and serious, but with a steely intrepidity and perseverance. It is capable of exalted idealism and can be greedily mercantile at the same time, just as it was in the Calvinist countries of the Old World, Scotland and the Netherlands.

Virginia brought another type to maturity: the aristocratic planter, socially more distinguished, but even poorer in elementary intellectual culture than the New Englander. Virginia had not produced a single intellectual work of any importance when the first work which, however clumsy and strange, can bear the name of American literature had already emerged from the Puritan environment of New England: Cotton Mather's *Magnalia Christi Americana* (1693–1697), a remarkable mixture of historical tales and the lives of preachers and magistrates.

It was only slowly that the colonial society began to feel a need for some intellectual culture of its own other than religion. But even then the motherland continued to be the honored model, and the colonists tried to follow the respected English forms as faithfully as possible. In the meantime, however, a lag had occurred; the colonies were not up to date in taste and knowledge in the fields of literature and philosophy, and this backwardness was not completely overcome. Milton, Locke, and Shaftesbury reached America too late and too weakly to exercise their influence to the full. Aware that he was behind the times and somewhat too simple intellectually to master every subtlety, the colonial man of letters sought by meek submission and lack of originality to conceal his failure to assimilate completely the spirit of the motherland.

The process of civilization in the colony was therefore a triple one. In the first place, an effort was made to preserve in as pure a state as possible the valuable cultural possessions which had been brought over, the old political attitudes, the old faith, the old mores and customs. In the second place, an effort was made to keep pace with the spirit of the mother country by respectfully imitating the innovations which it offered. But there was also a third process of civilization at work, one which was almost unconscious and not yet expressed in writing or art, but which in the long run would bring the most noble fruit to maturity—the free development of the new country in nature and work. While conservative piety and obedient imitation nourished traits of tame conventionality, the living and individual element of the national character grew in the struggle with nature.

Because he neglected this last element, H. C. Emery ends his study "The American Intellect"[5] by characterizing the growth of civilization in the colonial period exclusively as a lagging behind England. And this thesis, once stated, provides him with an ingenious explanation of the American rebellion against England. For how can we understand, he says, why the colonies in 1776 reacted so vigorously against the mother country to which they were tied by so many bands of interest and affection? The tyranny of England was really not so severe that by itself it would explain such passionate resistance. The rebellion remains more or less of a riddle. Well, Emery's argument continues, it can be solved in this way: The American of 1776 had really remained an Englishman of the previous century and kept the English spirit of 1640. New England might have been better called Old England. America reacted to its treatment by the mother country according to principles and in a spirit no longer understood in England itself: the spirit of 1640, the old-fashioned sense of law and the simple feeling for freedom which had inspired Cromwell and Hampden. In this respect it was not England which was the conservative force, but America; not England which had remained unchanged, but America; and therefore America lost its ability to understand the modern policy of the mother country.

[5] *Cambridge Modern History,* vol. VII, *The United States,* chap. 23.

An ingenious paradox, but one which faces a number of difficulties. No doubt the old English sense of law and freedom took a leading place among the motives for the rebellion. But does this constitute the essence of the American of 1776? Can one really maintain for a moment that Franklin and the Adamses resemble Cromwell and Hampden? Indeed not, for they have not the slightest resemblance. Or could we confuse for a moment the sound of Patrick Henry or of *Common Sense* with that of the Long Parliament? "O ye that love mankind; ye that dare oppose not only the tyranny but the tyrant, stand forth; every spot of the old world is overcome with oppression." That is no longer the sound of the Puritan; it is the sound of the eighteenth century, and the Americans of the Revolution are Yankees.[6]

How did the Yankee grow out of the seventeenth-century Puritan of New England? This is not a story to be told in a few words; at most a few of its lines can be sketched. In the first place, there were already various Yankee traits latent in the mercantile Calvinist. We need only think of our own Dutch forefathers, who would voyage to hell if there was business to be done, even if they burned their sails on the way. In America economic forces had especially free play: The conditions of material culture prevailed more and more over the starved old spiritual culture. All was speculation in the trade of America in the seventeenth and eighteenth century. Prices were uncertain, losses through shipwreck and piracy great. The great chances and great dangers, the freedom from all the limitations which the traditional forms of economic society placed upon the merchant in the Old World, developed in

[6] It should be kept in mind that the American uses the term "Yankee" only for the New Englander. As for *Common Sense*, it should not be objected that Thomas Paine was an Englishman. His work is characteristic of the spirit of the American uprising.—J.H.

America a type of colonial merchant in whom the speculator, the adventurer, and the smuggler were merged. He saw nothing wrong in buying a pirate's cargo on the sly; the slave trade and rum manufacture helped each other like one hand the other. The godly citizens of New England shipped rum to the coast of Africa, where it was converted into slaves; the slaves went to the West Indies; from there molasses was brought home to make new rum—and the pious fatherland had not seen one slave.

Meanwhile the tone of culture was no longer set exclusively by Calvinism but also by the spirit of the Enlightenment. It seems to me to be one of the most important elements in the development of American civilization that, notwithstanding what happened in Europe, the Enlightenment in America did not combat faith or at least make it impotent but only pushed it a little to one side. Although we cannot determine exactly how it happened, America displayed all the traits of the Enlightenment even before the revolt: the belief in human reason, in the good nature of man and his perfectibility, the humanitarian strivings, the reverence for sound intelligence, in brief, all the optimism which had been so alien to the Puritan fathers. The rhetorical eloquence and phrasemaking of the eighteenth century flourished rankly in America, but at the same time a strongly realistic and practical sense prevailed, such as we have heard, for example, in the economic ideas of John Adams. The American Enlightenment thinkers of the eighteenth century were a type unto themselves. A difference as wide as the poles distinguished it from the French variety; Rousseau, Voltaire, and Diderot were virtual strangers to it. In the person of Benjamin Franklin it exercised its own not unimportant effect on the development of ideas in Europe itself.

But in America the great struggle for those ideals of the Enlightenment was waged not against the old spiritual forces, not against the church, the Court, noble privilege, the hierarchy of officialdom, but against a foreign power. The old religious beliefs continued to live on, even if somewhat weakened. The great abyss between the godless and the believers did not develop in America. As a consequence, America also missed the great struggle of revenge against the Enlightenment; this is a point to which I shall return presently. Of course there were freethinkers in America too; but not only was the unbalanced Thomas Paine mocked for being one, but even the noble Jefferson was reviled. The American typically assimilated in a remarkable good-natured way his forefathers' sturdy faith with the more recent ideals of freedom and love of mankind, as well as with matter-of-fact profit seeking in everyday life.

There are therefore a number of conditions which enable us to explain the American national character of the nineteenth century. These are the Puritan soil; the economic conditions of small business or farming; the strong spur of the drive for material prosperity; the colonial attitude of meek imitation so far as higher culture is concerned; the ideas of the Enlightenment; and in addition the acquired political equality and democratic rights. These conditions worked together in various ways toward intellectual leveling and conventional uniformity. From Puritanism were retained the sense for conformity and the respect for law and rules. The petty-bourgeois spirit which marks American society until the present day is descended both from Puritanism and from the old isolation of the population in small groups. A little settlement amid loneliness and perils needs strong cohesion. When contact with the outside world is difficult and infrequent, an individual knows his neighbors all the better and people are interested most of all in each other. In America a certain small-town attitude still holds sway on an immense scale. The unabashed curiosity with which a stranger is met, which always so impressed earlier visitors, has not yet completely died out. Everything appears in the newspapers, even the most personal matters; local patriotism is as naïve now in Saint Louis as it was earlier in Salem.

The Enlightenment itself nourished a certain tendency to mediocrity. From its general philanthropy, linked with its respect for sound understanding, there logically resulted a high esteem for the average mind. Political equality, the smallness of class differences, and the democratic forms of life, worked in their turn toward a level uniformity. Thus developed the solidarity of mediocrity which permeates American life. As a result of universal education, the intellectual life of the public is high enough for everyone to understand each other. Men are accustomed in every field to encounter a certain consensus of convinced persons of like mind, and because of such harmony of opinion to feel justified in readily rejecting whatever deviates from it. "Although open-minded," says Bryce,[7] "they are hard to convince, because they have really made up their minds on most subjects, having adopted the prevailing notions of their locality or party as truths due to their own reflections." Public opinion responds as if to one signal. A general preference prevails for what is popular, for what is understandable by all men and immediately displays its morality and practicality to everyone. Hence the receptivity for slogans and for characteristic slang terms which for a brief time characterize the general attitude to one or another question. And hence, too, the love of "public speaking" with all its oratorical cheapness.

Mechanization of industry has contributed in large measure to the intensification of these traits. It makes everything on a large scale and delivers only one model of hat or collar, only one fashion in furniture.

The feeling for conformity is revealed with particular clarity in the attitude toward religion. It is only too well known

[7] Bryce, *The American Commonwealth*, II, p. 293.

that Americans are a nation of churchgoers. The willing acceptance of the church as an institution seems to exclude all spiritual individualism. It was already remarked by Tocqueville: "Religion holds sway there much less as a doctrine of revelation than as a commonly received opinion."[8]

Now for the opposite side: the passionate American energy and the dogged personal independence in the actions of individuals. Just think what a wealth of courage and perseverance of uncounted nameless men and women went into the building of America! The men who conquered the continent bit by bit from the wilderness and the natives; the women, often alone with their children, who brought them up and kept home amid constant dangers. When one leafs through the pages of an American biographical dictionary and watches the passing lives of a good number of Americans, and not just those of great men, then one is repeatedly impressed by the intense energy, the inventive originality, the unflinching devotion to the chosen life task, the enthusiasm and often also the violence which served the pioneer and the merchant, the inventor and the politician in their life struggles. Take, for example, the group of lawyers, preachers, merchants and landowners who, in the course of destiny, were present at the Congress in Philadelphia in July 1776, when independence was declared. The "Signers of the Declaration of Independence" enjoy in the American national mind the same kind of reverence as the Helpers and the Companions of the Flight of Mohammed in Islam. Although these members of a political assembly by their very nature belonged to the circles of men who were settled and worked quietly, one is nonetheless repeatedly struck by the adventure, the violence, and even the personal choice of career

[8] *De la démocratie en Amérique*, vol. III, p. 18. [*Democracy in America*, vol. II, p. 12.]

which marked their life stories. Or take figures like Andrew Jackson, the wildest of presidents, John Brown, the bloody fanatic of the liberation of the slaves, or that other Jackson, the Confederate general nicknamed Stonewall, and a Dutchman will always say to himself: "These are different lives from those of a Van der Palm or a Nicolaas Beets."[9] There is a motley variety of types, one of the most unusual being that of the artist-inventor like Robert Fulton and Samuel F. B. Morse; but almost all impress by their individuality, their striking and vigorous enthusiasm. It comes as a surprise that Americans during the colonial period were characterized as phlegmatic, for their lives speak of everything but phlegm, both among the old and the young. Or did the observers mean by phlegm not sluggishness and apathy, but courage and strength of spirit?

In the culture as a whole we see first of all what has been brought down to a level, the tame, but in the persons taken individually one is repeatedly impressed by the intensely personal traits. It is in them that the growth of an individual American civilization, of which I spoke before, finds expression: the influence of nature and work, the education by hard life itself, which opened all spiritual capacities and put them under tension; in brief, here lies what America itself has taught its children, separate from the cultural possessions it brought over or imported.

Some anthropologists hold the opinion that the clear sky, the dry, strongly electrified air, the great temperature variations have in fact created a new physical and psychical type

[9] Johannes Henricus van der Palm (1763–1840) was a Dutch theologian and man of letters, a Patriot, minister of education during the Batavian Republic and professor at Leiden; his principal achievements were improvements in elementary education and spelling reform. Nicolaas Beets (1814–1903) was a Dutch writer of the second or third rank, whose work is marked by sentimentalism and high-flown rhetoric. —H.H.R.

in America, with a more delicate skeleton, a more colorless skin, smaller hands and feet (proved, according to what they say, by the current sizes of shoes and gloves), projecting cheek-bones, deepset eyes and a heightened nervous activity and stamina. If this is true, then it is an encouraging idea for America's future. For if it is nature itself which creates and maintains the energetic American type of man, then there is no need to fear that this type may well die out, even if many of the conditions disappear under which almost all the well-known figures in early American history grew up: in the wilderness, in nature, in struggle and hard labor, and not in school. The types like Abraham Lincoln and Henry Clay, who were day laborer, village schoolteacher, storekeeper, journalist, lawyer's clerk, are numberless. Even Emerson, the thinker, and Thoreau, the dreamer, ran after the cows when they were boys. America has always trained its children for "the strenuous life." And there lies in this energy by itself, although the external forms of culture do not always betray it, an element of individualism which forbids us to think we have seen American civilization when we have observed nothing but its herd spirit.

The primitive life in the wilderness without doubt advanced in a high measure the development of violent energy and independence. But we must not therefore conceive the contrast of individuality and conventionality in America as meaning that the wilderness awakened personality and city life the herd spirit. Spontaneous vehemence can also appear as a mass phenomenon, and it was precisely life in the wilderness which developed it to the extreme. Vehement agitation and conventionality do not at all exclude each other.

The spiritual forces in American society have had as free

play as the economic. As a consequence of the relative emptiness of culture, the small stock of traditional cultural notions,
coupled with the great excitability heightened by lonely life
in a wild and perilous nature, the American was always open
to excitement by the new and the unprecedented. Alongside
the tame subjection to everyday church faith, there stand always the religious movements of spasmodic character, which
recur in America more frequently than elsewhere. As early
as 1734, even before John Wesley visited America, we find
talk of a Great Awakening spreading over the whole East
Coast. This movement was greatly overshadowed, however,
by the Kentucky Revival of around 1800, which convulsed the
primitive population of what was then the new West for a
number of years. It was one of the strangest of the many
religious fevers reported in the history of Christianity. The
camp meetings of Kentucky displayed all the universally recurring characteristics and practices of religious enthusiasm,
but in the wildest form. For the bodily signs of grace, "jerks"
and "rolls," pickets were set up to which those possessed held
on during their wild leaps; around the pickets, the ground
was torn up if as by horses' hooves. Besides "the holy laugh,"
the hysterical convulsions of laughter of the people, they stood
up and barked in chorus during the sermon, or around a tree
from which the devil had to be driven out.

Twenty years later the same events were repeated in
Tennessee. Among the numerous later outbreaks of odd sects
in America, that of William Miller stands foremost; he predicted the end of the world about April 23, 1843, and when it
did not happen chose a later date. Excitement spread throughout the Eastern and Central states; 700 preachers were said to
be active in the service of the Second Advent; the multitudes
met in great tents or tabernacles; storekeepers gave away their

stock while others advertised "muslin for ascension robes."[10] Afterward the phenomenon of revivalism, apart from the extremely eccentric sects which appeared here and there,[11] took on less extravagant forms. The revival of 1857, which occurred in the very midst of a financial crisis, formed the transition: Begun in exaltation, it became calmer and settled down to a long-lasting and serious deepening of religious life.[12]

It was primarily the West which remained always open to strange denominations and vehement enthusiasms. Tocqueville still saw in the West of 1830 conditions such as are reported in medieval history from the early times of the Franciscans: people streaming in by horseback and on wagons from great distances and camping for many nights to hear a traveling preacher, while the work lay still and all else was forgotten.[13]

But this same phenomenon of spasmodic religious excitement still exists equally in the cultivated urban environment, transformed by modern forms of life but really the same in spirit. Billy Sunday, the evangelist, who caused a stir in all the large cities of the United States about 1917, remained the typical revivalist of the present day until Mrs. Aimee Macpherson came to put him in the shade with her wonderful adventures. Tabernacles for 50,000 persons are erected for the modern preachers of repentance; no crudity, no blending of religion and advertising, is spared in order to arouse the masses.

Thus a primitive attitude of mind is continued in an economically highly developed environment. All the credulity,

[10] MacMaster, *History of the People of the United States*, vol. VII, pp. 134 ff.

[11] J. Mooney, *The Ghost-Dance Religion and the Sioux Outbreak of 1890*, pp. 944 ff.

[12] F. M. Davenport, *Primitive Traits in Religious Revivals*, pp. 6, 203.

[13] *De la démocratie en Amérique*, vol. III, p. 216 [*Democracy in America*, vol. II, p. 142].

uncritical attitude, and fantastic excitability, all the tenacity in once-adopted prejudices and the naïve sentimentality, with which we are familiar in the spirit of the medieval populace, still characterize the popular spirit in America today.

America has always been a fertile field for every possible "ism," and every kind of charlatanry and humbug has flourished there on a gigantic scale. A journalist like Horace Greeley (1811–1872) devoted his life to the "isms" with great seriousness and futility: Fourierism, spiritism, the movement against the death penalty, women's education, spelling reform, cooperation. Modern spiritism developed in America from Margaret and Kate Fox, and vegetarianism was promoted by Sylvester Graham. Nothing was more characteristic of the entire group of exaggerated movements in America than the history of the Mormons. We find in it the Puritan tradition mingled with Indian fantasies, energetic violence, and the most exalted quackery and a love of secret rites, a talent for spontaneous social organization independent of government and resisting its authority linked to enthusiastic Americanism. Madame Blavatsky found America to be the first fertile soil for her doctrine, and the teachings of Mrs. Mary Baker Eddy arose and flourished there. But the American spirit even in its miracles is directed toward achievement; the movement must have a practical social value or it is lost. The American spirit comes to full expression for the first time in Katherine Tingley's creation at Point Loma and in the large-scale edifice of Christian Science.

The need for "organized emotion" that permeates political, religious, and esthetic life in America was displayed in the most remarkable way during the years of the World War, especially after American entry.[14] In 1917 there literally broke out a general desire for a common, solemn, and festive uplifting into

[14] *American Year Book, 1917,* pp. 373, 710; *1918,* pp. 420, 428; *1919,* pp. 406–417, 765.

the ardor of the sacred national cause. This spirit was ready for expression in things of every kind which resulted from the state of war. It was not only army camps which were centers of enthusiasm and fraternization; the central kitchens became more than just places to feed men, but exercised a spiritual function: "They have been demonstration centers; they have had beneficial results far beyond the field of domestic science." The new social feeling was expressed most of all in choral singing. Community-singing instantly became a burning issue throughout the country. In addition, the new spirit found satisfaction in community pageants and community Christmas trees. The return of the victorious troops lent the movement new force. The years 1919 and 1920 saw the high point of this "great awakening in community spirit, the new community emphasis, a new form of spirit mobilization, developing a new civic consciousness." A central body, Community Service, Incorporated, took the leadership of the movement into its hands. Community days were celebrated, a community drama was established in the form of "roaming theaters" on the roads. In various cities the citizens voluntarily devoted a day to clearing a sports field, as the citizens of Paris had done in 1790 on their Champ de Mars. Noontime singing in factories and stores sometimes seemed the way to salvation from industrial unrest.

Meanwhile the movement put down deep and lasting roots. Popular recreation in the best and broadest sense is one of the national aspirations America devotes its best forces to.

The desire for common excitement finds on the one hand much satisfaction in the busy and full life of today, but also results in blunting and leveling of feeling. Newspapers and moving pictures enslave the people, to whose need for the catchy and the spectacular they constantly cater, but they do so in a purely mechanical way, touching not the essential personal life of men but only their superficial fantasy. The vigorous commotion then becomes at last nothing more than entertainment, and the fact that it is enjoyed strengthens to the highest degree the generally standardized and uniform character of American civilization.

The question "What is the highest value in American civilization?" can be put in a simpler form: "What has America's spirit contributed to the world and to mankind?" But even then it remains very difficult to answer. The influence of America on the civilization of the Old World has never been precisely investigated and hardly ever evaluated with accuracy. That it has been important is obvious. The first period of the influence of American civilization falls in the eighteenth century. The young commonwealth then provided Europe with a political model and a political ideal of the highest importance, and at the same time it made a not unimportant contribution to the formation of the ideas of humanity. There reside more Americanisms in the ideas of the European Enlightenment in the second half of the eighteenth century than we are ordinarily aware of. But their magnitude is immeasurable, and the way in which American ideas bore fruit in Europe cannot be traced in individual cases.

During the nineteenth century America gave to the world primarily a great mass of technical progress. Her contribution in pure science was also of some importance. But what was America's share in pure intellectual culture, the ethos of mankind, that is, in art, literature, religion, and learning? That may be determined with greater certainty if we accept at once the great judgment of the world—which accepts few minds and few works into the humanity's pantheon. What American minds or works have obtained that place? The general reply must run: for the visual arts, almost none; for literature, religion, and learning, a small number of works and figures, but those few of extraordinary importance.

Surveying the older American art and literature in general, it takes its place for the most part in that category of timid America which we described earlier. The tameness characterizing it was in the first place the result of society's colonial character, which, as we indicated, exercised a restrictive influence upon the creativity of the free spirit. People then have little time for or interest in a more refined culture, and where a desire for it exists, people are satisfied with what the mother country offers or anxiously endeavor to follow the model it presents. Before the War of Independence, there was no American literature to speak of. The country's own intellectual productions were principally limited to sermons and almanacs. Only after victory did a brand-new and most self-complacent patriotism cause the emergence, among other things, of a desire for an American national literature, worthy of a free people. But the spiritual dependence on England was not shaken off in a moment; for a long time a cautious concern for established forms remained one of the characteristics of American literature, such as one finds in a man who learns good manners late in life. Furthermore, English works long dominated American intellectual life. It did not occur to America, which was otherwise so fierce in protecting its own products, that the minds of its children also needed such protection. Until the Copyright Act of 1891, it was the American publishing industry itself which flooded the country with English literature in cheap reprints.

Most of what America itself produced until the end of the nineteenth century is distinguished in the first place by smooth, correct form, and then by its close involvement with public life and social utility. Writers and poets, most of whom came out of journalism, placed themselves at the service of a good cause, or of several good causes. The standard poets of the nineteenth century—William Cullen Bryant, John Greenleaf Whittier, and James Russell Lowell—all found their highest inspiration in the struggle against slavery. Whittier saw his newspaper plant plundered and burned down because of it. All three were enthusiastic patriots, and Whittier also possessed a genuine feeling for the people.

What is the quality of their poetry, which is next to unknown in Holland?[15] Here is, for example, a strophe from Bryant's "Our Country's Call" of 1861.

> Lay down the axe; fling by the spade;
> Leave in its track the toiling plough;
> The rifle and the bayonet blade
> For arms like yours were fitter now;
> And let the hands that ply the pen
> Quit the light task, and learn to wield
> The horseman's crooked brand, and rein
> The charger on the battle field.

If America's poets and writers have almost always had the welfare of the nation in view, and striven to be of use to society, their country for its part has always demonstrated that it did not look upon them as useless dreamers and had confidence in their knowledge of men and their characteristic healthiness. There was a certain tradition of sending men of letters abroad on occasion as envoys of the United States. Washington Irving was in Spain, Lowell went not only there but also to London; Lisbon was offered to Hawthorne.

That Longfellow should be known to the world while Bryant, Whittier, and Lowell are in comparative obscurity, probably has its cause in no small measure in the fact that he is less exclusively American in character. But he does not differ importantly from them in the kind of poet he is; he too is characterized by sweetness and virtue, the idyllic ambling pace of his hexameters, and the soft romanticism of his imagination.

These same characteristics of good form and a certain

[15] And, of course, in Europe in general.—H.H.R.

innocent originality also typify the visual arts. "The average American painter is distinguished above all by what may be called good table manners. For the most part he has learned his craft in Europe and knows how to handle it with modesty."[16] The tendency to imitation is equally true for architecture, in which a French education prevailed too for a long time. The imitation of the old styles fell into discredit even later in America than elsewhere.

Although the judgment sounds paradoxical, one may ascribe the good, correct form of American art to the absence of formal sensitivity and powers. Form means tradition. A lone man does not create any forms; the grand form is only developed where there is a spiritual heritage of centuries, where free artistic energy has profound maturity because it rests upon many generations. This is what America does not have, so that its art until now has lacked grand forms of its own. It has mastered form only by careful imitation. Whenever true and deep American spirits like Emerson and Thoreau wrote verse, it came out wooden and jerky, probably just because they were men too lofty for smooth imitation. And even in their prose, with all its admirable qualities, there is no ripple of moving, impetuous sound. Emerson's prose belongs to the second order; it has no rhythm but a certain monotonous gait. The brief demonstration in which Emerson excels has, however, a *vitium originis;* because of its origin it must be witty, and hence it falls into a kind of trinket-style.

The absence of a sense of form explains why the great genres are almost completely missing from American literature, especially the drama, which requires the highest formal power. Its strength lay in the minor genres in which the formal element is of little importance: the essay, the short story, occa-

[16] An American's judgment cited by Jan Veth, "Een Amerikaansche Schilder," *De Gids,* 1914, no. 4, p. 176.

sional verse, and table talk (Oliver Wendell Holmes). And even in these formal control sometimes falls short. Some essays of Emerson are tiring in their accumulation of aphoristic sentences without a clear overview. Among lesser figures, the small forms easily encourage feeling and imagination to move within the pleasant boundaries of geniality.

The imaginative element in American literature is primarily defined by dependence on Europe and the European past. What is the romanticism—the dreams of the past and the gardens of thought—through which American literature has strolled? In the first place, it is the romanticism of Europe. For America too, the medieval world, the Italy of dreams, or Spain and England in the Renaissance, have been the world in which romantic fantasy has flourished most luxuriantly. But the American spirit created its own national romanticism besides. The first of the categories into which it can be divided is ancestral romanticism. Along with *The Golden Legend* laid among the knights of medieval Germany, Longfellow composed the idyllic epic of Puritan New England in *Miles Standish* and another of old French America in *Evangeline*. There is in this ancestral romanticism an element of the strong and naïve ancestor worship which in its more banal forms is also characteristic of America. How could Hawthorne, who gave Puritan romanticism its liveliest expression, help but be obsessed with the magistrates and sea captains of Masschusetts, his forebears, who joined in sitting in judgment on the Salem witches and fighting the Indians? Even in Whitman's free brain the shades of the ancestors hovered round: especially of a half-mythical Dutchman "old Kossabone" (could his name have been Karseboom?). The Dutch variety of this ancestral romanticism was created by Washington Irving: the Knickerbocker figure Rip van Winkle, and the schoolmaster of Sleepy Hollow. With it romantic sentiment ceases to be wholly serious; the "Dutch" type is spiced with a dash of amusing ghosts and a sprinkling of irony. It satisfies the need for snug romanticism and peaceful idyllicism.

At the side of ancestral romanticism stands the Indian variety. Even while the struggle against the natives was still under way, America accepted romantic veneration of the Indians as an element of national feeling. The first families of Virginia were proud to be descended from Pocahontas, the Algonquin "princess" who married the Englishman Rolfe. Statues were raised to the great Indian foes of an earlier day: Red Jacket, Pontiac, Tecumtha, or children were given their names; Sherman, who in 1864 drove the Southerners to the sea, was named William Tecumseh. The Indian already figured as a national symbol on a model for a ten-dollar piece submitted by Gouverneur Morris in 1782: an Indian with his foot upon a crown, a bow with 13 arrows in his hand, and the legend: *Manus inimica tyrannis*.[17] Admiration for the wild and strangely beautiful sounds of the Indian languages can be heard already in Hawthorne and Whitman. The former has an Indian lad reading Eliot's translation of the Bible: "Then would the Indian boy cast his eyes over the mysterious page and read it so skillfully that it sounded like wild music. It seemed as if the forest leaves were singing in the ears of his auditors, and as if the roar of distant streams were poured through the young Indian's voice."[18]

And Whitman:

> . . . The red aborigines,
> Leaving natural breaths, sounds of rain and winds, calls as
> of birds and animals in the wood, syllabled to us for
> names,

[17] Latin for "A foe's hand [that is, foreign rule] is tyranny."—H.H.R.
[18] Hawthorne, "Grandfather's Chair," *Complete Works* (Fireside edition), vol. IV, p. 472.

Okonee, Koosa, Ottawa, Monongahela, Sauk, Natchez,
Chattahoochee, Kaqueta, Oronoco . . .
Leaving such to the States they melt, they depart, charging
the water and the land with names.[19]

Whitman's love for Indian names, which made him always
say Paumanok for Long Island and Mannahatta for New York,
was shared by many, who regretted the innumerable Uticas,
Bethels, Jacksons, and Madisons when they compared them
with the splendid geographical nomenclature of Indian origin.
"A prodigality of fine melodious names remains, the best legacy
which the unlettered red man could leave us before he vanished forever before the march of civilization."[20]

Indian romanticism makes its way into literature with
Irving, who wrote about King Philip of Pokanoket, the feared
foe of Massachusetts in the seventeenth century, with Bryant,
who composed an *Indian's Girl's Lament*, and most of all with
the novels of Fenimore Cooper and Longfellow's *Hiawatha*. But
despite the wild material it continues to be a traditional and
domesticated romanticism: The mythic idyll *Hiawatha*, however unusual its setting, remains an offshoot from a European
source of inspiration, for it is in form and style an imitation of
the Finnish *Kalevala*. The great and true spirit of America
does not reveal itself in romanticism of any kind.

At the top of the pages in which I try to come at this
spirit in all its fullness, I should like to write: "This, Here, and
Soon." These words would indicate the vigorous acceptance
of life, the commitment to this world and to the present and

---

[19] "Starting from Paumonok, 16," *Complete Writings*, vol. I, p. 30.
[20] A. R. Spofford, "American Historical Nomenclature," *Annual
Report of the American Historical Association*, 1893, p. 33. The author
mistakenly includes Hoboken among the Indian names.—J.H. [Hoboken,
New Jersey, is named after the town of Hoboken, a small city in Bel-
gium near Antwerp.—H.H.R.]

future time, in which the essence of America's spirit lies. It
may well be that modern Europe has also relinquished most
of the old *Jenseitlichkeit*[21] in its culture; nonetheless it remains
much more heavily laden with its past and is much more passionately given to retrospection. America runs toward the future much more lightly shod. "The mystery for them lies not
behind them but before them."[22] This is also true for Europe,
so far as its political and economic aims are concerned, but its
ideas and imagination are much more firmly fixed in the old,
dead cultures, in remembrance, in the monuments and arts of
the past, in the grim eyes of the heroes of another day. We
cannot give up our cathedrals or Shakespeare. But the American mind, apart from its modest romanticism and its light-
weight tradition, is free; it is not burdened with so many old
writings and so many old stones.

At every level of American intellectual life, from the
highest to the most everyday, we see an enormous zest for the
future, confidence in the improvement of man and society,
moral optimism, expressed in the most varied forms. When it
was first founded the city of Bismarck, North Dakota, built
an immense state capitol, because it counted firmly on being
a center of the world.[23] The enthusiasm over Roosevelt's and
Wilson's ideas of social reform, of improvement and renewal
of political and economic life, arose out of the mingling of
ethical and material idealism which comes about so easily in
America.

The whole tone of religious life in America is that of
"This, Here, and Soon." Morality and a regular life, practical
activity for the improvement of moral and social conditions,
are its main business. Hence the success of the strongly moral-

---

[21] German for "otherworldliness" or "transcendence."–H.H.R.
[22] Boutmy, *Eléments*, p. 78.
[23] Bryce, *The American Commonwealth*, vol. II, p. 898.

istic sects such as the Baptists and the Methodists. Tocqueville had already observed that despite the differences of dogma, all the sects saw their task under this same light of practical activity, and that even the Catholic church could not withstand this flood of the American spirit and makes less use in America of its rich treasury of historical tradition, as for instance in the veneration of saints.[24] Nowhere probably does there lie such a strong proof of the unity and uniqueness of American civilization than in the fact that the old church has assimilated to American life in every way; and where this was possible, without touching doctrine. For this naturally was a frontier that could not be crossed, and the church was strong enough to subject even America, apparently so at variance with its spirit, to itself in this regard. As soon as a hint of "Americanism," the tendency to allow doctrine to be softened in some points under the influence of an optimistic evaluation of modern civilization, and to consider some virtues as merely *pro memoria*, was revealed in the church in the last years of the nineteenth century, Rome spoke[25] and at once found full obedience from the flourishing American Catholicism. But where the purity of the faith is not involved, what authentically American characteristics are displayed there by Catholic life! The "Knights of Columbus" is the name of a far-flung society of the kind we have named so many of before; its purpose is "a practical Catholicity," and for it the church even permits an exception to its general ban on secret societies. It works zealously on the national problem of Americanization. Cardinal Gibbons, who in his purple opens a party convention of the Republicans with a prayer; a prelate who hires a theater;

24 *De la Démocratie en Amérique*, vol. III, p. 44 [*Democracy in America*, vol. II, pp. 28–29].

25 In the Apostolic brief *Testem benevolentiae* of January 22, 1899 to Cardinal Gibbons; see *Catholic Encyclopedia* s.v. Testem b. and Hecker, Isaac Thomas.

an auto chapel which travels around in order to strengthen the
faithful by special delivery[26]—these are all signs of how the
need for efficiency expresses itself.

The churches accept the most strict business forms in
order to attain their social objectives more effectively.

In 1908 all the Christian denominations except the Catholics formed their own "trust": the Federal Council of the
Churches of Christ. Its program of activities extended over
evangelization, Christian education, the temperance movement, the advancement of peace and international arbitration,
observance of the Sabbath, and social work. The last is phrased
in almost Christian Socialist terms: "to improve social and
civic conditions, to secure justice for the masses, to eradicate
vice and to bring the church into the closest possible relations
with humanity."[27] The strivings of the Inter-Church World
Movement in America, which was launched in late 1918 and
began activity in 1920, went much further. Nineteen and one
half million Protestants of thirty denominations joined together
to Christianize America and the world. The work was begun
with the construction of a complete card index of all inhabitants of the United States; in this way the entire spiritual status
of the continent could be registered and analyzed and the
conversion of the country begun after men and means had
been accurately assigned. It was to be ready in five years.[28]

The unshakable confidence in the results of an education
equipped with every resource is part and parcel of the optimistic belief to which I am referring. "Equality suggests the
theory of the indefinite perfectibility of man."[29] The stream

[26] Dr. G. Brom, in *De Beiaard*, 1919, p. 93.
[27] *American Year Book, 1916*, p. 724.
[28] *Daily Telegraph*, March 8, 1920; *American Year Book, 1919*, p. 747.
[29] Tocqueville, *De la démocratie en Amérique*, vol. III, p. 52. [*Democracy in America*, vol. II, pp. 34–35.]

of money for schools and libraries flows incessantly. These are the public buildings par excellence in American towns. In this confidence in "the saving grace of education" there probably lies some peril of overestimation of outer culture, which is not wholly alien to Europe either.

The demand for efficiency permeates the spirit of America at every level, from questions of town government to the highest problems of pure thought. What is the pragmatism of William James but this very attitude carried over into the sphere of philosophy, so that it is a characteristically American philosophy? According to some writers, it is not so much James's personal conception as actually a general direction of American thought. "The religious philosophy of the sensible American has long tended in the direction now ticketed by philosophers as Pragmatism. Whatever will work in the conduct of life, strengthening it, enriching it, giving it a higher trend, must, so far as it goes, have elements of truth. If it were not true, it would not work."[30]

In the American mind efficiency and democracy are closely related concepts. The endeavor to democratize the idea of God goes hand in hand with pragmatism, and both arise out of the spirit of "This, Here, and Soon." "Smitten as we are," says William James, "with the vision of social righteousness, a God indifferent to everything but adulation and full of partiality for his individual favorites, lacks an essential element of largeness; and even the best professional sainthood of former centuries, pent in as it is, to such a conception, seems to us curiously shallow and unedifying." "The God whom science recognizes must be a God of universal laws exclusively, a God who does a wholesale, not a retail business."[31]

[30] D. S. Jordan, "The Religion of the Sensible American," *Hibbert Journal,* VI (1908), p. 860.
[31] James, *Varieties of Religious Experience,* pp. 346, 493.

If we want, we can see in all this optimism, this confidence in our total perfectibility, this sense for what is useful in practice, this ideal of pure humanitarianism, the evolution of spiritual currents which we are wrongly in the habit of considering to be long past—namely, the humanitarian ideals of the Enlightened eighteenth century. The historical line may be drawn as follows. America did not experience the great reaction against the Enlightenment. Faith, being involved in humanitarian idealism, remained virtually intact. There did not arise in America, as in Europe, an absolute enmity of Voltaireans, liberals, and advocates of the Revolution against those who sought a basis for their fiercer and more torrid ideals in history and became the followers of De Maistre and De Bonald, Von Haller, Stahl and the Réveil.[32] From the beginning the forces from which the escape from superficiality and jejuneness had to come could make themselves felt in America within the very framework of life that had been brought from the eighteenth century. The Enlightenment itself was able to develop without disturbance and with continued fruitfulness in America. The deepest and most enduring value of the Enlightenment as a cultural current must be measured much more by its growth and results in America than in Europe. Very early the humane idealism of the Enlightenment had a finer, nobler sound in America. William Ellery Channing (1780–1842), the enthusiastic preacher of the worth of human nature and belief in social progress, can be considered as the link between eighteenth-century humanitarianism and its modern version. Emerson follows directly after him, and in his ideal of man we hardly descry any more of the shallow benevolence of the

[32] The first four are theorists of the early nineteenth century, the last a Dutch movement of the same character, all emphasizing hostility to the ideals of the Enlightenment and the French Revolution, the restoration of authority and tradition, and the primacy of religion.—H.H.R.

eighteenth century; he envisions his picture of the new gentle-
man more according to the norms of knighthood and the
Renaissance than those of the salon and utility. It is "made of
the spirit more than of the talent of men, and is a compound
result, into which every great force enters as an ingredient,
namely, virtue, wit, beauty, wealth and power."[33]

Emerson's optimism, perfectibility, and individualism are
raised to transcendental heights. "I am primarily engaged to
myself to be a public servant of all the Gods, to demonstrate
to all men there is good-will and intelligence at the heart of
things and ever higher and yet higher leadings. These are my
engagements. If there be power in good intentions, in fidelity,
and in toil, the north wind shall be purer, the stars in heaven
shall glow with a kindlier beam that I have lived."

This is the "healthy-mindedness," the belief that "all's well
with the universe," which James, who had plumbed other
depths of consciousness, could easily mock. But it is James
himself, although unlike Emerson he does not give his testimony without reservation, who is another unmistakable representative of this optimism. And America has the same quality;
its spirit is "healthy-minded." No one has felt this as strongly
and expressed it as exquisitely as William James's amazing
brother Henry, whose figures of Americans all share to a
greater or lesser extent in Christopher Newman's "air of being
imperturbably, being irremovably and indestructibly at home
in the world."[34]

Emerson's namesake Ralph Waldo Trine has transmitted
this attitude of moral optimism to thousands in the Old World
as well by his *In Tune with the Infinite or Fullness of Peace,
Power and Plenty*. It reads almost like an advertisement for
soap or cigarettes; but that is what America is like, and that is

[33] Emerson, "Manners," *Works* (Routledge, 1883), p. 108.
[34] Henry James, *The American*, p. 115.

also how the wise men of ages when religion was more naïve praised their own insights. His aim is strictly practical; he provides the "method of entering into this higher realization." The credo with which Trine concludes another book is so characteristic for "healthy-mindedness" and at the same time displays so tellingly the relationship with eighteenth-century ideals that I wish to quote a good portion of it here:

> To live to our highest in all things that pertain to us, to lend a hand as best we can to all others for this same end;
> To aid in righting the wrongs that cross our path by pointing the wrong-doer to a better way, and thus aid him in becoming a power for good; to remain in nature always sweet and simple and humble, and therefore strong;
> To open ourselves fully and to keep ourselves pure and clean as fit channels for the Divine Power to work through us; to turn toward and keep our faces always to the light;
> To do our own thinking, listening quietly to the opinions of others, and to be sufficiently men and women to act always upon our own convictions; to do our duty as we see it, regardless of the opinions of others, seeming gain or loss, temporary blame or praise; . . .
> To love all things and to stand in awe or fear of nothing save our own wrong-doing; to recognize the good lying at the heart of all people, of all things, waiting for expression, all in its own good way and time;
> To love the fields and the wild flowers, the stars, the far-open sea, the soft, warm earth, and to live much with them alone, but to love struggling and weary men and women and every pulsing living creature better. . . .[35]

Do you feel how close this is to Whitman?—Now the essence of American individualism in its higher significance, assembled as it is from optimism, cultivation of the personality for higher action, reverence for spiritual and bodily health,

[35] Trine, *In the Fire of the Heart*, p. 359.

admiration for the noble and vigorous deed, slowly begins to have force for us. But Emerson, Whitman, and Trine, it will be said, are the few, the best; the rest are no less a herd because of them. Do you think that the contemporaries of Leonardo or Goethe were any less a herd? If the standard must be that everyone was a personality, then we would never have the right to speak of an individualist period or environment.

Yet everyday America does really share in these characteristics that I have summarized. It is always but a short step from the lofty revelations of philosophy or poetry to the everyday expressions which come from the same spiritual fountainhead. Trine's individualism, with its honest moralism, has closely related parallels in a series of systems which are more or less quackery; they present themselves as "mind-cure," "new thought," "higher thought," "menticulture," "soul-culture," "joy-philosophy," "higher health," "new mysticism," "new or cosmic consciousness," and have in part found their way from America to the Old World. For the most part they are the crudest parodies of real mysticism or spiritual exercises. Not only are their goals directed to the individual, they are an egoist materialism. What they promise is money and comfort; compassion for others merely disturbs the arousing of one's own soul to contentment and repose.

"Inhale slowly, but not too slowly, just easily; as you inhale, say mentally, with eyes raised under your closed lids, I AM—say it slowly, and distinctly, and try quietly to *realize* that the Infinite is really *you*. . . . This same exercise, used with the words 'I AM *money*," is the finest treatment for opulence."[36] Is a more exquisite mixture of the style of an Upanishad and a quacks's formula imaginable?

[36] E. Towne, "*Just How to Wake the Solar Plexus*," quoted by Mrs. E. Stuart Moore, "The Magic and Mysticism of To-day," *Hibbert Journal*, VI (1908), p. 384.

Next to such weeds of culture, we have, however, a general, truly social, and passionate reverence for physical health which has become a kind of public religion in America. I find somewhere the report of the proceedings of a sociological conference in the Southern states in 1915; it carries the title *New Chivalry-Health*. We see how the ideal of health immediately assumed the character of a cherished object, a new form of life. In the childish elation of his active spirit, everything that the American favors at once becomes a slogan, a movement. The displays of the health cult illustrate this. In March 1916, the celebration of a Baby Week began throughout the country. The movement "literally swept the country," even reaching the Philippines and, in 1917, the Indian reservations. The aim was national instruction for parents in infant care. The methods employed were meetings, exhibitions, conferences, stage performances, tableaux, school themes, and the distribution of flags to houses where there were babies. In Kansas the governor offered a badge of honor to the healthiest district in the state. In 1918 this celebration was lengthened to a Children's Year, with the presecribed goal of saving 100,000 children from death by preventable illnesses. "The drive began on April 6, the anniversary of America's entrance into the war, with a nation-wide measuring and weighing of babies and children of pre-school age." Later followed a "recreation drive and patriotic play week" in order to decide what each town was doing in the interest of children's play facilities, which finally concluded with a "back-to-school drive."[37] Meanwhile this festive competition provided a stimulus for a permanent health-care system which is not to be disparaged.

On the lower, common level of the popular mind of a naïve hero-worship corresponds to Emerson's reverence for the

[37] *American Year Book, 1916*, p. 390; *1917*, p. 376; *1918*, p. 430.

free, strong personality. Lord Bryce, who was not at all in the habit of praising Americans beyond measure, testified that their imagination and emotions are especially susceptible to impressions of the noble and the sympathetic. "They are capable of an ideality surpassing that of Englishmen or Frenchmen."[38] American hero-worship is expressed in a number of ways. The lowest of these forms of expression is movie romanticism, which still is confined mainly to American culture. The honor given to success, the admiration for self-made strength, are only a part of hero-worship. What is admired above all in George Washington are his quiet strength and his patience in adversity; in Lincoln all the qualities dear to the American come together, and it is not in the least his rise by his own abilities which have made him such a national symbol. History is deliberately taught in American schools by honoring heroes. "This emulation of heroes . . . has become in the United States the tie which brings the races together and fortifies spiritual unity. American patriotism is composed in the first place of admiration . . . it is naïve and categorical, more than elsewhere."[39] The need for a common, continuous worship of their great men is expressed by putting the portraits of former presidents on postage stamps and naming cities after national heroes. In 1893 (there must be more now) there were 49 places with the name of Washington, as well as 47 Jeffersons, 63 Franklins, 43 Monroes, 44 Madisons, 61 Jacksons (Andrew, the President, the hero of the West!), 30 Hamiltons, 25 Websters, 13 Calhouns, 7 Clays. And also a modest 9 Emersons and 6 Hawthornes.[40]

Children too are named after the heroes. Washington

[38] Bryce, *The American Commonwealth*, vol. II, p. 293.
[39] Suzanne Moret, "Le patriotisme à l'école Américaine," *Revue de Paris*, November 15, 1917, pp. 382, 397.
[40] Spofford, "American Historical Nomenclature."

Irving was born in the year of victory, 1783. Jefferson Davis, the president of the Confederate (Southern) States during the Civil War, illustrates in his very name the worship for the old ideal of independence once proclaimed by Thomas Jefferson.

There is another form of hero-worship which is of exceptional importance for history; I have in mind the extraordinary interest and ability in biography which mark the American as strongly as the Englishman. As a result, the life stories of all great men as well as those of lesser rank are written in a profusion which we Dutchmen, who often lack the most necessary things in this field, can envy. But we also find at the lower level of everyday affairs the interest newspapers devote to the personal life and daily welfare of all respected citizens.

By hero-worship the crowd pays its own tribute to individualism; it pays homage through great men to an ideal of personality which it feels to be beyond its own attainment but nevertheless admires. Hero-worship and individualism are closely related. It was not for naught that Emerson, the individualist, was a friend of Carlyle, the godfather of hero-worship. Emerson saw as *Representative Men* those in whom he recognized the jewel of great personality which is indispensable and irreplaceable for the world. If Emerson's hero-worship always moves more on the intellectual plane, Whitman also possesses a direct *feeling* for the importance of the individual deed of heroism, however simple and ordinary. Somewhere in *Specimen Days* he relates the death of a young sergeant who refused to surrender during a Confederate attack. "When I think of such things," he concludes his account, "knowing them well, all the vast and complicated events of the war, on which history dwells and makes its volumes, fall aside, and for the moment at any rate I see nothing but young Calvin Harlowe's figure in the night, disdaining to surrender."[41]

[41] *Specimen Days. Complete Writings*, vol. IV, p. 116.

The *conviction* of the importance of the individual deed is expressed with special force in these words of Emerson's:

> There is a great responsible Thinker and Actor working wherever a man works; . . . a true man belongs to no other time or place, but is the centre of things. Where he is, there is nature. . . . Every true man is a cause, a country, and an age; requires infinite spaces and numbers and time fully to accomplish his design;—and posterity seem to follow his steps as a train of clients. A man Caesar is born, and for ages after we have a Roman empire. Christ is born, and millions of minds so grow and cleave to his genius, that he is confounded with virtue and the possible of man. An institution is the lengthened shadow of one man; as, Monachism, of the Hermit Antony; the Reformation, of Luther; Quakerism, of Fox; Methodism, of Wesley; Abolition, of Clarkson. . . . All history resolves itself very easily into the biography of a few stout and earnest persons.[42]

Although historical scholarship no longer dares to profess such extreme individualism, the spirit always strives to go back to it. For the common mind continues to affirm: "The world is upheld by the presence of good men. They make the earth wholesome."[43]

As it is used, the idea of individualism ceaselessly shifts ground. Now it is the conviction that individuality resides in the man who gets the job done. Then it is the compulsion to live one's life according to one's own ideas. Channing provides the note of religious individualism: "We must start in religion from our own souls. In these is the fountain of all divine truth." And Emerson put it into practice; he resigned his position as a minister in 1832 because he had ceased to gain inspiration from the practices of his church, and he became the preacher of

[42] Emerson, "Self-reliance," *Works* (Routledge, 1883), p. 14.
[43] D. S. Jordan, "The Religion of the Sensible American," p. 854.

individual idealism par excellence: "Know thyself and Study nature become at last one maxim."

This is the soil in which American individualism grows: life in and with nature. Henry David Thoreau isolated himself in nature so as not to have to subject his individuality to that of others. Nature at Walden was anything but wild: Thoreau heard the train and received many visitors there. It remained a picture full of contradictions: Thoreau's perfectly sincere feeling for nature and his tiresomely affected thought and form, in which the most sparkling treasures of profundity and simplicity sometimes lie hidden away amid masses of clever chitchat.

The experience of the recluse at Walden (1845) was only one example among many. The others were not hermits but practitioners of life in common, like the Fruitlands of Amos Bronson Alcott, Louisa's father, and Brook Farm, a community intended "to insure a more natural union between intellectual and manual labor than now exists; to combine the thinker and the worker, to guarantee the highest mental freedom." It was, therefore, an organized individualism. Hawthorne looked in on Brook Farm, describing it in his *Blithedale Romance*. Emerson lightly mocked Brook Farm. "We are all a little wild here with numberless projects of social reform; not a reading man but has a draft of a new community in his waistcoat pocket."

What in the middle of the nineteenth century were the individual endeavors of a few took on its general, everyday form in the course of time. The camping out of a later time meant that Thoreau's gospel had become a general faith. We may call it the modern form of the old ideal of the shepherd, with nature more true and love less sweet.

Until relatively recently it might seem to the European that almost all American literature worthy of the world's attention had come into existence in one place, at one time, in one circle. This was just where the old Puritan culture had also flourished and borne fruit and where the first episode of the war for freedom had occurred—in New England, and within even narrower limits, the Boston vicinity. One cemetery holds Emerson, Thoreau, and Hawthorne. The three of them and Channing, Alcott, and a number of lesser known figures were all tied to each other by personal bonds. Hawthorne was a classmate of Longfellow's and a friend of Motley's. He wrote *Mosses from an Old Manse* in the house where Emerson had lived before him. Lowell followed Longfellow as professor of modern literature at Harvard University. Or, if we want still more coincidences: Emerson was an old friend of Henry James, Sr., the father of William and Henry; he resided in the very hotel in New York where the philosopher was born on January 9, 1842, and was "proudly and pressingly taken upstairs to admire and give his blessing to the lately-born babe."[44]

It might be thought that it was an arbitrary trick of fame that made just this one group renowned—that America, even in these earlier times, must have produced much more important literature in addition to and besides what these men wrote, in the South and in the shifting West, but that we Europeans are not sufficiently aware of it. But we should not suspect fame of such one-sided favoritism toward Boston. The few great men who arose outside this circle—Irving, Poe, and Whitman—also became equally well known.

Is there some quality which binds the important figures of this earlier American literature together in some way, so that we may consider it a quality essential to the mind of America? I think that there is such a quality—the gift which

[44] Henry James, *A Small Boy and Others*, 1913, p. 8. William's birthday is usually given not as 9, but as 11 January 1842.—J.H.

we may call, with a word they themselves often used, "insight." The word "insight" has retained in American speech, because it is used less often, a much more pregnant and transcendental significance than the ordinary Dutch word *inzicht*. It can serve to indicate the enormously lucid perception of the inwardness of things, that sense-organ for what lies beyond ordinary reality, which distinguishes these American writers.

It is expressed in Poe and Hawthorne as fantasy, the painfully sharp and bright force of imagination. In many respects Edgar Allan Poe (1809–1849) was an untypical American. He was too decadent, too unbalanced for that; he had too much in common with Oscar Wilde and Villiers de l'Isle Adam; he was too lacking in quiet strength and "healthy-mindedness." He plays his own inspiration: In *The Raven* a half-comic element is so mixed with weirdness and mystery resting for the most part on the distasteful jingle of the verse, that we wonder whether the poet did not permit this admixture of comic effect because he felt that the poem was otherwise too full of faults to be taken with full seriousness. In his tendency to the bizarre and the extravagant, he gives descriptions which sometimes merely produce an artificial motley effect but at other times create a flush of wild grandeur, like the bridal chamber in *Ligeia*, where the somber fantasy makes one think of Huysmans's *À Rebours*. Poe's talent is very cerebral and somewhat artificial. But what is very American in Poe is his acute imagination and the vigorous intelligence with which he constructs his tales. Poe is probably most original and therefore most imitated by later writers in the rational puzzle-stories by which he prepared the way for the detective story: *The Gold Bug, The Purloined Letter, The Murders in the Rue Morgue*. The effect of horror at which Poe aims follows older traditions. About 1800 the feeling for the English style of wonderment and fright, to which E. T. A. Hoffmann gave the sharpest expression in Europe, already had a representative in America. He was Charles Brockden Brown, whose *Sky Walk or the Man Unknown to Himself*, and *Edgar Huntley or the Memoirs of a Sleep Walker* display their mood in their very titles.

But Poe wanted to do more and go deeper than merely give his reader a shudder. His spirit always roamed back to the unfathomable, cloud-covered abysses of the riddle of personality, identity, of life after death, of the fading of consciousness. Powerless to solve these riddles, he gives pictures which present them to our eyes in thrilling materiality: the personality which is repeated in another individual in *Ligeia, Morella, The Black Cat*, the simultaneous double personality in *William Wilson*. In Poe we find, as it were, the same powerful and intensely sensitive interest for the deepest individual life which is heard in Emerson's work, but in a totally different key conveyed in a fever of fantasy.

Nathaniel Hawthorne (1804–1864) created what might have been expected from Poe, had he had a more fortunate upbringing and been able to develop all his gifts in balance. Hawthorne may have lacked the hyperbolic sharpness of Poe and his eccentric sweep toward the extremities of human thought; but how much richer and well-considered his work is! Hawthorne seems to me the finest and most harmonious among the older representatives of the American spirit. Like Irving and Poe, he excelled in the short story; his *The Scarlet Letter* is hardly longer than a novella. He shares with both Irving and Poe what seems to be the typical American liking for mystifying the reader with an elaborate fiction of old documents he claims to have taken his story from. He has all the entertaining good nature of Irving, but at the same time his view of the local past is much more serious and intimate, much more visionary, and without any of Irving's idyllic humor. Puritan New England arises in him in all its strict simplicity and somber seriousness, yet illuminated by that warm glow of Indian Summer which is Hawthorne's particular atmosphere.

He has as acute an imagination as Poe, but is much more serene, harmonious, natural, richer, warmer, finer, and more colorful. He combined the dreamy motley pomp of Gottfried Keller with the childish tenderness and naïve sentimentality of Andersen. Sometimes he becomes a bit too sweet. He commands the weird element as well as Poe, but in a more subdued way and without the deliberate effect of horror. *The Birthmark* and *Rappaccini's Daughter* are equal to the most striking things that Poe could produce. And Poe could never have written the *Wonderbook* and *Tanglewood Tales*, which retell the classical tales for children.

"I never did anything so good as those old baby stories," wrote Hawthorne, when he had completed *Tanglewood Tales*,[45] and it is not impossible that in this case posterity will exceptionally agree with a writer in the estimate of his own work. The fantasy of these tales of Perseus, Midas, the apples of the Hesperides, Proserpina and the rest is so pure, so strong and direct, that only the *Moralités Légendaires* of Jules Laforgue and the *Sieben Legenden* of Gottfried Keller can be named at their side. The humor is so muted, there is such a fullness of inward feeling, that the old myths radiate as with a new warm light. The view of things is almost that of Dante, for example in the conversation of Hercules with Atlas or in the growth of the giants in the moonlight from the dragon's teeth sowed by Jason. And with all of this, the perfect childlike tone which makes them remain true children's stories. It is as if Hawthorne had already felt what the latest *Forschung*[46] into myth has discovered, that it is not the fairy tale which is a

---

[45] *Complete Works*, vol. XII, p. 514.
[46] German for "research," which has here a slightly ironic tone of pedantry that the plain Dutch *onderzoek* would lack.—H.H.R.

by-product of myth but the myth which is a stylization of the fairy tale.

One of the most important tests of the true humanity of a literature is the question of the place taken in it by animals and children. Think of *The Little Clay Wagon*,[47] think of Telemachus who "was not alone" because he had two dogs with him.[48] If American literature is subjected to this test, it emerges very well. It treats animals and children with exceptional love. Out of a notebook from Hawthorne's youth comes a conversation with a "solemn-faced old horse," which foretold all the humor, the fantasy, and the great heart of the storyteller of Tanglewood.[49] Whitman said: "I think I could turn and live with animals, they are so placid and self-contained." And he sees himself screaming and wheeling slowly in the air as one in a multitude of thousands of gulls, or fishing as a heron.[50]

Our admiration for the animal stories of Jack London and Seton Thompson may be large or little but they are of importance as an expression of America's spirit. And if the true test of children's stories consists in the question whether adults can also enjoy them, then Louisa Alcott and Mark Twain may be named along with Hawthorne, and their influence on the development of European children's reading is probably greater than we usually realize.

The feeling for animals and children is part of what I should like to call the strong element of sympathy in American literature. This sympathetic element relates not only to living fellow creatures but most of all to nature. We hear it *fortissimo*, in Whitman, in Hawthorne singing in the sweetest *cantilena*. From his easy, unconstrained pictures of nature there remains

---

[47] *Mrcchakatika*, a Hindu drama of the 6th century A.D.—H.H.R.
[48] Odyssey, II, 10.
[49] *Complete Works*, vol. XII, p. 459.
[50] *Song of Myself* 32, vol. I, p. 71; *Our Old Feuillage*, p. 211.

above all the impression of the hazy sun and soft still warmth of a September day, with the bronze colors and elegiac fragrance of leaves about to wither. But beyond simple descriptions of nature, Hawthorne seeks to penetrate it with his mind, to attain the unity of spirit and environment. He has for everything around him above all a sense of that quality of meaningful reality beyond the immediately given, which is so strongly emphasized by William James. "We suspect," says James, "that our natural experience, so called, our strictly moralistic and prudential and legal experience, may only be a fragment of reality. . . . The believer finds that the tenderer parts of his personal life are continuous with a *more* of the same quality which is operative in the universe outside of him, and which he can keep in working touch with."[51]

It is this which Hawthorne often sets forth directly. In *The House of the Seven Gables* the introduction of an atmosphere of mystery is too deliberate; in *The Scarlet Letter* the effect is more genuine and immediate. But more striking than these literary effects is his perception of the outer regions of the mind, unconscious action, depersonalization. Few have depicted so vividly how ordinary things sometimes acquire "a strange remoteness and intangibility," like the room with the doll and the rocking horse in the moonlight.[52] Here is an observation in which he foretells the later developments of psychology. "Truth often finds its way to the mind close muffled in robes of sleep, and then speaks with uncompromising directness of matters in regard to which we practise an unconscious self-deception during our waking moments."[53]

Hawthorne is deeply persuaded of the insufficiency of

[51] James, "Pluralism and Religion," *Hibbert Journal*, VI (1908), p. 723; cf. *Varieties of Religious Experience*, passim.
[52] *Scarlet Letter, The Custom House*, vol. V, p. 55; ibid., pp. 117, 249, 260.
[53] *Mosses from an Old Manse, Complete Works*, vol. II, p. 52.

words, "the burden of mortal language, that crushes all the finer intelligences of the soul. . . . Who has not been conscious of mysteries within his mind, mysteries of truth and reality, which will not wear the chains of language?"[54] He quests like Poe, but is more resigned in his impotence, "beyond the shadowy scope of time, and, living once for all in eternity, to find the perfect future in the present."[55] That is the most extreme recognition "insight" can achieve into the nature of things.

When we speak of "insight," of the endeavor to express more than the immediately given reality, can we pass by Henry James (1843–1916)? Despite his love for old Europe, which, like Whistler, he cannot forego as a residence for his refined mind, he remains an American to his fingertips. This is true not only because of his deep and masterly insight, by which he saw the contrast between the Old and the New World, proclaiming in his heart the superiority of the latter, but for the very core of James's literary power—the constant revelation of arrière-pensée, the hidden grounds of his characters' thoughts, and the razor sharpness of his psychology. I should like to consider this as a more recent expression of the same striving that inspired Poe and Hawthorne, or as the application of literary methods to what his brother William described in the words just quoted. The lack of dramatic structure in James's tales, which as a consequence require so much attention and even exertion from the reader, can also be considered an American characteristic. In one of his shorter tales, *The Turn of the Screw* (a favorite metaphor of James, who always wants to turn it a little more), he has, it might be said, sought in a specimen work deliberately to equal, combine, and excel Poe and Hawthorne. Unlike the usual atmosphere which interests

---

[54] *Tales and Sketches*, vol. XIII, p. 68.
[55] *Mosses from an Old Manse*, p. 69.

him, he seeks in this tale to create a maximum of horrible
spectrality. It is the story of the spiritual apparitions experienced by two children; in it he joins a mastery of Poe's icy
sharpness with Hawthorne's melancholy and tenderness. The
line of American literature undoubtedly runs from Poe and
Hawthorne directly through Henry James. How far it was
continued thereafter may be permitted to rest here in this historical study.

Superficially there is no greater contrast than between
Emerson and Whitman.[56] The wild shaggy Walt, the Rabe-
laisian idler who mixed with the whole people, and the genteel
Emerson, the center of a circle of most refined culture, exquisite to the point of artificiality. But it is a contradiction
only in appearance. The true Emerson, full of open wisdom,
independence, and strength, is very closely related to Whitman.
Emerson was the first to see Whitman's importance. "I am not
blind," he wrote to him in 1855, "to the worth of the wonderful
gift of *Leaves of Grass.* I find it the most extraordinary piece
of wit and wisdom that America has yet contributed. . . . I
give you joy of your free and brave thought, I have great joy
in it. I find incomparable things said incomparably well, as
they must be. I find the courage of treatment which so delights
us, and which large perception only can inspire. . . . I greet
you at the beginning of a great career."[57] Whitman for his
part long had a very vigorous admiration for Emerson. "He has
what none else has; he does what none else does. He pierces
the crusts that envelop the secrets of life. He joins on equal
terms the few great sages and original seers. He represents the
freeman, America, the individual. He represents the gentle-
man. No teacher or poet of old times or modern times has made

[56] Emerson, 1803–1882; Whitman, 1819–1892.
[57] *Poems of Walt Whitman (From Leaves of Grass),* ed. E. Rhys,
p. xviii.

a better report of manly and womanly qualities, heroism, chastity, temperance, friendship, fortitude."[58]

What Emerson and Whitman have in common is their will, the consciousness of their duty to speak as the voice of America to America, words that the world had not yet heard. Both are inspired by the passionate desire for an individual American expression of spirit, which will display an absolutely American individuality. Here is Emerson: "If the single man plant himself indomitably on his instincts, and there abide, the huge world will come round to him. We will walk on our own feet; we will work with our own hands; we will speak our own minds."[59] "Why should we not also enjoy an original relation to the universe? Why should not we have a poetry and philosophy of insight and not of tradition and a religion by revelation to us, and not the history of theirs? . . . The sun shines today also."

We find this feeling on almost every page of Whitman. "America (I to myself have said) demands at any rate one modern, native, all-surrounding song with face like hers turned to the future rather than the present or the past. It should nourish with joy the pride and completion of man in himself. What the mother, our continent, in reference to humanity, finally means . . . is *Individuality* strong and superb, for broadest average use, for man and woman: and that most should such a poem in its own form express. Of such a poem (I have had that dream) let me initiate the attempt; and bravos to him or to her who, coming after me, triumphs."[60]

[58] *Preparatory Reading and Thought*, vol. IX, p. 159; cf. *Specimen Days*, vol. VI, pp. 22, 26, 37. A less favorable judgment of Whitman on Emerson in *Complete Writings*, vol. V, p. 265.

[59] "The American Scholar," in Emerson, *Works* (Macmillan, 1884), vol. I, p. 91.

[60] "Meaning and Intention of 'Leaves of Grass,' " *Complete Writings*, vol. IX, pp. 11, cf. *Complete Writings*, vol. V, p. 128, and *Specimen Days* (London ed., 1887), pp. 225, 235.

The tame America which pridefully took Emerson into its pantheon long remained somewhat shy of Whitman. When you see the name Whitman on the map in Oregon and Idaho, do not think that it is Walt to whom honor is being paid; it is the pioneer, Dr. Marcus Whitman, the legendary rescuer of Oregon, who was murdered by the Indians with his wife and children in 1849. H. C. Emery, in his essay on American culture, apologized, as it were, for Whitman: The European readers ought not think of Whitman as so much the authentic American.[61] A. B. Hart took verses about the Civil War by Bryant, Whittier, Lowell for his *American History Told by Contemporaries;* but we look in vain for anything from Whitman's war poetry or from his "Specimen Days." In his enumeration of the leading minds of America, Hart does not mention Whitman at all.[62]

Americans, moved by the Anglo-Saxon prudery which they too usually share, felt some embarrassment over the great American poet whose shamelessness went even beyond the pagan; and they were also annoyed by Whitman's spirit of disobedience. But, good people, Emerson said the same thing: "Wherever a man comes, there comes revolution. The old is for slaves. Go alone. Refuse the good models."

The fundamental idea in both Emerson and Whitman is the unity of the world and the self, complete expression and consciousness of individuality and complete penetration by the spirit of nature. Through nature they see beyond to something that is more than nature. "Nature always speaks of spirit, suggests the idea of the absolute." It is what we find at every turn in Poe, Hawthorne, and Thoreau too, but in a less general way, expressed in more deliberate images, but fundamentally with the same meaning. Thoreau stands close to both Emerson and Whitman.

[61] *Cambridge Modern History*, vol. VII, p. 747.
[62] Hart, *National Ideals Historically Traced*, pp. 226, 262.

Isn't this parallel attunement to individualism and to nature worship in America's greatest poets enough to prove that
Whitman, who proclaims it most noisily, most absolutely, is
thereby the most American of them all? Whitman is the embodiment par excellence of all the qualities which comprise
the spirit of America. This, Here, and Soon.

How intense Whitman's feeling for the future is:

> Poets to come! orators, singers, musicians to come!
> Not to-day is to justify me and answer what I am for,
> But you, a new brood, native, athletic, continental, greater
>   than before known,
> Arouse! for you must justify me.
>
> I myself but write one or two indicative words for the
> future, I but advance a moment only to wheel and hurry
> back in the darkness. . . .[63]

Who but the Whitman of "Crossing Brooklyn Ferry" felt
so at one with the men who would come after him?[64]

What of Whitman's formlessness? We have expressed the
opinion that one of the characteristics of American literature
is that it has no sense of form, no formal strength. This is confirmed by such younger writers as Sinclair Lewis. But Whitman was the most formless of all; he despised form. And it
was just this which enabled him to be authentically American.
This total formlessness does not at all consist merely in the
totally loose structure of his verse. That concerns only the
external form. It is the thought itself which is formless. There
is hardly any attention to syntax or style; it consists in enu-
merations and exclamations, set in coordination, not in subordination. But it is precisely subordination which is the most
essential element in every creation of higher form. Other poets
choose a subject that may be grasped in a thought and give it
form, they make it into an idea or an image. Whitman never

[63] "Leaves of Grass," *Complete Writings*, vol. I, p. 15.
[64] Ibid., p. 191.

takes a personal subject, he never speaks of personal suffering. He does not give the subject that inspires him a definite attitude; he portrays no figure or group with specific gestures; he never paints a specific scene. Everything remains undefined. An industrious philologist could calculate whether or not Whitman's work displays a great shortage of definite articles. He gives everything in a raw state of immediacy; he piles the conceptions upon each other like a huge mass of rocks. He is elementary. And hence he can give *everything*, because he does not care to give *anything* with clear outlines and style. Is this chaos or cosmos? It is definitely cosmos. In this roaring, staccato flood of ideas which run into and through each other, Whitman gives the same thing that a few years ago the so-called Futurists, with their pictures of fragments, jostled together into a minor system.

Whitman's art also expresses its elementary character in the predominance of the noun. Things force their way into his consciousness in their own simple essence. He forbids himself any decorative elements. "Also no ornaments, especially no ornamental adjectives, unless they have come molten hot and imperiously prove themselves."[65]

The mighty acceptance of life, the passionate enjoyment of all things, material and spiritual, the humanity which streams out to all men, the joyful optimism—are not all of these things precisely the traits which are the essence of America?—Whitman devoured life. His attitude toward life cannot be better expressed than as the absolute opposite of *Weltschmerz*.[66] We weaker souls all know the feeling that we must bear more affliction than just the burden of our own personality. Whitman had the opposite quality: He always carried with him in

[65] "Meaning and Intention of 'Leaves of Grass,' " no. 55, *Complete Writings*, vol. IX, p. 32.
[66] German for "world pain."—H.H.R.

jubilation the enjoyment and the splendor of everyone and everything. Thundering and overawing, the images roll on in his poems: the lists of names and things, each full of a vehement life and a great joy. "The universe is in myself—it shall all pass through me as a procession."[67]

> See, steamers steaming through my poems,
> See, in my poems immigrants continually coming and
>   landing . . .[68]

And all America rolls out, the lakes, woods and prairies, the cities and machines, triumphantly, like the brass instruments in a finale.

The shapes arise!

—and all the things stream through again which the merry axe chops down,

> shapes of the using of axes anyhow, and the users and all
>   that neighbors them,

once again all America ringing and roaring with work.[69]

> O to make the most jubilant song!
> Full of music—full of manhood, womanhood, infancy!
> Full of common employments—full of grain and trees![70]

And all the bright joy of life and the sun, the wind and water, glide by in a rippling sequence, St. Francis' Song of the Sun brought up to date.

Nature, labor, health, the beauty of men, strength, "power of personality just or unjust"; freedom, humanity, brotherhood, democracy, friendship, love—all flow together.

There is the constant returning of the masses of fellow

---

[67] *Meaning and Intention*, no. 49, *Complete Writings*, vol. IX, p. 31.
[68] "Starting from Paumanok, 18," *Complete Writings*, vol. I, p. 31.
[69] "Song of the Broad-Axe," *Complete Writings*, vol. I, p. 233.
[70] "A Song of Joys," *Complete Writings*, vol. I, p. 213.

men who people his poems, like the strange multitudes one meets in a dream—a perpetual swarming of figures. How could he have loved them all? Whitman never knew that feeling of desperate loneliness which sometimes overcomes other men just when they are in the midst of great crowds. He found a friend in everyone. In his last weeks he expressed his regret that he had not said more on behalf of criminals and outcasts. For he was always concerned with the effect of his poetry, its result for the life of his people and mankind. This too is truly American. No one stood farther from *"l'art pour l'art."*[71] "In these States, beyond all precedent, poetry will have to do with actual facts, with the concrete States, and—for we have not much more than begun—with the definitive getting into shape of the Union."[72] "Poems are to arouse the reason, suggest, give freedom, strength, muscle, candor to any person that reads them—and assist that person to see the realities for himself in his own way, with his own individuality and after his own fashion. . . . The great poet . . . It is not that he gives his country great poems; it is that he gives his country the spirit which makes the greatest poems and the greatest material for poems."[73]

The word for Whitman's poetry is cosmic. It is immensely primitive and pagan; it has found once more the authentic sounds of the dithyrambic and the conception of the mythical. "I speak the pass-word primeval."

I am he that walks with the tender and growing night,
I call to the earth and sea half-held by the night.
Press close bare-bosom'd night—press close magnetic nourishing night!

[71] French for "Art for art's sake."—H.H.R.
[72] *Complete Writings*, vol. V, p. 274.
[73] "Meaning and Intention," nos. 48, 49, *Complete Writings*, vol. IX, p. 30.

Night of south winds—night of the large few stars!
Still nodding night—mad naked summer night.
   Smile O voluptuous cool breath'd earth!
Earth of the slumbering and liquid trees!
Earth of departed sunset—earth of the mountains misty-
topt!
Earth of the vitreous pour of the full moon just tinged
with blue! . . .
Smile, for your lover comes
   Prodigal you have given me love—therefore I to you
give love
      O unspeakable passionate love."[74]

It is all permeated with cosmic love. This is also the source of the shameless directness of *Children of Adam*, which may be compared only with some Vedic hymns.

Where Whitman appears to be bluntly individual and material, he is in truth cosmic and transcendental. "I say nothing of myself which I do not equally say of all others, men and women." "All through writings preserve the equilibrium of the truth that the material world and all its laws are as grand and superb as the spiritual world and all its laws. . . . How shall I know what the life is except as I see it in the flesh?"[75] But this appreciation of matter is not materialistic but pantheist and mystical. Tocqueville had drily decreed that democracy has a tendency toward pantheism.[76] Emerson and Whitman are the living proof that he was right.

In each thing there lies an absolute miracle.

And (I will show) that all things of the universe are
perfect miracles each as profound as any.

[74] "Song of Myself 24, 21," *Complete Writings*, vol. I, pp. 62, 58.
[75] "Meaning and Intention," nos. 49, 8, *Complete Writings*, vol. IX, pp. 31, 5.
[76] *De la démocratie en Amérique*, vol. III, p. 49 [*Democracy in America*, vol. II, pp. 32–33].

Elsewhere:

> Why, who makes much of a miracle?
> As to me I know of nothing else but miracles,
> Whether I walk the streets of Manhattan,
> Or dart my sight over the roofs of houses toward the
>   sky . . .[77]

But men want to understand the meaning of a miracle. Once again Emerson comes before us. "What we would really know the meaning of? The meat in the firkin; the milk in the pan; the ballad in the street; the news of the boat; the glance of the eye; the form and the gait of the body! Show me the ultimate reason of these matters; show me the sublime presence of the highest spiritual cause lurking, as it always lurks, in these suburbs and extremities of nature; let me see every trifle bristling with the polarity that ranges it instantly on an eternal law. . . ."[78]

But no answer follows the question. The unutterable, inaccessible remainder is always left. Whitman again: "Common teachers or critics are always asking 'What does it mean?' Symphony of fine musician, or sunset, or sea-waves rolling up the beach—what do they mean? Undoubtedly in the most subtle-elusive sense they mean something—as love does, and religion does, and the best poem; but who shall fathom and define those meanings? . . . At its best poetic lore is like what may be heard of conversation in the dusk, from speakers far or hid, of which we get only a few broken murmurs. What is not gathered is far more—perhaps the main thing."[79]

With all his acceptance of life, Whitman's attitude is that

[77] "Starting from Paumanok, 12," *Complete Writings*, vol. I, p. 25; *Miracles*, vol. II, p. 163.
[78] "The American Scholar," in Emerson, *Works* (Macmillan, 1884), vol. I, p. 91.
[79] *Specimen Days* (London ed., 1887), p. 306.

of purest mysticism, no less than Emerson's. Even the de-
vourer of life knows the feelings of doubt and despair which
are indispensable on the path toward the highest knowledge
and repose. "Of the terrible doubt of appearances . . . ,"
"Whispers of heavenly death murmur'd I hear . . ." "Yet,
yet, ye downcast hours, I know ye also . . ." these are among
Whitman's most gripping poems.

> Darest thou now O soul,
> Walk out with me toward the unknown region,
> Where neither ground is for the feet nor any path to
>   follow.[80]

Emerson speaks of the highest region which all mystics
strive to reach and which they express in words, which is
ecstasy: "For the sense of being which in calm hours rises, we
know not how, in the soul, is not diverse from things, from
space, from light, from time, from man, but one with them,
and proceeds obviously from the same source whence their
life and being also proceed. . . . The soul raised over passion
beholds identity and eternal causation, perceives the self-
existence of Truth and Right, and calms itself with knowing
that all things go well."[81]

---

[80] "Leaves of Grass," *Complete Writings*, vol. I, p. 145; vol. II,
p. 221 ff.

[81] "Self-Reliance," in Emerson, *Works* (Routledge, 1883), pp. 27,
29.

LIFE AND THOUGHT IN AMERICA

Stray Remarks

Foreword

Stray Remarks. . . I could also have said Contradictory Observations. America flings you from one hour to another between acceptance and resistance, and a complete resolution of all the contradictions is not achieved even in rethinking. The writer of these pages did not originally intend to amplify further the historical observations about American civilization which he had already published. But he continued to feel a need to give his impressions order and form.

What is it that compels us Europeans in our criticism to take such a firm stand against America? It is just because it has compelled our admiration by its firm grasp on life, refreshed us and gladdened us with its great, simple, joyful humanity. It is just because we know, furthermore, that our observations among a people of a hundred million cannot be much more than the play of a child who takes a few small shells, shrimps, and a starfish and puts them in his little pail.

Probably it is the necessity to define our distance which impels so many of us to have our personal say about America.

We find, along with much outward similarity and close kin-ship, that America still thinks and lives in a different way. At the same time, however, we constantly hear the *Tua res agitur*.[1] Modern civilization is on trial in America in a simpler way than among us. Will Europe be next? More than once the reader will say regarding what follows: "But is that spe-cifically American?" No, but it is American par excellence, American in its fullness.

If an American who reads Dutch were to ask me: "Can't you find anything more in my country to which you can give unconditional praise?" I shall reply to him: "Weigh more heavily what I praise than what I seem to blame. We prefer to speak least of what is best."

October 1926　　　　　　　　　　　　　　　　　　　*J.H.*

---

[1] Latin for "You too are concerned."–H.H.R.

Progress is a terrible thing.
William James

Chapter I

SOCIETY

DEVELOPMENT AND RESOLUTION

Prosperity and Progress

A year of unprecedented prosperity lies behind them, and the prospect looks favorable. The immense difficulties on the way ahead do not frighten them. The question of capital and labor, the crisis in agriculture, the urgent necessity of reforestation, the problem of irrigation, the Negro question and that of the assimilation of foreign immigrants, the increase in crime—we shall gain control over them just as we shall over the problems of transportation and automobile parking in the big cities.

Fear that natural resources will be exhausted in the near future seems to have relented rather than intensified among the leading thinkers in the world of technology. Not long ago Senator La Follette predicted "dollar a gallon gasoline" within a few years. That won't be necessary, the engineers replied reassuringly. The improvement of machinery already saves about 25 percent compared with before, and better methods have increased the production of gasoline from crude petroleum from 20 to 50 percent. And if petroleum runs out, we will make other fuels.

Technology advances with giant strides in the quantity

of goods produced, in the savings of labor and materials, and in precision and safety. We stand as yet only at the beginning of technical development based upon exact science. By the use of exact scientific methods the machine builder achieves results which far exceed the most optimistic expectations of less than ten years ago. There are locomotives which work under a pressure of 350 pounds, and steam turbines of 80,000 horsepower; a single one of these, the American says triumphantly, is big enough to provide all the electric power needed for one of Europe's smaller countries. There are measuring instruments which permit an accuracy of 1/200,-000,000 of an inch, machines which operate at a speed of 660,000 revolutions per minute.[2] Men dared scarcely even to think of such things a few years ago. The use of powdered coal as fuel permits unprecedented convenience and savings. The old question of the utilization of the tides seems on the way to solution: In Passamaquoddy Bay, on the border between Canada and the State of Maine, Dexter S. Cooper wants to control the flood tide and put it to work.

No wonder that a newspaper, the *enfant terrible*[3] of the American spirit, has expressed unshaken confidence in the domination of nature in this headline: "Man will conquer the Earthquake, Scientist says."

Waste

The constant squandering of materials and power that strikes and annoys the European visitor obviously occasions

[2] I take these figures from the chapter "Engineering and Construction" in *American Yearbook, 1925*.
[3] French, literally "terrible child," more loosely, "a little terror." —H.H.R.

little distress to the Americans themselves. Along railway tracks where men are at work, the fires of old ties burn merrily: it does not pay to haul them away. Every day enough food is thrown away in the big cities to feed a town, but this cannot be helped because of the way a metropolis has to be organized. The accumulation of beautifully wrought and costly products in a few places is unavoidable. Commodities which are a miraculous achievement of skilled technology and human labor are hardly touched or left unused. Valuable forests are felled every day for paper manufacture, and the newspapers are thrown away after a careless glance and flutter through the streets and upon the subway platforms. And anyone who walks home at night along Fifth Avenue past the store windows illuminated at the late hour would grow elegiac over all the light that burns without giving joy to anyone, all the time that is frittered away on aimless amusements, all the words which are never read, all the shoes which will never be worn, all the silk which will never cover a shoulder, all the flowers which wither behind the show windows.

Mechanization of Culture

The doubt as to whether all is quite right with modern civilization, the feeling of being past one's prime and on the brink of decline, which has become so common in Europe since 1918, is still hardly to be observed in America. A translation of Oswald Spengler's *Untergang des Abendlandes*[4] has just been advertised as "A History of the Future," with a laudatory comment by the well-known historian Charles A.

[4] *Decline of the West.*—H.H.R.

Beard. He calls it "a magnificent challenge to the great American people on their way to counting houses, golf links, factories, corn fields, colleges and delicatessens, inviting them to pause a moment and reflect on the nature and destiny of culture."[5] Pause and reflect? Will they, can they?

Spengler's brilliant and icy words of prophecy had not yet been spoken at the time when I endeavored, in an essay on "The Mechanization of the Life of Society,"[6] to sketch what seemed by all appearances to be the inevitable course of contemporary civilization, with America as its most perfect example. I sought to show how each technical discovery shackles human energies as much as it liberates them, how all organization leads to mechanization, how society compels men to disappear into an impersonal equality of action and thought.

The progress of technology compels the economic process to move toward concentration and general uniformity at an ever faster tempo. The more human inventiveness and exact science become locked into the organization of business, the more the active man, as the embodiment of an enterprise and its master, seems to disappear. Every organization of human energies works both to spare them and to confine them. The means of transportation abolish distance and eliminate geographical and intellectual frontiers at both a profit and a loss. The means of exchange and distribution of work of the mind—the telephone, the newspaper, the cinema—bring about a level uniformity of the spirit never before known. The methods of recording thought and of intellectual coopera-

---

[5] In the *American Mercury* of June 1926, Beard's words, "in spite of its majestic nonsense and its dubious conclusion," were left out of the advertisement "owing to an inadvertence." The mistake was corrected by an inserted slip.—J.H.

[6] *Mensch en Menigte in Amerika*, first ed. Haarlem, 1918, 2nd rev. ed. 1920 [see above, pp. 61–118].—J.H.

tion subject the mind to the constraints of preestablished patterns and pigeonholes. In all these things America has gone ahead of Europe.

The mechanization of culture has increased immensely since 1918. We may name only two things which then were only in their swaddling clothes—radio broadcasting, and the development of the automobile from a luxury vehicle to a general means of transportation. The importance of the radio is still scarcely to be overestimated. Its intellectual effect in bringing men to a single level will probably appear even greater than that of the cinema. The family in the isolated farm, the invalids in their compulsory isolation, share by means of the radio some of the life of the great city. But no one who listens to it any longer chooses for himself the stuff upon which his mind feeds, or at most he does so in the way in which one chooses a meal *à la carte*. Broadcasting feeds an entire nation in the manner of Oliver Twist's poorhouse. And the food must be such that every stomach can tolerate it. Everything which does not correspond to a general standard of acceptability and satisfaction is excluded. Radio shares with the moving picture the quality of compelling us to exercise our attention strongly but superficially, completely excluding reflection, or what I might call reflective assimilation.

The big city is no longer a place to live but a mechanism, a machine for the movement of traffic, transportation, and communication. It has become completely dynamic. It does not serve primarily to give a person a particular place to live but rather to enable him to move, physically or intellectually, inside and outside the city. Its essential organisms are the means of travel, elevators, telephones, radio stations, the press, and adding machines. Houses only form the skeleton. A deep significance lies in the name "The Shuttle" given to the little subway train which runs back and forth between Grand Central Station and Times Square in New York. A shuttle in a great loom, nothing more.

"Standardizing"

Eight years ago "standardization" was by far not so generally required nor such a common slogan as it is now. The standardized product is met everywhere in daily life, in fruits and breakfast cereals, in the complete predominance of two or three brands of cigarettes, in the power of the mail-order houses and the chain stores which, like a physiological organism, provide an entire continent with wholly similar goods.[7] Standardization in industry means a vigorous effort to increase productivity, utility of the product, and reduction of costs. The automobile industry calculates its annual savings from organized standardization at $750,000,000. Organized standardization means establishment of a uniform, well-described technical nomenclature, generally enforced tests of the quality of materials, equality in dimensions to make possible interchangeability of parts like screws, pipes, and many more things. It can be applied by individual firms, by industrial associations, on a national footing and, finally, internationally. Everything is now ready for the necessary transition from the first two of these stages, which are almost completed, to the third, the national stage. After the engineers and business leaders, it is now the public administration which is promoting standardization, for the sake of savings to the treasury, advantages for industry, and benefits to the general public. The Federal Specifications Board has been at work since 1921, and

---

[7] For all these matters, read the absorbing book of Arthur Feller, *Amerika-Europa, Erfahrungen einer Reise* (Frankfurt, 1926).

it has already laid down precise specifications for 350 articles used by government departments. There are also the Bureau of Standards and the Division of Simplified Practice. The Department of Commerce and the Department of Agriculture each work for national standardization in their own fields. Alongside the government bureaus there exists an American Engineering Standards Committee, in which more than 250 industrial and commercial organizations are represented; it concerns itself with the drafting of national standards in the fields of bridge and road construction, building trades, machine construction, electrical engineering, automobile and aircraft industry, transportation, shipbuilding, iron manufacture, other metallurgies, chemical, textile, mine and wood industries, and paper manufacture.

It is clear that this movement, whose immediate goals are strictly technical, once it has achieved extensive uniformity, must bring with it vast transformations of a general economic character.

Everyone who has experienced the Americans' feeling for conformity and similarity will understand that standardization for them means not just an industrial necessity, not to say a necessary evil, but also an ideal of civilization. The American *wants* to be like his neighbor. He only feels spiritually safe in what has been standardized, apart from the fact that standardization means efficiency. A course was announced at Leland Stanford University in California in 1924 in "scientific yell-leading," open only to sophomores. This summer [1926] a newspaper in San Francisco poked fun at an extreme example of voluntary standardization at the University of California in Berkeley, where a new gymnasium building for girl students was under construction. The question came up how the shower facilities should be arranged. The girls decided themselves that after the exercise period was over each girl should not turn on her own shower faucet in each of the 150 (as I believe the number was) stalls but the refreshing spray should be turned on simultaneously from a central point.

We may laugh at this. It was probably a completely practical decision. But whoever sees at another state university, in this case that of North Carolina at Chapel Hill, the intelligent and loving way in which the Extension Division has promoted knowledge of literature, interest in the stage, and love of music among the scattered population of this agricultural state, which is a quarter the size of France, will begin to suspect that standardization and uniform practices can be necessary and salutary.

If the Americans, in addition to the eagle and the Stars and Stripes, and the more unofficial symbols of bison, moose, and Indian, should ever need another emblem, one which is friendly and pleasant, then I think that they should choose the grapefruit.[8] Or rather the half grapefruit, for this fruit only comes in halves, I believe. Practically speaking, it is always yellow, always just as fresh and well served. And it always comes at the same, still hopeful hour of the morning.

An Outward-Looking Culture

The picture of American society that forces itself upon the meditative observer may well be called, to borrow a term from Jung's school, an extroverted culture. The unbounded ease of communications and spread of knowledge, combined with the commercial interest that to an important measure dominates this activity, makes a certain level of civilization a

[8] We may observe that Huizinga here uses not the Dutch word *pompelmoes* (= Fr. *pamplemousse*), but the English word, capitalized and hyphenated.—H.H.R.

public culture in the highest sense of the word. Individuals hardly appear to be any more the transmitters and cultivators of culture. Culture is available to everyone, displayed in the newspaper, at school, or in the museum. It is brought to individuals ceaselessly and with great energy. The ideal of continuous education fills America to the marrow. An American museum strives to educate through objects. The whole range of fauna, the whole history of the earth, are displayed in dioramas and model landscapes. The science of nutrition is demonstrated by wax still-lifes of foodstuffs. Tables, statistics, and graphic representations aid the understanding. In a big showcase stands a naked young man made of papier mâché. Next to him are a number of large and small jars with fluids and solids. In his hand he carries a sign with an inscription that begins: "I am fearfully and wonderfully made," and then indicates the elements from which the human body is constructed (shown in the flasks), and it ends: "Reduced to a familiar form, I am in the main made of charcoal and water and the total value of such of my constituents as are shown here is about eighteen dollars." This is education of the people.

All during the spring [of 1926], America was filled with news of the mysterious disappearance of an evangelist, Mrs. Aimee Macpherson, who had maintained a tabernacle at Los Angeles with many . . . I almost said, customers. The case apparently aroused little stir in Europe. Mrs. Macpherson drowned while swimming at the beach. Or did she really drown? That was the question. In any event she disappeared, and her mother continued the business for a while on the same footing. When she had been gone long enough so that her return was doubtful, a memorial service was held in Angelus Temple, her building. The subject of the addresses was that so many of God's chosen have been taken from earthly life in mysterious ways. Her mother, Mrs. Kennedy, told how Enoch walked with God, and God took him away. How no one had been a witness to Moses' death, how Jesus' body had disappeared from its grave, and how the apostle Philip had suddenly been transported to a distant region. Dr. Charles A. Shreve then observed how much Mrs. Macpherson's disappearance recalled these and other biblical examples, and how profane history also furnished other examples, like the disappearance of Lord Kitchener.[9] The service was made "more realistic" by having each of the biblical figures named appear upon the stage in proper garb, except for Christ, whose disappearance was represented by angels. Finally, a student of the Temple Bible School read an article on the disappearance of Christ's body as it would have been reported in a present-day newspaper if there had been newspapers published in Jerusalem at the time, with the aim of demonstrating the futility of the work of reporters. A "monster memorial service" was announced for fourteen days later. Whether this was held or not I do not know, for about that time Mrs. Macpherson returned in person, with a tale of being kidnaped. But she disappeared at the same time from my field of vision, for by then I was at sea and did not see any more American newspapers.

Democracy

Anyone who wishes to understand America must first carry over his concept of Democracy from the political and social field to the cultural and the generally human. The best way to do this continues to be reading Walt Whitman.

[9] H. H. Kitchener (1850–1915), Earl Kitchener, British general, vanished at sea without a trace en route to Russia in 1915.—H.H.R.

There is no stronger promoter of democracy in this sense than the cinema. It accustoms the nation, from high to low, to a single common view of life. As a result of its limited means of expression, its accentuation of the external, and the necessity for general understandability, it places numerous areas of intellectual life beyond its scope. It thrusts forward a reduced number of patterns of life interpretation which then dominate the multitudes. It gives the city resident a chance to see the life of the countryside, or a picture of it, and similarly for the countryman city life, for the poor the life of wealth, for the rich that of misery, but all highly stylized pictures such that they can easily take hold of the mind. It does it all in a way that reconciles class hatreds more than it creates them. The repeated illusion of the life of the wealthy gives the poor man a certain communion with riches and refinement; the picture in his fantasy becomes a portion of his own existence. In the hero he honors himself; furthermore, the film star in his real life gives him a new model of emulation, a new assurance of the opportunities for everyman, more appealing and consoling even than the dream of the White House.

The Function of the Newspaper

The true expression of the mind of present-day society is the newspaper. Although it will be easier in the future to obtain a copy of the works of Robert Frost, the poet, which will still be reprinted, than of the *Atlantic Monthly*, for which one must go to the library, and easier to obtain the latter than *The New York Times*, which will be kept only in a few libraries, at the present moment the situation is the reverse: it is the newspaper which rules supreme. The poet reaches thousands, the journalist millions. Although their name is Legion, the great newspapers may really be considered as a single newspaper; they are one loud outcry repeated every day everywhere in the country. The differences between the news of Chicago and New York, and between the content of one day and that of another, vanish into nothing since all the newspapers become completely equivalent and homogeneous if we consider them as a social phenomenon. As is well known, the great American newspapers no longer possess a political creed. Their importance as a business does not permit them to direct themselves to only a part of the public. And it is also not their task any more to engage in politics.

The European traveler scoffs at the American newspaper as long as he has to grapple with it. He recognizes with admiration and a sigh that there lies concealed in the unwieldy supplement of the Sunday edition an excellent illustrated picture book and a first-quality literary supplement. But he hates this daily flow of crimes, political scandals, divorces and marriages recounted so loudly, these colorful and fragmentary bits of political news, and this shortage of news about what is really happening in the world (and he means the Old World, forgetting that he is in the New World). He soon no longer gives himself the trouble of unfolding the monster when he sits down to breakfast; even the most exciting story cannot get him to turn the page if it is "continued on page 4," and he rails to a companion from his own hemisphere against the trashiness of the American press. Only when he has returned to his own country and can read down to the last detail in his own, painfully missed, and solid newspaper just how much the population of Sliedrecht[10] has grown, or the speeches

[10] A quite secondary industrial and trading town in the western Netherlands, which only attained a population of less than 14,000 by 1939.—H.H.R.

in celebration of some senior civil servant's fiftieth year in office, does his feeling toward the American newspaper grow milder. He becomes aware that, in the final analysis, even the material which did not interest him always had its own importance. He catches himself with shame in the fact that he every day really skips almost completely the extremely complete but unreadable dispatches from Geneva.[11] And he probably even asks himself the heretical question whether basically the case of a gang of young criminals in Chicago, well told, does not teach him more about his fellow men and their society than the most serious dispatches concerning ministerial statements and political negotiations.

The fact is that the newspaper fulfills a wholly different function in America than among us Europeans. As for the question whether this will come to pass in Europe too, I let it stand as it is: but in any case this function is much further developed there than here. Let me put it this way, no matter how hazardous it may sound: The newspaper in American society has become real literature in the essential sense of the word. The newspaper fulfills in America the cultural function of the drama of Aeschylus. I mean that it is the expression through which a people—a people numbering many millions—becomes aware of its spiritual unity. The millions, as they do their careless reading every day at breakfast, in the subway, on the train and the elevated, are performing a horrendous and formless ritual. The mirror of their culture is held up to them in their newspapers, with more emphasis and persistence than in any novel. The newspaper itself does not pass judgment. The young jailbird appears in the same halo of heroism as a sports hero. No stone is thrown at the woman who has been divorced twelve times. An election scandal is painted in the colors of a fabulously successful trick rather than as an act

[11] I.e., from the League of Nations.—H.H.R.

of depravity to be vehemently condemned. Moral reaction is generally left to the public. The moral attitude of the newspaper, so far as it has one, is healthy, simple, and without sternness. The democratic society, with something of Whitman's all-embracing charity, takes the attitude "This is how you are" toward all kinds of success, courage, and corruption.

We [Europeans] feel human interest stories to be the lowest element of a newspaper. The American newspaper is human interest news and that is all it wants to be. The striking and shocking events of the day have an entirely different importance for it. They are symbolic in the full meaning of the word. Practically speaking, one can be sure in a big Dutch newspaper of finding a report of every broken leg and every youth run over by a car, but in a strictly factual and plain way, just as it happened. The event in this case possesses its own individual importance, which dims in direct proportion to the distance the reader is from what happened. The American journalist chooses from an abundance of events those which lend themselves to a picturesque or romantic presentation, "for their human interest rather than their individual and personal significance. In this way news ceases to be wholly personal and assumes the form of art. It ceases to be the record of the doings of individual men and women and becomes an impersonal account of manners and life."[12]

"It is the truth shop," the newspaperman says when he is reproached for the mercantile character of his product. Is this really so? Is this mirror of culture so plain and clear? Or does the act of giving symbolic form for the purpose of picturesque or romantic effect, and in such a way that everyone can be expected to understand it and be interested in it, create nothing but a huge, horribly colorful, and vulgar lie? Even

[12] Robert E. Park, "The Natural History of the Newspaper," in *The City*, by Park and Burgess, Chicago, 1925.

then the newspaper would be the mirror of a completely developed, democratic, and extroverted culture.

But we can kick against the walls of time and cry out, "This is not what I want, give me as my social sacraments the tragedy, or the mysteries of Mithras, or a snake dance," but it will be to no avail. "Progress is a terrible thing."

The Art of Journalism

The status of journalism as an art undoubtedly differs somewhat in America and the Netherlands. I imagine that a reporter who indulged in the kind of literary exuberance we Dutchmen have to swallow on occasion would be fired at once by an American editor. For an "artist in words" cannot enthrall anyone whose attention and interest are of the slightest. A certain conformity to the literary taste of the day is naturally desirable. Now and then an unexpected or overcolorful adjective or fashionable turn of phrase catches the eye. But mysterious and fancy writing wearies and annoys the educated and the uneducated reader alike, and it probably does not even interest the half-educated man. For an American editor, boring the public means sinning against the Holy Ghost of democracy. What finally matters is to get and hold attention.

This aim has shaped a very important development in the writing style of American newspapers. There is a very deliberate striving to reduce the effort of thought required, and to capture attention. In practice, therefore, the overwhelming bulk of reading matter becomes very limited in character. A newspaper no longer is intended to be read through—but that is true in Europe too. Anyone who would read every page of a daily newspaper attentively (and reading really ought to mean attentive reading) understanding and absorbing what he read, would have to be both a marvel of information and a fool. We peck here and there in a newspaper, that's all. But the technique of catching and guiding attention is vastly better developed in every American newspaper, including the weeklies and monthlies, than among us.

This technique consists in the journalist's applying what Herbert Spencer called the essential principle of the art of writing. "The art of writing is economy of attention." Or as a contemporary American author whom I shall name more than once[13] expresses it more generally: "The power of all art is the power of selective emphasis."

Headlines and Advertisements

The art of choice and emphasis, the art of guiding attention, is applied unawares by every story teller or debater. It constantly dominates and defines the form of the news report or the argument. It is almost the only thing necessary in two very important forms of expression of our day, the headline and the advertisement. With the latter, we leave the terrain of the press, for culturally illustrated posters on walls and billboards are as important as advertisements in newspapers and magazines.

Composing striking headlines has become almost the most important part of newspaper work and is the task of specially trained copy editors. The methods they employ have to be simple. The headline must draw the attention of readers gen-

[13] H. A. Overstreet, *Influencing Human Behavior*. (New York 1925), p. 57.

erally. This can be accomplished by the use of current slang, or by alliteration if this has become fully acceptable. But slang terms and alliteration are not enough. The headline must make the reader curious and arouse his expectations. It must not say everything in the story but only stimulate him to read, or really only to buy the paper. When headlines are very well chosen, reading is often reduced to reading of the headlines, with a hasty assimilation of what they mean. Reading a newspaper becomes a kind of puzzle game, and the headline itself becomes a literary form with its own style and qualities of language. One of its peculiarities is absence of the article. "Baltimore Wife-Beater Given Five Lashes at Whipping Post." "Man Found Dead. Gas in Room Turned On." This probably also contributes to another peculiarity of the American language, the capacity to form combinations, which already distinguishes it from English and brings it closer to German in a very important respect.

The art of advertising, as is well known, is taught in America at institutions of higher learning. It has its own professional journals and brings into its service the best of what the graphic arts and the science of psychology have to offer. Advertising has become one of the most important means of influencing society. The leading universities of the nation do not consider themselves too good or too dignified to make use of advertisements. "If You Cannot Come to Columbia, Columbia Will Come to You," runs the announcement of its home study courses in a magazine by the great university in New York. The advertisement is an extraordinarily important and at the same time entertaining way of learning to know the mind of America. What the news story does by a lively account of crime, politics, sports, adventures, voyages of discovery, and society, that is, reflect the whole daily life of the community, the advertisement does by sounding the praises of goods and services. "Make-Believe Land Come True," is the way the Union Pacific Railway advertises the natural wonders of Utah and Arizona. All American life—its technological perfection, its aspiration to knowledge and power, its covetousness and its amusements—is constantly unfolding in the advertising pages of every periodical. As much as the headline or even more, the advertisement becomes an art form of an independent kind, in which a treasure hoard of inventiveness, judgment, and skill is put out at interest. In this case, the reduction of the readers' mental work is coupled with intensified persuasion on the part of the advertiser. He reduces the argument to a single effective element and then colors it with every hue he can find. Selective emphasis is paramount. In New York this spring a poster was put up for a campaign on behalf of a Jewish charitable fund. All it showed was an old Jewish woman with a tired, careworn face. "Tired of giving?" were the words above the picture, and below, in smaller letters, "You don't know what it is to be tired."

Are advertisements going to take over one of the functions of literature, as the news dispatch has already done? What I have in mind is the way that advertisements, in addition to their commercial value and practical results, become the spiritual nourishment of the masses. An important function of literature is to take us out of ourselves and make us dream. Advertisements create illusions of wealth, comfort, and enjoyment of nature, not with the repellent sternness of a price list but with all the means of allurement. They employ enchanting colors, a poke in the ribs, a pull on the lapel.

Advertising operates as a cultural factor not so much in the press as on the billboard. Along every road and street the posters for cigarettes, soap, and human breakfast fodder hold before the eyes of the public an ideal of felicity and harmony, refinement and enjoyment. An advertisement, it goes without saying, must be democratic. Its presentation of an ideal may go beyond the purse and the heart of the masses but not over their heads. In the high-fashion trades, we may see the snobbery of the rich flattered by the conventionalities of modernism, with its chemical effects of carmine, yellow, and hard green; advertising for the common man requires a pleasing, "natural," and palatable presentation. It must avoid every appearance of the extravagant or the perverse, and preach public morality in its own way.

Advertising therefore plays upon every healthy aspiration and patriotic virtue. A pink-cheeked lad with a broad laugh, and next to him three boxes of breakfast cereal. "For that million-dollar boy of *yours.* Puffed wheat." We see the pride of parents, the feeling for the dollar, and the ideal of health, all reached by one stroke.

The woman in makeup, which European advertising art (which does not understand its craft as well) is so fond of, may be seen on the street in America but not on billboards. Advertisements give their preference to the healthy, happy girl who comes down from Charles Dana Gibson, although now with some variation. Advertisements display sexuality in a more chaste form, but with a fairly sweet feeling that still tries to avoid sentimentality. Their atmosphere and environment is that of an evening party, where young men in tuxedos offer cigarettes to girls, or the beach life of surf-riding and sun-bathing. Think of the soap advertisement with the head of a happy and serious woman, listening to a telephone. This is what she hears: "Remember! Keep that schoolgirl complexion!"

Don't you find it unbelievable that hundreds of thousands of people on the way to factory or office, on the bus or streetcar, feed themselves, probably only half-aware, with such consoling idylls?

Another question would be how far advertisements, with their forceful suggestions and their strong impress upon memory, initiate adaptation and imitation by the model of life which they present to a whole nation.

It would be the triumph of commercial culture if, sometime in the future, advertising swallowed up literature, and praising the good, preaching of morality, and satisfaction of fantasy all merged into one. Just look for once through an entire number of *The Ladies Home Journal* with attention. It will make clear to you what I have in mind.

The Pictorial Quality

The function of literature is no longer exclusively bound to words. A visible picture is paired with words and often is stronger. Even someone who finds the proposition that the advertisement is on the way to becoming literature too paradoxical must admit it is true for the film. For it is clear that the art of the moving picture—which no one can deny any longer as such, and for which we must seek a Muse or patron saint one of these days—is not destined to find a place among the graphic arts but belongs with dramatic art at the side of literature. Despite all its emphasis on the visual, the film does not work by creating images, which endure too briefly for their ghostlike figures to take hold upon us. Although it must be called "pictures" in a broad sense of the term, the film misses the essence of graphic art, which is to create permanent and closed forms. The scenes of the film do not work like sculpture and painting, by means of esthetic form, but as powerful communication, as the speeded-up suggestion of thought or feeling. To see a film is functionally much more closely related to reading a story than seeing a painting.

The "Movies" are only a part, although the most important part of all, of an important process of transformation in our civilization—the movement from reading to looking. Technical progress in photography and the art of reproduction has made this shift possible, but it also corresponds to a spiritual need. In the modern urban environment, the mind, which is swamped with printed words, requires a shorter and easier way of assimiliation and finds it in pictures. In a certain sense pictures therefore restore a function—the ideographic—which they also fulfilled in ancient times.

The American accepts these tendencies without any reluctance. Saving time is one of his passions and he therefore makes "picturizing" one of his ideals. Why spend two minutes reading a text when one can grasp what is intended in a single minute with the help of a picture and a few words? In America the teacher and the advertiser therefore worship pictorial quality more fervently than they do among us. Give diagrams and curves to the pupils, teach them to think in graphic representations, in a word in "conceptual shorthand." Let children learn to express themselves in drawings. The overwhelming success of Hendrik Willem Van Loon[14] in America is fully understandable. His unpretentious scribblings, which the least-educated man can understand, meet the minimum commitment which a public of millions has left over for knowledge.

If the picture really meant a new way of giving form in present-day culture, a selection and combination of the essen-

---

[14] Dutch-born American writer (1882–1944), author of numerous popular histories and biographies, including *The Story of Mankind* (1921) and *The Story of the Bible* (1923).–H.H.R.

tial and the significant out of a mass of intellectual works so immense that it is beyond mastering, we probably could consider it something that civilization could make use of, even if it breaks us of the habit of thinking. But in fact the picture has long since become the object of mass production without point. The effects of photographic reproduction for the last forty years have been utterly deadening. The great majority of illustrated papers nowadays are filled with an endless sequence of uniformly meaningless scenes. A photographic record of the opening of a public meeting, a welcome for government ministers, and a hundred other daily recurring events, ordinarily means that it is just those things which do not really matter which are depicted. How different it was when an artist could still put something of his own imagination into a drawing and give it form! But now, even when imagination must be given full play, it works in the service of business and technology. Do you know anything that in all its innocence is more humiliating than the funny pages of a Sunday newspaper in America?

Concentration

Pictures break us of the habit of thinking and they heighten the superficiality and inability to concentrate that ceaselessly threaten modern intellectual life. The European traveler finds it almost impossible to concentrate when he is in a big American city. The telephone becomes a curse. The variety of personal assistance and technical devices causes as much diversion of attention and loss of time as it saves work.

One of the leading economists of Columbia University sang the praises of his country to me in triumphant tones. "It is our high standard of living that is making us great," was his text. Every good investment of wealth brings a profit in living. It permits us the excellent equipment in our schools, brings the automobile into general use, and gives men free time, all of which increases efficiency. And he saw before his eyes those conferences of "leading men in banking and business," in which the highest interests of the country were decided by young men between 30 and 40 years of age, with thin lips and bright, strong eyes. I asked him: "But doesn't the technique of modern living deprive them of the gift of concentration?" No, he replied: The automobile, golf, the movies "keep a man more on the job," they give him the possibility of concentration when he needs it. Can this be true?

Slogans

The rule of the slogan, the brief and pithy catchword, is a sign of how much the popular mind in America needs abbreviation and condensation of thought. The slogan is closely related to headlines and advertising. "Say it with flowers" or "Safety first" can be called national or public advertisements. The slogan is the subject of deliberate cultivation as much as the headline. Schools hold competitions for the invention of "safety slogans," preferably with alliteration. The slogan offers a counterweight to the general dispersion of thought by holding it fast to a single, utterly succinct and unforgettable expression, one which usually inspires men to immediate action. It abolishes reflection: the slogan does not argue, it asserts and commands. It has a high measure of unifying effect. It dissolves all individual nuances of opinion in the fortifying catchword. It indicates that the scope of thought has become much smaller.

The slogan is completely identical in outer form and as a cultural function with the motto and the device of much earlier times. It is a form of crystallized thought which holds a group together and spurs it to common action. In it we face regression of civilization.

Men of Letters

If it is true that the news dispatch and the film are taking over some of the functions of literature, does this mean that attention is diverted from literature itself? Not necessarily. In the first place the newspaper and movies have accustomed a very large section of the people to literary nourishment who previously were virtual strangers to it. The public reached by higher literature has never been more than a small group.

But actually such a group does not exist; it is only a fiction of our understanding which takes things apart. Even the individual reader is a complex and heterogeneous creature. He is not just a reader, but a businessman, a scientific researcher, a father, a churchgoer, a fisherman, an automobile driver, and a moviegoer as well, probably all together. Each of these areas of his life defines a part of his culture. Literature seldom occupies more place than an ornament, even for persons of refinement and art-lovers. For most people it involves neither faith nor interest; it does not become any part of their being. I can imagine an inquiry into the effect of contemporary literature in which the question is put to a hundred thousand readers of a specific group of works, not, as the Apostle Philip put it to the Moorish chamberlain, "Do you understand what you are reading?" but, "Do you accept what you read?" For the great majority the answer would necessarily be: "I understand and enjoy it somewhat, I accept it about half way, and I do not apply it." The average reader—and, socially speaking, it is he with whom we are concerned—no matter how much literary pessimism, revolutionary thought, romanticism, amoralism, or mysticism he reads, remains a good citizen, a sober businessman and a more or less dutiful person. He will stand up from reading the sourest and harshest naturalist books by Theodore Dreiser and go to bring his offering of incense to all the gods of fatherland, prosperity, the home fires, and poetry. And it is fortunate that this is so.

Although still perceptible boundaries therefore exist between the literary public and the *profanum vulgus*,[15] between literary art and works of entertainment, we continue, like the incorrigible Neo-Platonists we all are, to speak nonetheless of Literature as a reality, and of a literary culture as the culture of a group or elite who are to be found behind and above the general civilization as it is represented by the newspaper, the school, the pulpit, the political platform, and the movies.

That happens to be the way our minds are organized; we must work with such ideas if we want to understand each other. We know in any case that Literature is a factor, an agent, and that it constantly causes rearrangements in the mind of the nation. But as soon as we make these qualifications, we accept the anthropomorphism which is indispensable to us. It would really be much simpler just to think of it straightforwardly as a Muse.

This way of thinking is all the more necessary for a judgment of contemporary America because a remarkable contrast may be observed between the attitude of the nation in general and the tone of its literature. The spirit of American culture in general continues to be steadily filled with bold confidence in life, confidence in education and progress, and

[15] Latin for "the vulgar herd."—H.H.R.

respect for the established moral and national institutions. In brief, it is healthy-minded, positive, and optimistic.

None of this, or at least much less of it, is present in the dominant tendency in contemporary literature. We could probably say: "But is literature ever in complete harmony with the general ideal of life? Isn't it always more or less a protest?" To this we must reply: No, literature in all the great ages of civilization was precisely the perfect expression of the dominant ideals of life, with the exception of the period of Romanticism in which we Europeans have been living for a century and a half. And the remarkable thing is that American literature, even when Romantic influence was strongest, maintained this harmony, this confirmation of the general ideal of life, until fairly recently. It is to be found in Walt Whitman no less than in Hawthorne and Longfellow, in Henry James no less than in Mark Twain. It is probably still present if one penetrates more deeply into contemporary American literature, but on the surface it has the character of aversion, protest, and accusation in its most striking and distinguished works. Aversion to the all-too-cheap optimism, the national self-overestimation, and the Puritan ideal, a protest against vulgarity and the hollowness of society.

Sinclair Lewis has become very well known in recent years in Europe, but what Europeans know Willa Cather, Joseph Hergesheimer, Theodore Dreiser, James Branch Cabell, to speak only of the prose writers?

Lewis illustrates in the first place the passionate aversion of the younger generation (he was born in 1885) toward all the hopeless ugliness of city and country, all the ludicrousness of spongy pseudoculture and national bumptiousness. The importance of the creation of Babbitt as a mirror of the nation has been compared by an English critic with that of Don Quixote, so richly and with such high humor and vitality does it represent the national character. The Americans can no longer get rid of Babbitt as a warning example. He is more than a literary figure, he has been a force. Nobody wants to be a Babbitt, and most people in fact detect in themselves traces of "babbittry." "One-hundred percent Americanism," although it is still seriously professed by countless Americans, has become part of Babbitt's ludicrousness.

In the second place, Lewis illustrates an important event in the literature of the English-speaking countries, namely, the abolition of the "sex taboo," the freer handling of sexual life. This transformation is not limited to literature in the narrower sense. It is an event of general importance. It is reflected in the daily press by frequent use of words from Freudian terminology. "Inflated mother-image" and various "complexes" are current coin.

Lewis could also serve as an example of the small talent for a closed form which still characterizes so many American writers. The judges who awarded him the Pulitzer Prize for *Arrowsmith* (which he refused) had evidently laid down no standards of strict and controlled composition.

The triumph of virtue and the happy ending had already had their day before Edith Wharton painted the pitiful fall out of society of a somewhat too distinguished girl without fortune in *The House of Mirth*, and the success of the professional divorcee in *The Custom of the Country*. The accusation against the sins of society remains soft and moderate in her. The later rise of literary realism has caused much harder notes to be heard. America honors her most significant naturalist writer in Theodore Dreiser (of whose work I could still not find a single copy in London this very spring). His first work dates from 1900; only in recent years has his influence broken through. In it a complete and apparently very un-American pessimism is having its turn at being heard.

Dreiser believes in the extinction of mankind; he sees no purpose in existence, only endless change, and man as a futile
creature between enigmatic and frightening forces, with the
sexual drive as the most powerful motive force. He has no
heroes; one man is as useful for his protagonist as another,
for blind passions, vain hopes and disasters are the lot of all of
them. Critics have called his attitude "animalism."

It is no wonder that American naturalism turns out to be
especially stiff and hard. The background of cities without
style in their crying ugliness, and villages without form or
charm, is cheerless.

The turn away from the banality and vulgarity of the
present day can also be displayed in other ways. Joseph Hergesheimer expresses it in the garb of a personal neo-romantic-
ism. In *Balisand* (1924) he creates in imagination a national
historical figure, a aristocratic Federalist from Virginia in the
days of Washington. Where Sinclair Lewis handles his coun-
trymen homeopathically through Babbitt, Hergesheimer uses
an allopathic treatment, offering as a contrast to democracy,
city life, comfort, diversions, gentleness, and prohibition, the
duellist, hunter, and drinker with fierce urges and great passions. The whole scene is bathed in a sweet atmosphere of
over-refined, perfumed beauty, suffused with immense quantities of rum. It is all a hankering after what one does not
have.

Aversion to the Western civilization of his own time
seems also to be the ground tone of the fantastic illusionism
of James Branch Cabell. An attack against the falsehoods of
society is most certainly the principal motif of Eugene
O'Neill, who is praised as America's greatest playwright. In
the play from his pen which appeared this spring, *The Great
God Brown*, the influence of international modernism, with
its desperate floundering toward a new stage style, was too

overwhelming for it to be called characteristically American at all strongly.

The attack against everything that is hollow, woolly-minded or false in America is heard more deliberately, explicitly, and systematically in the journals of criticism than in the novel or on the stage. This applies to the best known, which are the weeklies *The Nation* and *The New Republic* and the monthly *The American Mercury*. H. L. Mencken, the editor of *The American Mercury*, holds a position midway between a Mephisto and a Grand Inquisitor. A dissenter to the tips of his fingers, he calls his purpose "to combat by ridicule and invective American piety and stupidity and tin-pot morality." It would almost appear that he had renounced his fatherland; in his "On being an American," he speaks of the multitudes who constantly flee over the ocean "to escape the great curses and atrocities that make life intolerable for them at home." But it only looks that way. Mencken is a good American, as is shown by his angry outbursts against the English critics who do not know America or have a low opinion of it, in the June number of his magazine this year. He hates the idea that for the self-satisfied Englishman Babbitt has now become the sum and total of America. Even Mencken, despite all his denials, has national ideals. If he did not, America would have expelled him spiritually, for America tolerates everything except pure denial. Now it swallows him and his monthly crop of "Americana." It does not take him wholly seriously, for his criticism is all too premeditated; it makes his name an everyday word and calls certain circles "Menckenized"—and undergoes his influence. Mencken is very popular especially among the younger generation.

This spring his name temporarily rose to a greater notoriety than usual because of a typical American event. The April number of *The American Mercury* published a short story describing how a girl from educated circles somewhere in the Mid-West fell into prostitution as a result of circumstances. A champion of the old, puritanical standards in literature—shocked most of all, I fear, because the protagonist was a person of social standing—accused the editor of spreading immoral literature. Mencken gave him the opportunity to prove his case by personally selling a copy to him. In order to add color to the transaction, he bit the half dollar he received in payment, according to the popular custom. The result was that the sale of *The American Mercury* in railway stations was forbidden. What better could Mencken have asked for!

We have hastily considered here a few figures from the present-day literary world in America, more in their relation to the nation and their importance for culture than from the viewpoint of strictly literary appraisal. That is why I have placed them under the rubric of Society rather than of Thought.

Youth

The growing generation! America, with all its pervasive sense of the future, worships the young. The sense of the future, parenthetically, is betrayed even in little things. A student is known as soon as he arrives by the year in which he will finish college four years later, and the end of the academic year is called Commencement.[16] The weight of the coming generation rests upon the American mind with steady

[16] Huizinga obviously confused the end of the academic year as such with the fact that academic degrees are granted at that time. —H.H.R.

and extraordinary strength. Youth stands in the center of thought, the child is ruler. At the dinner table in New York, I heard the French sociologist Marcel Mauss, who was asked to communicate some impressions of America, give a witty discussion on the theme: You sacrifice yourselves to your children, or rather to your wives and through them to your children. You put up with the difficulties of commuting to work in order to enable your children to grow up outside the city, you spend your earnings on expensive colleges for your daughters, and maintain an automobile for the whims of the family.

There is unrest among the youth and concern over the youth. Adults anxiously wonder what their sons and daughters are coming to. The monthly *Forum* announced an enquiry into the question: "Has youth degenerated?" At the back of a number of *The New Republic* I find four books advertised: three of them concern problems of education. The first is called *Concerning Parents,* the second *Youth in Conflict,* and the third *Our Enemy the Child,* and the latter two are by women. The older generation looks for guilt primarily in its own bosom. Does the family satisfy its task of shaping men? Is the school still inadequate? We must keep in mind the enormous importance of the idea of education in America in order to realize how much these are burning questions for everyone.

There is much discussion in America of the intolerably free-and-easy ways of the children and the increasing laxity of relations among the young people. We learn of American mothers who send their daughters to Europe in order to get them away from the atmosphere of youthful life in America. European women who reside in America assure you: I would not want to bring up a daughter here.

If the general freedom of relations between boys and

girls in America is in fact much greater than what recent
years have brought about in Europe, and in many cases leads
to loose conduct, two things seemed to have played an important part in it—the automobile and Prohibition. Along
with many other things, the automobile has become *the* instrument of adventure and crime. It also replaces the knight's
steed and the castle towers with an extraordinarily increased
efficiency. The watchman has long since retired on pension.
In addition to many other results, Prohibition has had the
unintended result of making getting a drink a youthful sport,
and the drink itself, even more than the means of pleasure, its
very symbol. A party without whiskey is considered incomplete; it seems to have become quite common for girls of sixteen or seventeen to become drunk after such "petting parties."[17] But one also hears less alarming judgments, particularly
at coeducational universities. There is a youthful marriage
now and then, but also venereal disease has disappeared almost
completely among male students. The question remains how
far the woman has become the victim of this shift in morality.

In any case, the phenomenon cannot be considered exclusively with the eyes of the appalled moralist, but also in its
social and cultural significance. It might be supposed that a
movement is under way here which is fundamentally a consequence of the general mechanization of social life. The
extraordinarily increased ease of local transportation brings
about that of personal intercourse as well.[18] The general
leveling of culture also affects love life. Just as intellectual
enjoyment becomes available for everyone in a thousand
ways, and hence loses the quality of something conquered,
something which represents success and to which one pays

[17] Presumably his American friends failed to explain to the staid if
inquisitive Dutch visitor the difference between drinking and petting.
—H.H.R.

[18] Huizinga uses the one Dutch word *verkeer* for both transportation and intercourse.—H.H.R.

worship, so there also arises a form of sexual satisfaction which signifies the dissolution of old forms of civilization. Won't the modern intercourse of the sexes make the generation which grows up with it immune to the great passions? It is not probable that the coming generation will sing of Werther or Tristan.

Personality

In the *American Mercury* of May 1926 I found a remarkable article under the title "Anon is dead," by Henry Seidel Canby. "Anon" means Anonymous. The writer calls attention to the surprising fact that at the very time that the general leveling of minds threatens the public with nameless impersonality, publication without a name or under a pseudonym has almost completely vanished from the customs of writers and publishers. He illustrates this with a striking example. "The Pickwick Papers by Boz" would now be impossible. We would now have "Charles Dickens writes in the current *Green Book*," and with portrait, of course. Canby pursues the idea of the disappearance of anonymity in several other areas, and interprets what has happened as "an almost hysterical attempt to escape from the deadly anonymity of modern life, and the prime cause is the craving—I had almost said the terror—of the general man who feels his personality sinking lower and lower into a whirl of indistinguishable atoms to be lost in a mass civilization."

Once one's attention has been called to this characteristic longing for personality, we find it recurring constantly. The lost individual hungers both for the recognition of his own personality and for contact with that of others. Poor deluded fellow, he wants still always to see a man behind everything the great machine offers to him each day. The advertisement, which in this is again a sensitive indicator of the feeling of the community, comes forward to meet this need in a thousand ways. We Dutchmen are accustomed to seeing the portraits of modestly garbed writers in book catalogues. In America every advertising section swarms with a pageful of portraits. A method for remaining young by the use of certain spinal movements is introduced by presenting the inventor as a man, a friend. "My meeting up with Bradstreet, I count the luckiest day of my life," declares the advertiser, who at the same time presents himself with a familiar sounding name. And so forth, and so forth, and before you realize it, you have read the whole story: how Bradstreet came to make his discovery, how the narrator was cured of constipation in an almost miraculous way, thanks to his system, and the rest. Or instead the advertisement remonstrates with the reader: "Mark Twain wanted to be your friend. Here are the books he planned for you."

Sports and the cinema have opened up an immense garden of delights for the requirements of personality; the whole nation can romp daily with its heroes, who give a more familiar, accessible, and congenial impression than the notables in the Capitol and the banks. And he who finds no consolation in the feeling of knowing other persons can find it in the promise of his own greatness: "See How Easy It Is to Quickly Become a Powerful Speaker."

A Contrast

Do the obtrusive bombast, the loudness and loquacity of the printed word in America, reflect the average American as he shows himself when he goes for a stroll? Absolutely not, it seems to me. It is dangerous to rely on an impression, but if I must describe the American, I would say: He is not loud and he is not loquacious. He speaks without strong emphasis, indeed in an offhand way. It was an American who called my attention to the stillness that prevails in an American gathering. The American does not force himself upon you. He is not at all in a hurry, as is often imagined; quite the contrary. In brief, there is a continuous contrast between the general habit and the tone of the printed word. If this is true, how are we to explain that it is this very man who produces these words and feeds upon them? Is the word itself no longer the product of the man but of the machine? And if so, where does culture reside, in the man or in the word?

*All action is an invasion of
the future, of the unknown.*
John Dewey

Chapter II

THOUGHT

TRANSPOSITION AND RE-CREATION

Intellectual Watchwords

When one has been in the company of intellectuals in America for several weeks, one becomes aware that certain words constantly recur in their conversation. These are words which betray a definite intellectual aspiration. There are, for example, the words "outlook" and "approach," the latter preferably in the form "a new approach." Is the "outlook" for a certain piece of research promising? What is your "approach" to a certain field of knowledge? Both questions indicate an attitude on the part of the thinker: He is on the look-out, he reconnoiters, he moves in closer, in short he is a hunter. A field lies before him which he wishes to search and conquer. The notion of purpose seems to speak more strongly in the scientific thought of Americans than among us.

The word "problem" has recently become a cliché among us because of its unthinking use, and as such it suffers the persecution of Charivarius.[1] It is used even more fre-

[1] Since there is no such person or god in classical mythology, the name Charivarius is obviously Huizinga's jesting transformation of the famous French satirical journal *Charivari*, on the model of a classical god.—H.H.R.

quently in America, but, it may be said, with more genuine feeling. The sense of standing together against a powerful mass of questions which imperatively demand solution appears more lively among them than among us. "The outstanding problems of today" is a turn of phrase that occurs repeatedly, and it is not a hollow phrase.

Of more weight even than the words I have named, which only reflect an attitude of mind, is another word that is in the air, the word "behavior." In this word the credo of intellectual America lies locked up, as it were. In what follows I have in view preeminently those sciences with which the purpose of my journey brought me in closest contact: the social sciences, by which the American chiefly understands economics, political science, sociology, cultural anthropology, and psychology. All social and individual actions and events are grasped by the American thinker under the aspect of "behavior." A good understanding of the phenomena of society lies in explaining them as results of human behavior. The idea is not unknown in Europe, but is placed somewhat less in the foreground here than in America. "The city," says Robert E. Park, "is a state of mind, a body of customs and traditions, and of the organized attitudes and sentiments that inhere in these customs and are transmitted with this tradition."[2] The study of urban society must therefore be directed not to the discovery of economic or demographic regularities, not to speak of political formulas, but to "human behavior." What holds for the city holds for all other human groups and social phenomena. The sociologist Ernest W. Burgess attempts to study the family "as human behavior," and to do the same with crime.[3] Biological and economic theories are abandoned. The anthropologist Clark Wissler visualizes civilization "as

[2] Park and Burgess, *The City* (Chicago, 1925), p. 1.
[3] *The American Journal of Sociology*, 28 (1923), p. 662; *The Family*, March 1926.

human behavior."[4] And even the engineer sees his most urgent task as the acquisition of exact knowledge about the "behavior of materials."

So far as I can tell, neither the word *gedrag*[5] in Dutch, nor *Verhalten, Benehmen,* or *Betragen*[6] in German, nor *conduite*[7] in French, and not even *behaviour* in British usage have taken on the marked, pregnant and almost symbolic meaning which the word "behavior" possesses today in American thought.

A portion of American intellectual history is imbedded in the attitude toward the world process which it expresses. I believe that connections could be traced as far back as Emerson. It is safer to place at the head of this chapter the name of the man who today counts as the country's leading thinker, John Dewey.

Behaviorism

I say John Dewey, not John B. Watson, who is the prophet, or probably more precisely the provost sergeant, of the system of psychology that calls itself "behaviorism." If I understand rightly, "behavior" did not become a fashionable term because "behaviorism" won such a vogue as a theory, but on the contrary "behaviorism" was elevated to a

[4] *Man and Culture* (Harrap, 1923).

[5] Literally, "conduct." The translations in this and the following footnotes are obviously inadequate to convey the semantic subleties in Huizinga's mind.—H.H.R.

[6] Literally, "conduct" or "demeanor."—H.H.R.

[7] In addition to its primary meaning of "guidance," literally or in the figurative sense *conduite* also indicates, like the foregoing, "conduct" or "manner."—H.H.R.

system because "behavior" as an expression of a certain attitude towards things was in the air.

The doctrine of behaviorism consists in the principle that all psychic processes have to be traced back to the concepts of stimulus and response. Together these result in the acquisition of habits, on which all psychic life rests. If behaviorism limited itself to a claim to be a working hypothesis in psychology, we would gladly leave it to psychologists to judge its worth. But it claims to be more. Through the mouth of its prophet[8] it declares that it is called upon to dethrone and succeed all philosophy in the near future and create a cultural doctrine and world view which will have sole and complete sway. It therefore compels everyone who recognizes that noology[9] has a value which reaches beyond the realm of experimental psychology to resist Watson's doctrine. The behaviorists make short work of all epistemology. They do not encounter the categories of knowledge in their investigations; they have no place for them in their system and in their radical naïveté therefore assert that they do not exist or have no value. Consciousness, says Watson, is just like soul and spirit, a mythological conception from obsolete schools. What the psychologists thus far (but soon they will all be behaviorists) have called thinking or thought was nothing more than "talking to ourselves." In Watson's eyes, what talking consists of if there is no thinking does not require any further explanation. He is wholly satisfied with labeling speech and thoughts both as "laryngeal habits," customary behavior of the throat, just as all emotions are adequately characterized as "visceral habits," or such behavior in the entrails. Com-

---

8 J. B. Watson, *Behaviorism* (New York: The People's Institute Publishing Company, 1925).

9 The science of understanding. Huizinga's deliberate use of the recondite term is probably a subtle baiting of Watson and company as philosophical ignoramuses.—H.H.R.

pelled by his psychological terrorism to ban summarily, or, better, to destroy, all terms from the domain of the spirit, he clears the ground out of hand. To attach meaning to any thing is superstition. "Meaning is a historical word borrowed from philosophy and introspective psychology." If people want to continue to speak of "motives" or "social values," fine, Watson will wink at it, but it would be much more correct to call them "verbal stimuli," for that is all they are. "The behaviorist never uses the term 'memory.'" For no such thing exists. What happens, then, when we keep an appointment made the day before? "We have in our verbal habits a mechanism by means of which the stimulus is reapplied from moment to moment until the final reaction occurs, namely going to the Belmont at one o'clock the next day." What is all this but to explain an incomprehensible fact by putting an absurd fiction (just imagine the continuous repercussion of all our memories) in its place? As a sample of exact expression, Watson says for *I will:* "I have had my own laryngeal processes stimulated to work upon this problem from another angle."

Although behaviorism continues to be under vigorous discussion[10] and to exercise a strong influence on America thought, of which it is a very characteristic expression, nevertheless it does not at all represent the totality of that thought. American psychologists whom I asked if their method had some relation to "behaviorism" smiled with pained irony. Obviously they are quite aware that behaviorism is a bit like a peasant in wooden shoes who strays into a gathering of thinkers. In the *American Journal of Psychology* of 1925[11] I found an expression of doubt whether there still exist adherents of the doctrine in its radical form.

[10] See the survey "Psychology" in *American Yearbook 1925*, p. 970.
[11] Ibid., p. 350.

The Science of Society

Even considered as a cultural phenomenon, as an effect of "human behavior," behaviorism appears to be one of the less talented offspring of pragmatism. Pragmatism, as a cultural phenomenon, is in its turn the expression of this inherent spirit of America, which I previously tried to characterize by calling it the spirit of "This, Here, and Soon."[12] William James himself called pragmatism "a temper of mind, an attitude," "the attitude of looking away from first things, principles, categories, supposed necessities; and of looking towards last things, fruits, consequences, facts."[13]

This direction and tendency permeate American thought in all its fibers. It is relatively rare in America to encounter the notion of a science which does not pursue something that can be of practical value. The American will seek a right to exist even for those sciences concerned with the past by reference to their educational value, either in cultivation of the mind or in the good understanding of today produced by knowledge of previous developments. The idea which threatened historical scholarship in Europe about thirty years ago,[14] that is, the demand that it should merely do the hoeing and the plowing for sociology, is prevalent in America. Iconoclasts[15] are being enlisted to introduce it as "the new history." But it

[12] See *Mensch en Menigte in America*, 2nd ed., p. 219 [see above, p. 195 ff.].

[13] *Pragmatism*, p. 55.

[14] I.e., about 1895–1900.—H.H.R.

[15] *Beeldstormers*, "image-breakers," in Dutch history the rioters who destroyed Catholic church ornaments in 1566 in a movement which helped to set off the Revolt of the Low Countries.—H.H.R.

will not be so simple, for a flourishing historical profession exists in America which differs little from Europe's, in spite of theory.

The social sciences in the narrow sense have been strongly unified in recent years under the banner of the welfare of society. The aim is to learn how to understand society in its economic, social, and anthropological forms in order to be able to cure it. The watchword and the slogan is: "Intelligent control of human behavior," "Intelligent control of the social process." If all cultural phenomena are questions of "behavior," then the strategy of this alliance of sciences—for it is truly a "campaign"—must be based upon psychology. Social psychology is therefore the task which they all share.

We will be asked: Don't we in Europe have such an enterprise? Of course we do, but there is a difference. You do not feel such an intellectual fervor in the air in Europe as in America. The cry does not ring forth loud and joyfully as a national intellectual slogan; social science here is not laden, as it is there, with the élan and the solidarity of everyone. The same forces which bring about the mechanization of culture—the easy exchange of ideas, the improved technology, the all-controlling organization—have created there a linkage between scholarly thought and social purpose that Europe does not know in the same measure. There is at work here an element which Spengler, when he predicted the great ice age of civilization, did not see; there burns a spark that probably still promises to light a new blaze.

The following are some of the special characteristics of social science in America.

First is its convinced pluralistic standpoint. In it the memory of William James again forces itself upon us. Social science is reluctant to affirm a single ground of explanation. The unending variety and complexity of phenomena and their continuing change and flux make it impossible to penetrate to the basis of things with a few distinctions, classifications, and abstractions. All theories seeking to explain complicated areas of life by placing them under the rule of an instinct or a group of instincts, says Dewey,[16] have worked to mislead and harm. Whether, with Hobbes, we seek to explain political life solely from the motive of fear, or with later thinkers to reduce all social facts to imitation and invention, or to derive all economic phenomena from profit and labor, or now with Freud and Jung to premise sexuality, we always end with misconceptions, in a blind alley. So long as social science is satisfied with such simplifications, it still moves in the stage which the natural sciences occupied before the inductive and experimental method was invented, when it still worked with general "forces" as a principle of explanation. Burgess[17] rejects all general theories of crime, the biological theory of Lombroso, the social theory of Tarde, the economic theory of Bonger, and the combined theory of Ferri, in order to present the strictly inductive study of cases and individuals as the first requirement for a sound and precise criminology.

A very important characteristic of America's sociological thought is, again in Dewey's words, "the intelligent acknowledgment of the continuity of nature, man and society." All action of living things is interaction, mutual actions. It never arises out of an isolated intellectual process but is always determined as well by natural conditions and environment. The character and the actions of a single person are always "coterminous" with those of other people, that is, everything that he is or does, he is or does in relation to other things or

[16] *Human Nature and Conduct: An Introduction to Social Psychology* (New York, 1922), pp. 132, 153.
[17] *American Journal of Sociology*, 28 (1923), pp. 657 ff.

men; his character is not his own "attribute" but the result of the mutual operation between the outer world and personality. Human actions and customs, just like physiological operations, are "functions" of the environment as well as of the individual. Breathing is as much a "function" of the air as of the lungs. In absolutely the same sense, sculpture is as much a "function" of the block and the tools as of the artist. The same is true of morality, economic life, scientific thought: they are all social functions.

This obliteration of the boundaries between the individual and the environment, this interchange of object and subject, if I see things correctly, opens up the possibility of a reconciliation with a mechanized, leveled-down society, in which productive energy is transferred from the living arm and fixed in the dead tool. But I shall not attempt to elaborate this idea here.

The consequence of this principle is that social psychology in practice becomes the understanding of habits and different types of habits. Although the operation of instinct and intellect may serve in a certain sense to explain individual action, both are, even in the individual man, subject in the highest measure to habit and they function, so to say, only as secondary agencies. "So that mind can be understood in the concrete only as a system of beliefs, desires and purposes which are formed in the interaction of biological aptitudes with a social environment."[18] Once again we approach the point at which we had put behaviorism aside; it is here that Dewey has his roots in pragmatism.

"An idea gets shape and consistency only when it has a habit back of it. . . . The act must come before the thought, and a habit before an ability to evoke the thought at will." "Every ideal is preceded by an actuality; but the ideal is more

[18] Dewey, *Human Nature and Conduct*, p. iii.

than a repetition in inner image of the actual. It projects in securer and wider and fuller form some good which has been previously experienced in a precarious, accidental, fleeting way."[19]

Morality is an acquired good, instilled not by education and encouragement, but by the impersonal operation of the social environment. An individual normally acquires morality from his social group, just as he inherits its speech. Encouragement, advice, and education are a weak stimulus compared with those which constantly emanate from the impersonal forces and depersonalized habits of the environment. "Virtues are ends because they are such important means. To be honest, courageous, kindly is to be in the way of producing specific natural goods or satisfactory fulfillments."[20]

These ideas of John Dewey fully and truly reflect, it seems to me, the conceptual basis of contemporary social-science thinking in America.

Now we come to the question how these general insights determine the development of the specific social sciences.

"Groups"

At this point one of those "frequency" words recurs upon which I have based this observation: the word "group." The constant need for this word extends far beyond its use as a term in social science. The awareness of the all-surpassing importance of social groups is now general property in America. We too have become accustomed in recent years to directing our attention to group phenomena—think, for ex-

[19] Ibid., pp. 23, 30.
[20] Ibid., pp. 22, 47, 58.

ample, of the studies of Van Ginniken[21]—but the operation of this concept of "group" is not so intensive by far in our thinking as it is in the American. This is natural, indeed, even apart from pragmatism and social science. For the social group itself, that is, the tight combination of a limited number of persons of the same attitudes and opinions, and facing the same dangers, has long had a very special importance as a factor and an entity in the building of American society. Under weak government, in a wide, thinly populated country, in the struggle against the raw natural environment and with the free play of economic forces, unified social groups became the transmitters of culture. I earlier attempted to demonstrate this in an article which, with more linguistic purity than clarity, I called "Independence and Unification," but which I now, with less sensitivity to the praise of purists, I will call "Individualism and Association."[22] It was my opinion that I could bring together the various forms of social association known to American history into a single cultural-historical process— the primitive societies of the "Regulators," the "Compacts" in the Carolinas of the eighteenth century, the "Land Clubs" of Iowa, the "caucus" in all its forms, the secret orders and societies America swarms with—all the way to the organization of the political machine of the major parties. In a study which would also include the present, the gang of young or adult criminals in the big cities should be added as one of its most important forms.

It seemed possible to consider an individualism that hungers for self-assertion and makes itself felt in and through

[21] See above, p. 94.
[22] *Mensch en Menigte in America*, chap. I [see above, pp. 6 ff. In the third edition of 1928, therefore before he wrote *In the Shadow of Tomorrow*, Huizinga had already changed the title of this article, which had read "Zelfstandigheid and vereeniging"—Independence and unification—in the first two editions.—Ed. of Huizinga, *Verzamelde Werken*.]

association to be one of the most essential forces in America's growth.

Realization of the outstanding importance of such social nuclei has grown enormously in America since the war, not only among the sociologists but in all public life as well. "Community" has taken on a resonance in America which it hardly possesses in Europe. "Perhaps no greater advance," says Howard W. Odum,[23] "has been made in the after-war period than the increased recognition of the institution of community, whether it be community of organization, of fellowship, of industry, of arts and letters, of learning, of religion, or of citizenship." A great zeal for the encouragement of good local government and knowledge of local community among a broad circle is only one expression among many. "The State," says W. Y. Elliott,[24] "is ultimately a pluralistic arrangement of group forces." This is really only a modern way of expressing the denigration of government which was already present in Jefferson.

The sociologist recognizes as a foundation of groups neither conviction nor interest but feeling. They are "we-groups," and their foundation is "we-feeling." The character of the purpose that the group represents is secondary. Group awareness creates as its best and strongest products loyalty, cooperation, brotherhood, devotion to the interests of the leader and the group. These are the old principles of the clan, the guild, the fraternity, and the feudal system. "The people within the organization," says Robert E. Park,[25] speaking of political "machines" of the Tammany type, "their friends and supporters, constitute a 'we'-group, while the rest of the city

[23] *Constructive Ventures in Government,* University of North Carolina Extension Leaflet, IV, no. 1.
[24] "Sovereign State or Sovereign Group," *American Political Science Review,* August 1925.
[25] *The City,* pp. 35, 36.

is merely the outer world, which is not quite alive and not quite human in the sense in which the members of the 'we'-group are."

The impulse that drives the individual to join (unless he becomes a member of a group by the mere fact of birth or circumstances) is a need to feel himself bigger and stronger, to extend the range of action of his ego, "magnifying the ego." The members form an *Illusionsgemeinschaft*.[26] Even if they are lynchers or community terrorists, they burn with an ideal of justice, performing a duty or taking vengeance. It is the social goal which lends moral virtue to the other element which impels people to join: the need for trust and the liking of a host of comrades.

We know the "Elks" from Babbitt. America swarms with fraternal orders like the "Elks." The habitual dabbler in such organizations is called a "joiner." The revival of the Ku Klux Klan and the success of the Rotary Clubs indicate how vigorous this spirit of joining continues to be.

Nothing is more important in this respect than the fact that the organization of labor in America is undertaken much less as the pursuit of a class ideal than seeking the advantages of distinct and concrete group interests.[27]

Educators are aware that they can reach the youth only by making use of gang spirit and guiding it, not by working against it. As a result of the alarming rise of crime in the big cities, extraordinary attention has been given to the gang. Anyone who reads about the criminal gangs in New York or Chicago, with the mutual blood feuds, may well be inclined to believe that these are transplanted seeds of the primitive civilization of backward Old World countries, especially when foreign elements like Italians and Jews play an impor-

[26] German for "society of illusions."—H.H.R.
[27] See A. Feiler, *Amerika-Europa*, pp. 183–214.

tant part. But this is generally not the case, except probably for the Chinese societies. The gangs arise spontaneously from the very soil of a cosmopolitan city. The mutual enmity is based on professional competition, whether liquor smuggling or the sale of Italian lottery tickets. Very frequently the gang is a continuation of children's games. The sociologist recognizes their great importance just in this. The play-group, says Park, is one of the most important factors in the formation of the character of the average individual. F. M. Thrasher studied a thousand boys' gangs in the Chicago slums, where criminals grow up but where, too, the social force of the gangs can be developed to good purpose. These gangs, Parks continues, probably have greater influence on the formation of young people than the church and the school.

The sociologist therefore sees here a task which reaches outside the scholar's study. There is a conviction that the formation of habits is ultimately the factor which controls man and society, that habits are the only field in which "intelligent control of human behavior" can be preeminently effective, and that moralizing and exhortation will fail.

The Chicago sociologists desire to build the study of family life and crime on the foundations of group consciousness. Utilizing the notions of Dewey regarding the merger of man and society, they develop the following distinction between the individual and the person. The study of man as an individual, and therefore of the reaction of his organism to the environment, belongs to the field of psychology and psychiatry. The study of the person, the product of social "interaction" between him and his fellows, belongs in the field of sociology.[28] The person is an individual, possessing

---

[28] It seems to me that psychiatry too must continue to concern itself with the person.—J.H.

status, a place and position in society. Each individual obtains such status not by the biological fact of his birth but by his social origin, education, and circumstances. He inevitably belongs to more than one social group: the family, the school, a religious denomination, a factory, etc., and in each of these his status is defined by his relation to every other member of this group. Each smaller group in its turn has a status in a larger group.

Working from the principle of this definition of the person, Burgess finds that in many cases a sudden falling behind and skewing in the development of a child or his entry into crime is the consequence of a break in this personality relationship. The person "has suffered a degradation in status in his group." If this has been severe, it can cause "a collapse of one's social world," and the individual, no longer an undisturbed person, is uprooted from society and misplaced in it.

Burgess sees here the program of a new sociology. First, by this method it will develop from a philosophy of society into a science of society. Not only crime but the whole field of group behavior and social life must be subjected to an analysis which finds the explanation of a person's conduct in the relationships between him and the group. "Explanations of his behavior are found in terms of human wishes and social attitudes, mobility and unrest, intimacy and status, social contacts and social interaction, conflict, accommodation and assimilation." Burgess, in a later article, also puts forward "social images," that is, everyone's conception of his role in the group reflected in the role which he sees other people play, as an important element in the formation of personality.[29]

[29] "The Family as a Unity of Interacting Personalities," *The Family*, March 1926, pp. 8, 9.

Once More Democracy

"The man and women I saw were all near to me. Others the same—others who look back on me because I look'd forward to them. . . ."

Why do I again call upon Walt Whitman's "Crossing Brooklyn Ferry"? Why do the contemporary sociologists and psychologists irresistibly remind me of the poet of the past century? Because they are inspired by the same thing, because science now attempts to give exact form to what the poet kneaded in gigantic formlessness from the chaos of thought, to build high bridges of understanding between our ideas of man and of society, and to set aside the isolated man as negligible and see him disappear into his surroundings.

There are dangers in democratic method, as I would call this whole style of thought. Behind the democratic ideal rises up at once the reality of mechanization. By carrying through the argument from the axioms of behaviorism, we reduce the world to a meaningless and barren thing, at its best a fool's paradise of technology. The mechanization of the spirit attacks all thinking. I shall come back to this later, however.

Here only the burning desire to make science useful to men brings salvation. Immediately behind the study of social psychology there lies a permanent question: How can we improve all these unsatisfactory and defective things? The mechanistic conception of social life, with its exclusion of morality and exhortation, seems to leave almost no means for intervention. If we are all just the nearly helpless followers of fashions, manners, and habits defined by our group, the poor slaves of our personal habits, which together determine our

AMERICA

character, staring as if under a hypnotic spell at our own social images, is there any way to bring about *change*, to change
and to improve all that which *must* be changed? How do we
reach that great goal, "intelligent control of the social process"?

A remarkable book by H. A. Overstreet bears the title
Influencing Human Behavior.[30] His students asked him to give
a course "indicating how human behavior can actually be
changed in the light of the new knowledge gained through
psychology. We have in our group educators, social workers,
lawyers, business men and women, and those describing themselves as having no vocation. We have in common an interest
in understanding and improving social conditions. Besides this,
and perhaps first of all, we desire to utilize as a part of our
everyday technique of action such knowledge as modern
psychology can furnish us." This petition is to a high measure
typical of the attitude of the American intellectual, not only
by the completely clear, concise correctness with which it
expresses his purpose, but because we see in it almost in a
single moment the social ideal and the personal need for
influence and action over others, with emphasis on the latter.
These young people are sensible enough to apply not to the
advertisements in which the teeming "fakers"—or quacks—
promise to give you sway over the world in ten lessons of
mental gymnastics, but to an experienced psychologist-sociol-
ogist,[31] who is also a very lively and interesting writer. He
meets the request in superb fashion. Note the titles of his first
chapters: "The Key Problem: Capturing the attention. The
appeal to wants. The problem of vividness. The psychology of
effective speaking. The psychology of effective writing.

[30] The People's Institute Publishing Company: New York, 1925.
[31] Professor Overstreet was professionally a teacher of philosophy at
the City College of New York, but Huizinga's characterization aptly
defines his interests and activity.—H.H.R.

Crossing the interest deadline. Making ideas stick."

We see how the writer moves at the boundary of advertising technique, yet his tone and aim remain worthy and serious. In the second part he comes to his own subject. "How to change persons: the entering wedge" is the title of the first chapter. And although now, even more than before, we may repeatedly find ourselves resisting his ideas and world view, the main impression remains that we have in H. A. Overstreet a worthy representative of what I would call constructive democracy. Whitman again comes to my mind. I wish that I knew more of Robert Frost and other present-day poets. The fundamental tonality of the civilization which speaks through Overstreet is the realization of each man's task of altruistic communication (along with complete irreligiousness, of which more later). It means the duty to communicate,[32] that is, to take hold of other men and influence them; it means that the individual is in contact with environment and society, that the spark must be able to jump the gap, "to get across"— but not to every side. It is a question of This, Here, and Soon. The purpose is not transcendental. I should like to speak in this connection of a transitive culture, in opposition to transcendental culture and with direct reference to grammatical terminology.

The University as an Organism

Whenever a newspaper in America speaks of a professor whose field is not natural science, it usually calls him an "educator." In other words, the ordinary mind sees in him

---

[32] Huizinga hyphenates the Dutch verb, *mede-deelen,* so that by bringing out the roots the primitive meaning "to share with," which has disappeared in modern usage, is expressed.—H.H.R.

AMERICA

primarily the teacher, not the man of learning or the research scholar. The situation is a little different with regard to the natural sciences. The word "scientist" arouses the imagination. It promises new discoveries, new cures: health, happiness, comfort and dividends. But the word "scholar" gets a negative reaction in America; it smells too much of old books. The professor has his status in American culture only as an officiating priest in the religion of education.

The function of the university in America is not the same as among us Dutch. It is the seedbed of learning, there as here. But in addition the Dutch university is a training institution, where the American university is an educational institution. Its broad base, indeed its real body, the "college" in which the student spends four years, serves only to give him a stock of higher culture. It does not qualify him for positions in government. There is no university training whatever for government service; it is entered by means of politics. Most students are satisfied with the years they spend in college and go into business or some other activity. Doctors, lawyers, and engineers attend their professional schools, which are usually connected with a university. But when it speaks of a university, the public means the undergraduate college. You are a Yale or a Harvard man because you have devoted several years to a great deal of sport and some learning, whether or not you have been trained as a scientific investigator in one of the graduate schools and obtained the doctor's degree.

The university likewise does not limit itself to the education of its individual nurslings.[33] It is confident that it can educate the state itself. In so doing, it fulfills a function com-

[33] Huizinga again half-puns on the primary but ordinarily neglected meaning of a term. The Dutch for "education" is *opvoeding*, literally "raise by feeding," and *voedsterlingen* are both "foster [i.e., fed] children" and "nurslings."–H.H.R.

pletely different from that which we know in the Netherlands. The Dutch university, however much it moves with the
times, is nonetheless always more or less an island. But that is
not what it makes of itself, it was what public opinion makes
of it. Public opinion sees the universities as dignified and
pretentious bodies outside real life. Respect for their erudition
is mixed with ironic disdain. "The Professor," in the style of
those who write letters to the editor in newspapers, is a figure
from the unwritten comedy of social life.

It is the goal of the American university to be the brains
of the republic. It is as such that it receives gifts in the millions, a practice unknown among us. It is as such that it enjoys
the respect of the nation, which has the deepest and most
sacred belief in everything which is Education.

In the final analysis, to think for the republic, to guide
it toward higher cultural power, can be done by the university in a democratic and technological society only if it devotes itself to the problems with which the state or the nation
itself is occupied. The American university also trains with
heroic devotion those who specialize in fields which promise
not one cent's worth of prosperity or progress. In it will be
found excellent classicists, Sanskrit scholars, and medievalists.
But it sees its great task elsewhere.

I obtained the most vivid impression of what this other
function of public education is at the University of North
Carolina in Chapel Hill.

North Carolina was for a long time the poorest state of
the Old South. It has a territory a fourth the size of France,
with a population (1925) of 2,759,014, including 31.6 percent Negroes. More than 99 percent of the population are
native-born Americans. There are until now no big cities but
the growing cotton and tobacco industries are causing a
strong movement to the more populous centers. Yet the state

is in general type one of small landed property, consisting of dispersed farms in the hands of white and black tenants. Illiteracy is declining rapidly; among whites it fell in ten years from 12.3 to 8.2 percent, among Negroes from 31.9 to 24.5 percent.

The State University, which was established in 1793, has taken the goal, since the revival of the impoverished and defeated South in the beginning of this century, of building up the backward state in every respect, in close cooperation with the state government. It is not possible to describe here all of this splendidly organized activity. I shall select two parts. The Department of Rural Social Economics takes in hand all agricultural problems. It seeks to gain adoption of better methods of cultivation and better housing conditions, to promote the raising of dairy and beef cattle, to show the tenants the way to ownership (in which respect the remarkable phenomenon has occurred that the Negroes are climbing out of tenancy into ownership at a rate 1½ to 7½ times as fast as the whites). In a weekly distributed without charge, the Department instructs the farmers in agricultural economics in easily understood form (every American understands figures and statistics). Because the farms are so dispersed, there are really no villages in North Carolina, and hence no village life. Together with the poor country roads, this produces a high degree of illiteracy. The improvement of the roads, the merging of the one-room schools into Consolidated Schools, the introduction of school buses, is therefore a second chapter in the program. In order to promote the development of small towns,[34] the University also seeks to encourage the churches to consolidate, "to make the church a socializing influence."

[34] Huizinga here and just before uses the Dutch word *dorp*, literally "village," which corresponds best to the American term "small town," as distinct from the British equivalents of "city" and "town."—H.H.R.

This is easier to do because there are almost no Catholics and few Episcopalians in the state. From eleven weak, small Methodist denominations have arisen three viable churches, and out of seventeen Baptist denominations seven churches.

Behind all this work rests a fervent enthusiasm and a proud love of their own state. "Know your own State," the University constantly appeals to its inhabitants. It puts graduate students from every department to studying their own county; the historical, economic, and social monographs which are the result are paid for by advertisements or by the delighted "home folks" of the young writers.

In 1923 and 1924 the head of the Department for Rural Social Economics, Dr. E. C. Branson, went to Germany, Denmark, Ireland, and France to study the question of tenancy and ownership.

Three times a year the State Commission for County Government meets at the University in order to discuss the questions of the day with the leaders of scientific research.

Like the Department of Rural Social Economics, the School of Public Welfare of the university, established in 1920, works in close connection with the state government. Its director is the sociologist Howard W. Odum. Its first purpose is *education* in sociology and social problems, then *training* for social work and "community leadership," followed by direct social *activity*, what is called "social engineering"—that is, the designing of public and private institutions of a social character—and finally pure scientific *research* in the social field.

A third organization, the University Extension Division, works with the two already named; the administrations of all three are interlocking. University Extension is what among the Dutch finally developed into the People's Universities after initial endeavors to get the [established] universities to do it had failed. They do useful work, to be sure, but have a limited effect. In a country where every section of the people possesses its own established group culture, there is only the slightest demand for University Extension. How different in a state like North Carolina, where almost the entire land may be said to lie fallow in a cultural sense! There the university is really effective in constantly reaching the entire country with a splendid organization and a devoted army of cultural forces. The main thing, once again, is to form nuclei of community organization and to cultivate them. The division directs its attention principally to the women, because they have more time than the men to allow themselves to become cultivated. Three full-time employees constantly visit the farmers (more correctly, the citizens) with the wares of the university. They can grant credits (which are something like certificates regarding courses that have been taken) and even award degrees; we might call them suffragan bishops. Men take courses in accounting and advertising, the women in everything. In addition, the division works with correspondence courses. These too lead to regular academic degrees. The students are mainly persons who have only been able to attend college for a year and now want to go on to improve their abilities.

From time to time the division invites one or another group of professional men to visit the university, which also provides an opportunity for discussion of their professional interests. During my visit, the excellent Carolina Inn, which has been established by an alumnus on behalf of the university, was inundated by 400 visiting accountants. The next day 400 bankers and bank employees were expected; I found them at Durham on the way to Chapel Hill.

In Miss Nellie Roberson, the head of the Extension Library, I found the same joyful enthusiasm in putting the three theological virtues[35] to social use, which repeatedly makes the European ashamed of his small belief in such earthly perfection. She told me of still other activities of the division: How a full-time woman employee teaches amateur dramatic societies throughout the state to put on stage performances, for the most part "one-act plays." How the university published a Musical Monthly Magazine and forms music groups alongside the drama groups, and how these are assisted in the organization of local history pageants. When I glance over the titles and the content of the series of publications by means of which the division brings its innumerable subjects to the man (or better to the woman) from a distance, with brief introductions for guidance and practical exercises, I am filled with admiration for so much sound, intelligent, and rationally practical social concern and cultural feeling. I choose a few titles: "Town Studies. Know your own State North Carolina. Studies in Citizenship. Public Welfare and the Community. Studies in the History of Contemporary Europe. Studies in Southern Literature. A Study of Shakespeare. Great Composers. Recent Tendencies in the Theatre. Contemporary American Literature." There may be a naïve note in all of this, so that we should speak of childishness and sometimes of superficiality; at the same time it is permeated with impartiality, with a free, bold spirit able to see the things that are under one's eyes. Let there be no suspicion of a scholastic spirit or a cautiously puritanic and conservative design. The young ladies in the remote places of the South are informed about and helped to understand and judge Dreiser, Willa Cather, H. L. Mencken, Frost, Dunsany, Drinkwater, and Pirandello.

Who will be the transmitters of this culture which has been nurtured in the open fields? Miss Roberson gave me the

[35] Faith, hope and charity!—H.H.R.

answer: "We are not reaching the lower classes, unfortunately (but how could they, even for a moment?). Our real pupils are the married women, when their children have grown up." But can we conceive of anything more delightful than that it should be the grandmothers who will be able to hand on the culture they have acquired?

I have lingered somewhat on the work at Chapel Hill because I came to know it best, and because it was there that I first gained an understanding of the best of America's spirit. A number of other examples of similar activity emanating from the universities may be placed beside it. It would repay the trouble to speak of the State University of Minnesota, where an Institute for Government Research collaborates with a Municipal Reference Bureau and an Agricultural Experiment Station has been established, or of the Institute for Research in Land Economics and Public Utilities under the leadership of the honored veteran Dr. R. T. Ely, who was once the teacher of Woodrow Wilson, J. Franklin Jameson, and many others, at Baltimore and is now at Northwestern University near Chicago, or of the Food Research Institute at Leland Stanford University in California. But the scale that I set for myself in making these observations does not permit me to do so. These few examples will have adequately illustrated the activity of the American university as a very vital social organism.

It is characteristic that the attempt to find by means of academic research a strictly scientific basis for business management is nowhere pursued so zealously and on so great a scale as at the oldest and stateliest of American universities, Harvard, with its grandly conceived, superbly equipped, and richly endowed Graduate School of Business Administration.

The American university has said to itself: If the mountain of business does not come to the prophet of science, then the prophet of science will go to the mountain of business. Who has cause for satisfaction in this—science, business, or both—I shall not attempt to answer here.

This poor historian was once given a wonderful occasion for delight. A new form of the principle "Learn through play" was applied at one of the most famous girls' colleges. A competition in stock market investing was announced, for purposes of practice and instruction. What a thrilling party game! The girl who displayed the greatest skill in cool-headed speculation and made the largest imaginary profits after a certain period received a prize and praise. At the same time a young man who had just finished his studies wrote in a weekly with the greatest indignation that he still had not gotten a job: "The university is a failure. Why don't they economize on a few professors of Greek, philosophy and history, and appoint some men to give training for business?" I should like to sentence this fellow to stand behind Euclid every day in the Elysian Fields and carry his book for him, for Euclid, who is the patron of the commuting student, who ran every day the eight miles from Megara to Athens for the sake of pure wisdom.

And it made me feel good that several economists at Yale University expressed doubt whether business training had much usefulness and repeated the statement of a big businessman: "Give my boy some culture, I'll teach him how to run the business in six months."

Big business irresistibly draws abilities and attention to itself. In May of this year a meeting was arranged of the presidents of a number of leading universities to consider how to keep the good heads, those who had the ability to do research work, from going into the all-devouring business world and to hold them for continued scientific training. This is the same aim pursued by the Robert Brookings Graduate School at Washington, of which more in a moment.

The University and Big Capital

A few years ago the well-known writer Upton Sinclair, in a little book entitled *The Goose Step*, accused the American university of becoming more and more the servant of big capital. The same accusation was made earlier in a more moderate and considered form by Thorstein Veblen in *The Higher Learning*.

Although it is difficult to form an independent judgment on a phenomenon of this kind, it seems to me that we can be legitimately confident that there is much exaggeration and one-sidedness in this reproach. The spirit which inspires the practice of social science at the universities is certainly not that of Mammon. The subject of the concerns of Branson and Odum at Chapel Hill, of Kelsey, Bossard, Donald Young in Philadelphia, of R. T. Ely and his staff at Evanston, of Commons at Madison, of Allin, Chapin, Anderson at Minneapolis, of the entire Chicago school, just to name a few, is not "big business" but the poor tenant, the hard-working farmer, the Negro, the "hobo."[36] "Business Research" does not work for the accumulation of capital but for the spreading of prosperity. The sociologists emphasize "Problems of Poverty."

The term "social science" was more or less unpopular

[36] At Chicago the current term for those who live on the fringes of society in the cosmopolitan cities.—J.H. [The American reader will be amused to see how the Dutch historian read the work of the Chicago sociologists but failed to learn that the characteristic trait of the hobo was "riding the rails," traveling by freight car.—H.H.R.]

until recently. For the broad public it inevitably smelled of socialism. "It is a subject loaded with politics," the businessman said. "There is lots of dynamite in it." Little by little even big businessmen are coming to recognize the socially constructive character of the social sciences. As a rule they do not supervise in a narrow-minded way the way their gifts are spent. And the American man of science is as a rule not the man to bow humbly before capital. Wealth is considered as the natural mine from which the university draws its resources. The funds for some scientific interest or other threatened to run out, "so we began looking around for another millionaire." As if they were drilling for oil! The immediate result of the great Rockefeller gifts to the University of Chicago, I was assured by one of its first economists, was that he and others could not help but become somewhat more radical in order to remain conscious of their independence. Discussion at Harvard turned to the fact that now and then gifts were made with specific conditions. For example, the condition that the all-saving effect of high protective tariffs would be taught, or the threat of socialism. "And did the university (I do not know which one it was) accept the gifts?" we asked. "Yes," was the reply, "they easily found professors who really believed in these doctrines and then named others who did not believe in them."

The Laura Spelman Rockefeller Memorial distributes its gifts for research in the field of social sciences without conditions and leaves the responsibility for the result to the university which has chosen the subject. As against sensational cases like those of Laski and Scott Nearing a few years ago, when freedom of speech was hard pressed, there stand others, like that of a professor who turned out to be secretly on the payroll of a great railroad and had to resign immediately.

We asked: "Who are the great conservatives opposed

to the growth of the social sciences?" The answer was: "The representatives of engineering and natural science. They are skeptical and on the defensive."

In general, my impression was that there is little political or other interference at the state universities, that the great endowed universities remain free of specific influences thanks to their prestige and independence, and that interference in the small colleges is religious rather than economic in character.

The Kinds of Universities

It is well known that America possesses an immense number of universities and colleges, large and small, good and bad, public and independent, for men, women, and both, for whites and for Negroes, professional schools and general schools, all together almost 700, or according to a broader estimate more than 900. Here are some figures for the man who loves them. The number of instructors rose between 1890 and 1924 from 7,918 to 56,279, of whom about one-fifth are women, and that of the students from 156,449 to 726,124, of whom about one-third are women. The total amount of income climbed between 1910 and 1920 from $88,369,734 to $240,141,994.

Since the American university[37] stands entirely outside federal control and also largely outside the control of the states, it must define and maintain its own standing. An Association of American Universities, to which the 24 most important belong, recognizes 166 institutions as fully qualified. In practice these may be divided into three groups: the great

[37] I use here the Dutch word *hoogeschool*, "high school," to include the university and the college. "High school," it should be noted, means the intermediate school in the United States.—J.H.

independent endowed universities, the state universities, and the small colleges. The old, distinguished universities are all private institutions. They are found principally in the Eastern states. Harvard dates from 1638, Yales from 1701, Columbia (in New York, once King's College) from 1754. In Virginia, William and Mary, which dates from 1653 and is now a small institution, arouses warm memories. By the eighteenth century the states formed after independence[38] began to establish public universities, first in the South, as in North Carolina, and then in the nineteenth century also in the West, as in Wisconsin, Minnesota, California, etc. Various of these state universities are now among the most distinguished and eminent. Meanwhile the establishment and endowment of private universities and colleges has continued undisturbed ever since. Of the total of 670, there are only 109 under public administration.

The functions of these three groups are different. The small colleges, some of them of doubtful metal, serve in the first place as regional centers of culture. If one wants to call some of them advanced boarding schools, fine, but fundamentally they are better than that. They also willingly devote themselves to scholarly research and therefore, in the second place, form the seedbeds for the larger universities. The state universities are obliged to be the democratic cultural center for the whole state. Coeducation, which is still resisted at some of the older universities, reigns supreme at the state universities. In fact they must admit everyone; sometimes they grow to immense size, for instance, the University of California at Berkeley with 15,000 students. They must in the first place perform their educational task, and their instruction (not their scholarly research) must be tempered to the comprehen-

[38] Literally, *later opgekomen*, "which arose later." It slipped Huizinga's attention that North Carolina, which established the first state university, was also one of the thirteen original states.—H.H.R.

sion of the average student. The endowed universities, on the contrary, can determine the relationship between teaching and scholarship themselves, according to their own standards. In the long run they can offer a counterweight to the utilitarian and democratic tendency prescribed for the state universities. They can select their students and limit their numbers. If they wanted, the president of the University of Chicago told me, they could close their doors to students and declare themselves to be purely institutions of scholarly research.

The small colleges, often held in some disdain and which feel themselves to be left behind, last year took a dignified revenge upon their seventeen largest sisters. They conducted an investigation by means of a skillfully prepared list of questions to discover which of the seventeen great universities stood highest in the various branches of scholarship, to be determined by the opinion of the scholars connected with the smaller institutions. Each institution therefore could receive a first, second, third rank, etc., in a specific branch of learning and its overall performance was expressed in a score of so many points. The result was that the University of Chicago won the most first-rank places and the highest number of points. Which result it advertised in a modest and confidential way.

Intellectual Organization

The American expects to achieve the solution of every problem through organized technology and technical organization.[39] For him they are equivalent to intelligent action. The

[39] "Technology" here means engineering, applied science, and "technical" rational and purposive.—H.H.R.

factory and standardization mean for him not only a more intensive and favorable form of production but a higher form, in the full sense of the word. Nostalgia for the cottage and handicrafts he feels, if at all, during the evening hours, when he is weakest. He uses the word "homespun" metaphorically and contemptuously. He has no sentimental attachment to the way his forefathers kept house or farm. He can do everything better, faster, and more efficiently.

The thought that energy is wasted and chances are missed is intolerable to him, as if society were guilty of a great sin. It is not the squandering of material that annoys him but failure to use earthly powers, delay in development of the forces and the riches of nature and of human inventiveness in the service of production.

The drive for power over nature and society stands revealed as a passionate urge to subject every domain of social and economic life to intellectual organization with as much precision as possible, and to make them totally technological in structure so as to be able to control them. The ideal which provides the impulsion in this quest is not merely to increase material prosperity, but apparently also to create anew a world in which it will be good to live.

A good example of how scholarship is put at the service of national life is offered by the institutions which the St. Louis millionaire Robert Brookings established in Washington. Drawing upon the experience he had acquired as a member of a commission on economy and efficiency appointed by the President in 1910, Brookings conceived the idea which he translated into action by establishing the Institute for Government Research. Under the leadership of W. F. Willoughby, this institute pursues the aim of laying down strictly scientific foundations for the theory of public administration. Although it is not a university, it is nevertheless an educational institution in very high measure. The institute drafts systems for the

choosing of officials and for accounting procedures in branches
of public administration. It publishes "Service Monographs,"
which are short handbooks for new members of Congress.
For what does a new congressman know of the real function
of the Land Reclamation Service or the Census Bureau? The
practical little handbook teaches him what he needs to know.
But Willoughby and his institute did more. He is the real
creator of the budget system which has not only changed the
government fiscal structure since its introduction in 1921, but
also importantly modified the operation of the Constitution
by considerably increasing the power of the president and
making him a "general manager" of the government!

During the war, Brookings was the chairman of the
committee that set prices. It was once again practice which
gave him the inspiration for the establishment of an experimental scientific organism. The Institute of Economics under
H. G. Moulton developed from Brookings's conviction that
the problems of national economics are too complicated for
individual investigation and that scholarship and the country
are not benefited by theories but by the determination of
facts, the collection of data, statistics. Subjects are treated in
constant cooperation. The institute has a staff of thirty in-
vestigators of the stature of college professors. They work
through frequent group meetings, luncheons, and discussions.
The schooling they undergo here makes them more fitted to
enter a university career later. A foreign investigator who
comes for information also finds the institute ready to discuss
his subject with him. Cooperation enables it to work quickly,
before it falls behind events. A good deal of the preparation of
the Dawes Plan was done here. Now its staff is studying the
possibility of a way out of the depression in agriculture, although it is fully aware that the farmers' expectation of a
restoration of old conditions is vain. In brief, the Institute of

Economics works as the brain of the national economy. The National Bureau of Economics at Columbia University, which also developed out of war work, works in a similar way, with the aim "to supply basic information of great public interest," for example regarding unemployment and market conditions, immigration, the distribution of national income, and so forth.

Finally, Brookings established the Graduate School of Economics and Government named after him, which has the aim of giving to a small select group of advanced students, in the stimulating surroundings of a boarding school for pure science, especially favorable conditions "for professional and cultural training in the studies which have to do with the control of a developing industrial society. Its interest is to teach the art of handling problems rather than to impart accumulated knowledge; and its aim is to turn out craftsmen who can make contributions toward *an intelligent direction of social change.*"

There we find again as always the same idea of intelligent reform. Everything fits together beautifully, it is wonderfully organized, and it is run with stimulating inspiration and bold optimism. The school aims to be "vision-giving."

One of the things which reveal the firm belief in technical organization of intellectual life is the large place occupied in scholarship and practice by the methods of testing and enquiry. Although the all-too-bold expectations of the first testing methods have already abated, there are more new tests published every year for measuring every conceivable intellectual ability in all conceivable individuals or groups.[40] School and college, the civil service, the army and navy, the office, factory, and department store are filled with them. Behind the

[40] See the chapter "Mental Tests and Measurements" in *American Yearbook, 1925,* pp. 984 ff.

confidence in tests rests the idea to which I have already referred: No usable force should go to waste or be misapplied. This is the point of departure of the investigations of the psychologist Lewis M. Terman at Stanford University. Science has the task of timely discovery, development, and utilization of ability. In 1925 Terman published the first part of the results of his studies of a thousand gifted children selected from a million California school children by careful tests. *Genetic Studies of Genius* is the name of the book (the American language is somewhat more liberal in the use of the word "genius" than the languages of the Old World).[41] I take the following from the results: A slight excess of boys over girls, a superiority of the Jewish race of 50 per cent over the average, and above all the fact that the gifted child as a type is not withdrawn, irritable, or sickly but on the contrary is healthy, normal, and well developed. Terman's conclusion: Let no sentimental pedagogy stand any longer in the way of school education (the three-track plan). Organize the talent of the nation!

As a remarkable example of the application of the method of enquiry, I call upon the experiments of L. L. Thurstone at Chicago in the field of social psychology. The general question which keeps him, F. H. Allport, and others occupied is this: Can public opinion be measured on a quantitative basis? An endeavor to transfer psycho-physical testing methods to social phenomena is intended to find an answer. In order to determine the attitude of various groups of persons with regard to crime, Thurstone draw up an ingenious list of questions, in which two forms of crime are set against each other, but repeatedly paired with each other in different ways, for example: "Kidnaping–Adultery, Abortion–Libel, Burglary–Counterfeiting, Bootlegging–Arson, Burglary–Bootlegging,

[41] Cf. Terman's "The Conservation of Talent," in *School and Society,* 19 (1924), no. 483.

Adultery–Receiving-stolen-goods," etc., etc., so that in all there are 190 choices to be made. In this way, he was able to obtain (for students) an exact scale of the "badness" of crimes, which is probably socially important but is certainly psychologically significant. On the scale rape came out at the top. He held a similar enquiry into opinions about the death penalty, control of the Supreme Court by the Congress, and Prohibition. We again see the idea which lies behind all this: first to learn to know public opinion or any social sentiment by an exact means, and thus to be able to influence it in an intelligent way.

Thurstone himself considered his method to be an experiment, and was open to the doubts that we Europeans feel sometimes during scientific investigations of this kind. Doesn't just that result usually emerge, after much labor and cumbersome methods, which everyone would pretty much have expected? With an increased level of certainty, with a certain addition of detail where before vagueness ruled, but with slight increase in significant knowledge. But such skepticism is rare in America. They are intellectual *Draufgänger*.[42] The notion that there could exist anything like over-organization does not torment them.

The Spoken and the Written Word: A Contrast

The American man of learning is as a rule fluent, precise, simple, and clear in his conversation; he quickly grasps the intention of a question put to him, and he replies clearly and factually. His conversation is stimulating and informative. There is something happening, something to be done. One

[42] German for "daredevils" or "plungers."—H.H.R.

feels oneself carried along in an élan of desire for knowledge and love of research.

I find that the quality and the tone of their conversation is only exceptionally reproduced when they write. More than once I could not recognize in what he wrote the living man who had held my interest. Frequently repeated experience makes me hold the view that my personal reaction to American scholarly prose still must rest upon the qualities of the prose itself. I read it with the greatest difficulty; I have no sense of contact with it and cannot keep my attention fixed on it. It is for me as if I had to do with a deviant system of expression in which the concepts are not equivalent to mine, or are arranged differently. I ask myself: Is it sometimes too deep for me? Then I must reply: On the contrary, it seems to me meager and thin of thought. It is full of technical words which always make me think of the dentist's forceps, hard instruments to use on a living thing. It seems to me that here the Anglo-Saxon element of the language is even more strongly restricted than in scientific British English.

It is in part a question of style. This prose does not paint, it has no rhythm and no shape. But that is not all there is to it, for even outside America, scholarly prose too often falls short. I cannot escape the conclusion which I have reached with hesitation, that it rests upon a certain thinness of thought, a certain superficiality. Titles often promise more than is given. A splendidly designed and carefully built edifice remains empty in the wind. There is scaffolding but no church. There are many indifferent sentences, many detached words, much that is self-evident and did not need to be said.

But there are also brilliant exceptions!

But if these difficulties did not all arise from my own unreceptivity (I checked my impressions against those of a few others), what can be the cause of this inadequacy which seems so difficult to square with the general tenor of American life?

A young Dutchwoman who had just spent two years working in the United States expressed this opinion: In America the spoken word, along with the experiment itself, takes a much larger place than writing in the working out of thought. Scholarship is in America a matter of planning and undertaking work as a team much more than among us. It is a job and a conspiracy. The thinkers put their heads together at lunch or in a conference. As they all talk together, ideas take shape. But ideas do not thrive in the study as they come from the pen, and the living spirit grows dim in solitude.

Or should the cause be looked for instead precisely in the fact that solitude no longer exists, that the pens lie rusting, replaced by dictation to a secretary to be typed, so that one becomes superficial and trivial? That, and the fact that the organization of thought has been carried too far and thinking is no longer aroused by writing?

The luncheon as a means of intellectual exchange has obtained an almost ritual importance in America. It is the modern symposium,[43] without mixing barrels, for there remains nothing more to be mixed, and the heads remain therefore clearer and cooler. Not all branches of learning lend themselves to the luncheon form; it is not right for history.

Transition, Transformation, Regeneration

We are concerned here not only with organizing what is still unorganized, but also with reorganization, transforma-

[43] In the ancient Greek sense of a drinking party with good talk. —H.H.R.

tion, and regeneration, especially of social forms. There is a profound feeling that everything is entering into rapid transition. Everything *can* become something else, everything can be done *better*, everything *must* be done differently. "That which man changeth not for the better, time changeth for the worse." Bacon probably was thinking of other things than present-day man has in mind, but he might have uttered this remark as a christening present for the child America. It is the same spirit as Dewey's when he says: "We can retain and transmit our own heritage only by constant remaking of our own environment." Only by reforming their environment can men change themselves. The American philosopher adopts a significant position lying between the purely moralist and purely materialist doctrines of social reform. "We can recognize that all conduct is *interaction* between elements of human nature and the environment, natural and social. Then we shall see that progress proceeds in two ways, and that freedom is found in that kind of interaction which maintains an environment in which human desire and choice count for something. There are in truth forces in man as well as without him. While they are infinitely frail in comparison with exterior forces, yet they may have the support of a foreseeing and contriving intelligence. When we look at the problem as one of an adjustment to be intelligently attained, the issue shifts from uniform personality to an engineering issue, the establishment of arts of education and social guidance."[44]

One is tempted to underline every word in this passage, so completely, so forcefully and so purely does it reproduce the confession of faith of the thinking America of today. Anyone who reads it correctly will understand why America can believe in moral preaching as little as in Marx, and why it will not believe in Spengler.

[44] *Human Nature and Conduct*, pp. 9, 10.

America is at the same time extremely averse to revolution and very revolutionary. Averse to the Revolution, with a capital letter, which Russia continues desperately to preach and predict. A social eschatology based on a class myth has not the slightest chance in America, in the first place because America's spirit is thoroughly pluralist, experimental, and opportunist, or indeed pragmatic. For them domination and transformation of social processes cannot ever be based on a doctrine, no matter which, but only on constant observation and intelligent experimentation.

They are averse to the Apotheosis of Revolution, but at the same time the opposite of conservative. Everywhere there is the awareness of rapid change and constant transition. Everywhere there is the endeavor to break loose from old methods, old forms, and to find better ones. Always again one meets the expression: "We live now within a rapidly changing order." Just read the chapter titles in the latest *American Yearbook* and you will be struck by the fact that in almost every field, in public administration, land utilization, science, and so on, a strong change in recent years and a constant experimentation can be observed. Everything is in movement. There is almost no scholarly treatise which does not assure one that the field is "undergoing a transformation." There is great unrest. Everything must become changed, nothing is satisfactory as it is. Every point is a question, and they are all burning questions.

Thinking America (not all Americans think, any more than Europeans) looks at the facts before its eyes with courage. If the divorce figures increase, if family life seems to be in dissolution, or at least in change, then a new form must be coming. If governmental bodies are failing in their tasks, then others must be created and the state organism adapted to real conditions. Government as such has never been the object of reverence in America.[45] It has always remained what Jefferson saw in it—a barely necessary evil. "We have great respect for traffic policemen but not for municipal councillors," said one of the representatives of political science at Harvard during a remarkable international discussion at which I was present. The monthly *Forum* recently announced one of its for-and-against discussions on the question: "Is it right to break unjust laws?"

The inadequacy of political forms in contemporary social and economic life has long since been recognized. The city manager, that remarkable grafting of business forms upon government, has already been followed by the county manager.[46] Political divisions and institutions, says Park, correspond to the social conditions and ideals of the eighteenth century. They are no longer able to satisfy the requirements of modern society. Everywhere the real groups function in disharmony with and despite government. These groups must be the subject of our inquiry and our great task of "social engineering." *Umwertungen*[47] are everywhere.

In the period from 1921 to 1925, 63 American cities changed their name. Practical reasons play a role in this as in other things. The large number of cities with identical names is inconvenient: There are 31 Franklins and 18 Genevas. But this desire for new names is also a characteristic of periods of great revolution, as witness Soviet Russia and the French Revolution.

The word "revolutionary" with a political ring is a mockery to Americans, but it must be admitted that they still are

[45] See *Mensch en Menigte in Amerika* (2nd ed.), p. 17, 131 [see above, pp. 20, 121].
[46] See Ibid., p. 152 [pp. 137 ff.], and cf. *American Yearbook, 1925*, pp. 175, 187, 202.
[47] German for "revaluations," a word created by Nietzsche.—H.H.R.

glad to hear it in another sense; otherwise, advertisers would not speculate on their readiness to buy by praising what they sell as revolutionary: "the revolutionary new science of Behaviorism"; "here is the revolutionary new principle," that is, teaching languages without grammar; "The Revolt of Modern Youth, a Problem That Parents Must Solve," specifically by giving them a billiard table.

"To build up a new type," "to overhaul their minds," "to be shaken up," these are some more of the phrases which characterize America's thought and aspirations. The radical improvers see everything as simple and clear. H. A. Overstreet does not doubt that "creative power" can be created in everyone. If anyone's personality is weak, "there is nothing to do but to change the personality."[48] Watson promises us as the fruit of his behaviorism, correctly applied, "a universe unshackled by legendary folklore of happenings thousands of years ago; unhampered by disgraceful political history."[49] His reviewer in the *New York Times* expresses this belief in the future and disbelief in the past in this way: "The human race is susceptible of improving to a higher state of excellence than the world has yet known. Man of the future need not be walled round with the emotional handicaps that limited man of the past."

A better mind says it with less certainty. "There are many who ridicule American faith in education, calling it a religion, which it often is, but treating it as a peculiarly jejune form of superstition. Yet it need not be superstitious, unless all faith in the possibility of a world better than that in which we live be condemned as unreasonable. Such condemnation seems to be itself peculiarly dogmatic. For until we have tried seriously

[48] *Influencing Human Behavior*, p. 232, 107–108.
[49] *Behaviorism*, p. 248.

and systematically (and I think only a few zealots would hold that mankind has yet tried intelligently and patiently) we do not and cannot know how far the world can be made a better and sweeter place in which to live."[50]

A New Ethics

If the ideal of education is in fact a religion, then it must bear fruit in its own ethos, a new self-sacrifice and a new charity, and it must ennoble the culture in which it works. The good and unprejudiced observer tests this improvement with each new experience. It is probably still only an elite, the thinking America of which I speak, but where in the world was the essence of a faith ever to be found on every street?

The European is easily inclined to pass judgment: Americans are superficial, they are big children, the individual does not think profoundly. In so doing he forgets two things. First, that we are inclined in everything to measure the average in America against the ideal in Europe. Secondly, that what appears to us to be individual superficiality also means social conformity. A spiritual coherence and a social striving in America such as we Europeans do not know. American men and women of learning work together as comrades on a number of well-put central questions. Each sacrifices something of his own personality in order to enter the serried ranks. Even if they do not know it, they are moving away from the castles of their own thought to plow for others. Their "like-mindedness" (a term of Dewey's) is a correlate of their cultural democracy.

Thinking America is turning away from the puritan ethic

[50] John Dewey, in *The New Republic*, May 19, 1926, p. 410.

in growing repugnance, and toward a standpoint of social ethics. "The intelligent acknowledgment of the continuity of nature, man and society will alone secure a growth of morals which will be serious without being fanatical, aspiring without sentimentality, adapted to reality without conventionality, sensible without taking the form of calculation of profits, idealistic without being romantic."[51] The American ideal of civilization is expressed in this group of contrasts in as pure a way as I have found anywhere.

A gentle judgment of one's fellow-man, a great feeling of shared responsibility for crime and misery, a living social charity, a tireless willingness to help—these are the blossoms of their new democratic and social ethics. And to these traits there corresponds in the intellectual sphere their higher measure of naïveté. They accept whatever is considered to be a product of modern science without much criticism, in a rather scholastic way—in the form of handbooks, as a formula. But at the same time they are very accessible to the new or surprising. They are more easily molded and bent than we. Their intellectual skins fit them less tightly.

One constantly meets the types in whom the new spirit of social ethics blooms. There is something radiant in the memory of all that mild, simple readiness for accommodation, that happy ease, completely unbiased benevolence, the lack of all pose and conceit. The picture of the individuals breaks up in the common remembrance, like trees in a rustling wood.

It is not only the younger people who embody this spirit. I think of that greybeard at Chapel Hill with the clear blue eyes of a boy, such as one sees so often in America; it was in conversation with him that I first grasped this spirit. Or the elderly lady who was the leader of a division of the School for Social Service in Chicago, in whom could be seen a per-

---

[51] Dewey, *Human Nature and Conduct*, p. 13.

fect union of enthusiasm and devotion, righteousness, gentleness, and humor.

This spirit is not limited to the representatives of the social sciences. The feeling of the sacredness of learning and of a true community of minds in the service of an ideal never became so clear to me as on the day I spent among the workers on Mount Wilson, the great observatory near Pasadena in California.

In Europe art has to a large degree taken the place of religion. In America it seems rather to be science.

Here are two more of the much-used terms which typify contemporary America: "goodwill" and "service." Together they form the substance of the new social ethics. What shall we say at length of the aspiration to create "goodwill," in Rotary Clubs and hundreds of other ways? Here is one recollection, no more. We visited a cotton factory in Durham and also the "community house" which belonged to it. The director was not there at the time but came running in rolled-up shirtsleeves as we are about to drive away. He put his arms through the door of our auto and literally held it fast so that he could tell us about his work. Courage and zest for work radiated from his ageless, happy workman's face. "It is the best behaved community I ever saw." They were just holding a "plant exchange," in which the visitors to the house came to exchange with each other the plants and flowers that they had grown themselves. "To counteract the spirit of cutthroat competition."

"Service" has long since become an overworked slogan, including the most sacred service of the community and the most prosaic business interests. We find it satirized in Babbitt, who noisily conceived his real-estate business to be a service to the community. But the popularity of the word demonstrates the seriousness of the idea; its misuse proves not that it is only a hollow phrase but that it has permeated men's aspirations deeply. The old, deeply ethical idea of service of the Middle Ages, which continues to exist today, shorn of its glory, in words like railway service, street-cleaning service, and so on, is awakened to new life. Whether the concept of service to the public really has an influence on the business ethic is difficult to determine, but only a hardened materialism would be able to maintain a priori that it could not do anything of the kind. I find two small writings among the printed matter that I brought home with me. One is a leaflet, taken from a taxi in Chicago: *The Tiny Taxigram*, vol. 3, no. 41, May 3, 1926. It is only an advertisement for Yellow Cabs. "Yellow Cabs are public servants." "Drivers perform many acts for common good." The claim is illustrated with many heart-warming examples. The other is a talk by Dr. E. C. Branson to a group of the alumni of the University of North Carolina. It bears the title "The University Serves," and is one of the most eloquent pieces of testimony to what the university wishes to mean and can mean in American life.

Today Is Good, Tomorrow Will Be Better

In the *Life and Letters of Walter H. Page* the story is told how once at a party at which Page was present, the question was asked of everyone by way of a game: "If you had a second life to spend, in what age would you choose to live it?" Page needed not a moment of reflection. In the future and in the United States, was his reply. Walter Page was one of the most vital and attractive Americans whose spirit we can reach. We learn to know him from his excellently written letters as a man of simple, warm heart, truly manly spirit, good humor and great love for his country. His words carry weight.

Except for England, of which he grew fond, Page did not want to take much from Europe. It had nothing which America had to envy, was his opinion. Many Americans share this opinion with him. Here is the peroration of an hour's lecture on American history: ". . . So that we don't wonder about America's being superior to all other countries, America, the best of the best, the fittest of the fit!"

How strange! Among us Europeans who were traveling together in America, in a striking solidarity of Latins, Teutons, and Slavs, there rose up repeatedly this pharisaical feeling: We all have something that you lack; we admire your strength but do not envy you. Your instrument of civilization and progress, your big cities and your perfect organization, only make us nostalgic for what is old and quiet, and sometimes your life seems hardly to be worth living, not to speak of your future.

And yet in this case it must be we who are the Pharisees, for theirs is the love and the confidence. Things must be different than we think.

There lies before me the manuscript of a still unpublished and very odd article by a young American sociologist, Elizabeth Ephrussi. It still awaits revision; it does not quite satisfy the writer. In this first draft it carries the title "Outlines of an Heroic Age." With a terribly bold reversal of the obvious patterns, she wishes to understand the present-day condition of America not as the extreme development of a far-advanced culture but as a beginning, a heroic era, in which the *"unausgeglichene"*[52] still clash violently, the crudeness is still dragged along, and power is spiritualized. A period in which, as it were,

---

[52] German for "unsettled," "still in dispute or change."—H.H.R.

there are still bear-hunts and men throw rocks at their friends. Monetary organization is only the *first* form of a new world process. Upon this foundation of iron materialism, mankind will climb upward. Leveling of the spirit, "likemindedness," is the necessary precondition in this struggle.

> Fundamental singleness of thought and feeling and action are the subjective or creative corollary of singleness displayed in vast unbroken lines and masses and enterprises of objective or created forms. For this singleness is of a strongly vital quality. It is bound up with an ever present activity bent on mastering the outer world, an activity that is strenuously transcending the individual inner life in favour of expansion and expression in the fabric of realities outside.
>
> Wherever one looks in American life, one finds this outward and onward thrust.

The writer continues: It is a misunderstanding to conceive of America as materialistic, because business activity, the organization of wealth, which is embodied in the skyscrapers, drives the country forward so mightily.

"The substance of this reality is materialistic, no doubt, but so vehemently, so insistently, so fervently materialistic that the very ardour of the devotion vouchsafed to material raises it to a new and strange kind of spirituality. The impulse, overreaching itself, becomes transcendent."

Once again I have the feeling that here is something wrestling to give form to what teems formlessly in the poetry of Walt Whitman.

Must we agree with this female Pindar of "progress"?— or must we see this new battle of heroes only as a hopeless gigantomachia? A battle against the killing force of the ever more perfect Tool? The content of culture grows immensely but the forms give way and are lost. Everything seems to be in development and there is no possibility of going back. The roaring world makes us grow deaf and withered. We look away from work, then, toward relaxation. Nature and art have never been so consciously and deliberately enjoyed, health never so worshiped and nurtured as in contemporary America. But what a bewildering triviality in the forms in which it is enjoyed! Golf and the auto, the film and light reading, life at the beach or out camping, and even concert-going, what are these *as forms of culture!*

Walking once in Cologne in the lost hours between two trains, I became indignant at the way the holy city on the Rhine had become ugly and banal. Toward dusk I left the indifferent bustle of the street to enter the church of Sankt Maria im Kapitol. A service was in progress. In the half darkness the sounds floated low and clear. I realized at once what a true ritual means in life, what it contains of cultural value, apart from its value for eternity. I felt the mighty seriousness of a time in which these things were the essence for all men, and I felt that nine-tenths of our present-day cultural life really *doesn't matter.*

No Flight from Today!

Even the most faithful Christian in America will deny in his heart one word of Scripture: For him Martha made the better choice. The American lives in the world of "This, Here, and Soon." He is, as Henry James expressed it so excellently, "imperturbably, irremovably and indestructibly at home in the world." Psychology has taught him that every flight from life, every withdrawal from the given reality that surrounds him, is only a reaction of his own weakness. Where man cannot satisfy his direct impulse, cannot achieve the desired place in life, he builds himself a better abode in imagination, he creates a world that recognizes him. These are "evasive satisfactions," "compensatory fabrications" of the mind, nothing else and nothing better than the pernicious daydreams of the unbalanced child. And he who does not shrink from consequences easily sees that among these fabrications are included all heavens and rewards, all visionary beauty and romantic fancy. For the man who is irrevocably at home in this visible world, all this cannot but be worthless. It is, in his opinion, "barren and illusory." It is "uncreative," it invents no new methods, tools, or useful things by which this world can be ruled. "We are seeking to escape from a dull world instead of turning back upon it to transform it." At most, it can have the value of an intoxicant or a diversion.

So speaks modern psychology. But as soon as one relates these evasions from the present day to something which lies outside or behind this world, they come into a completely different light. Most thoughtful Americans of today seem to have forgotten how strongly their own great and immediate predecessors, Emerson, Hawthorne, and Whitman, were still preoccupied with the essence behind things.

It is not even necessary to think transcendentally in order to withhold one's confidence from the disenchanted psychologist. It is necessary only to recognize that all that is real is already past, that only the past is real. He who wishes to maintain that the past of mankind no longer has any absolute value in life but probably only the utility of a warning and a lesson for the future, because in fact it no longer acts, must also be ready to deny his own life until the present moment, indeed in advance until the last moment, as worthless. He who realizes that culture is the giving of form will also see that the highest forms that it is given to the human spirit to recognize have always been, psychologically considered, such evasions from the present.

Considerations such as these do not at all square with the direction of America's mind.

Romanticism, as we just heard from Dewey, is for the American consciousness pure weakness and sin. But romanticism means a return to the metaphysical and is, well considered, the prerequisite for all art. The spirit does not create without withdrawing from the present.

I hear again the young sociologist who saw it all so clearly and simply. Yes, he granted me, it is possible that contemporary civilization is becoming more and more incapable of creating great art. It lives, gives, and strives in other ways. They are probably better ways. Why were the ancient ages able to produce great art? Because their means for dominating life and the world, in order to make life itself livable, were so defective that they could no longer tolerate the world without strong and constant evasions and imposing fabrications of their mind. The art of the ages is therefore fundamentally a symptom of sickness.

Then I told my young friend the tale of King Radboud of Frisia, who stalked away from the baptismal font and chose the country of his fathers above the new paradise, and declared that I wished to follow Radboud's example, preferring to live in the false and illusory abode of the old culture than in the promised land of social perfection.

My friend grinned and said (but now I was dreaming): "Watch what you're saying! You cannot eat your pie and have it. Modern culture must be accepted or rejected. If it doesn't fit what you hold valuable, you must like it or lump it."

Then I cried out, in confusion and despair: "But do you want to sell Eternity, then, for the appeal of welfare and the egg (your Columbus's egg) of technology?"

The Anti-Metaphysical Attitude

In the May number of the *American Mercury* I found a book advertisement covering a whole page. "Don't print this book!" This is the warning which the publisher said he had received. *The Bible Unmasked*. That is the name of the book. "A Monumental Fraud." That is what the writer will show us the Bible to be. "The Fighting Freethinker" is its freebooter's name. Earlier he had written "The Tyranny of God." A portrait shows a man with the thin lips of efficiency. We should not expect to find something of this kind in a European magazine of the first rank. That kind of audacity seems to us not only vulgar but a bit obsolete. In this too, we meet one of those differences in spiritual nuance between America and the Old World which have a deep background.

Conversing with representatives of contemporary Americans of scholarship or reading their works, one repeatedly meets a tone of mocking disdain for all faith, which, *ceteris paribus*,[53] we do not expect to meet in Europe, at least not any longer. All modern social psychology in America is far from religious in its commitments. It treats faith as virtually a defeated position. Overstreet, whom I have repeatedly cited and who is very typical, employs the phrase "the pietistic habit of mind" for religious feeling, "the heaven-adoring religionist" for the believer, and treats ideas of reward as pure infantilism. The Christian ideal appears to him "an effortless futurism, a

[53] Latin for "other things being equal."—H.H.R.

Micawber-like willingness to let the great and glorious thing 'turn up.' " J. B. Watson gives us the following in the beginning of his *Behaviorism:*

> No one knows just how the idea of a soul or the supernatural started. It probably had its origin in the general laziness of mankind. Certain individuals who in primitive society declined to work with their hands, to go out hunting, to make flints, to dig for roots, became keen observers of human nature. . . . These lazy but good observers soon found devices by means of which they could at will throw individuals into this fearsome attitude and thus control primitive human behavior.

Don't we imagine that we are back in the eighteenth century?

Now I know quite well that religious belief does not prevail among the scientific thinkers of Europe either. But one might be so bold, I think, as to take the position that the European thinker, unless his political belief compels him to be faithful to materialism, in general and in principle does not have an antimetaphysical "focus" (forgive me this indispensable borrowing from photography). Most of them, it seems to me, will be ready to admit that the foundation of all things is not to be seen with their experimental and inductive science, although they may take the view that all philosophy lying beyond it can still stay within the boundaries of this world.

On the contrary, American science in its dominant form appears to me to have a naïvely antimetaphysical focus. "Naïve" is much too bold a term for thinkers like Dewey but applies fully to many others whose ideas have the closest kinship with his. One can best come to know the general turn of mind from more popular exponents. The following comes, again, from Overstreet. Are these statements typical for America? And if so, do they also reproduce a general average of

European scientific conviction? Reply to this last question, "Oh most certainly!" and I shall pack up and go away.

> "To understand the material world and to organize it still more effectively to human uses, is the really high function of man."
> "The technique of experimentation may be regarded as the high-water mark of human achievement."
> "Where the primitive mind is acceptive, taking the world as it superficially finds it . . . the highly civilized mind is creative. . . ."

Oh wisdom of India, oh art of Egypt!

The antimetaphysical attitude of mind automatically includes an antihistorical one. Despite a flourishing and excellently organized practice of history, America's mind is fundamentally antihistorical. A history which wants to find in the development of mankind only the theodicy of progress or seeks in it only a mirror for today is not true history. And although history may be in practice for great numbers of Americans the food of life, and they may be bewitched by the past in the way which constitutes the historical attitude, the conception of its task and character as a field of learning by some of its leading representatives is a different one.

Their ideal of historical science is one which, by comparison, generalization, and synthesis, still puts exact description of the development of the state, culture, and society as such in the place of the events of particular times and places. That comes from H. Elmer Barnes in *The New History and the Social Studies*.[54] As the best specimen of such historical writing, he praises the work of his teacher James Harvey Robinson, *The Mind in the Making*.[55] This widely read and much praised book, in the concise form demanded by the

[54] New York: Century, 1925.
[55] New York and London: Harper, 1921.

American reader, gives a survey of the development of the
civilization of mankind, climbing up from the state of savagery
to the triumph of science. All older ages of civilization have
had their day. There is no awareness in it that they may contain treasures which mankind lost while hunting and winning
other things. What is most significant for Robinson's ideas
is probably the motto that he places before his introductory
chapter, a quotation from G. Stanley Hall: "Now, my thesis
is that all . . . fugues from actuality . . . are now, as never
before in history, weak and cowardly flights from the duty
of the hour, wasteful of precious energy, and perhaps worst of
all, they are a symptom of low morale, personal or civic, or
both."

One realizes with amazement that the word "mystery"
for Robinson only means the terrains still undiscovered by
science. The sense of the direct and constant presence of mystery in and behind everything, a spirit of which Emerson was
so vividly aware, has become totally strange to these thinkers.
"It is no longer," writes another, W. T. Bush, "the outer
sphere beyond which God abides that limits the range of
existence but the technique of grinding lenses." Doesn't he
therefore himself betray that primitive form of thought which
conceives the "beyond" as something farther away in the
same space?

In all these things, fashionable American thought gives
us the sensation of an outdated or backward Europe. Thirty or
forty years ago there were some in Europe who attempted to
impose on history the task of sociology and to compel it to be
exact and general. It was not without difficulty that the sciences of the mind or culture[56] resisted subjection to the norms

[56] The Dutch *geestes- of cultuurwetenschappen*, corresponding to
the German *Geistes- oder Kulturwissenschaften*, indicating the fields of
knowledge concerned with intellectual and cultural phenomena. The

and aims of natural science at that time. The most valuable gain won in that struggle was the realization that not every "science" strives always and exclusively for knowledge of the absolutely simple, for the extremes of analysis. Are men in America sufficiently aware of this methodological change? Or do they still hold the opinion that nothing can be understood so long as it is complex, that no term can be scientifically useful unless it is strictly exact?

In the last third of the nineteenth century, many in Europe thought that philosophy with all its adherents could be put away with the other junk in the attic. This is now the triumphant argument of J. B. Watson, the behaviorist. Philosophy and religion have had their day, and as for morality, he has, thanks to his system, "experimental ethics." He and his friends easily get rid of everything which constitutes theory of knowledge. They declare it to be a defeated standpoint. They guillotine with amazing readiness all terms of thought: consciousness, reason, meaning, memory, cause—they are all fiction and error! It does not occur to them that all their results must always in turn be tested and judged by the reason which they dethrone, and exist only in such reason. They do not want to see that the noetic has its own laws, despite all experimental psychology, and that their reduction of the world to meaningless mechanism will always be foiled in turn by the unassailable independence of the spiritual.

When one reads the writings of the radical representatives of the "new materialism," as its opponents call it, one detects in their facile explanations of psychological or social phenomena an appalling impoverishment of thought. These

term *wetenschap* in Dutch, like the German *Wissenschaft,* indicates not only "science" in the narrow sense of the natural or physical sciences, or even the somewhat broader range inclusive of the social sciences, but also the whole general notion of "field of learning."—H.H.R.

are all apparent solutions in simple terms, which in fact only push the questions aside. Something mechanical, something technological and schematic has entered their thinking. And there undoubtedly lies in this very abdication of reason an element in the large-scale process of mechanization of culture. There must be a more deep-lying relationship between such science and the novels of Dreiser. Strong feelings of social depersonalization must be at work. It is completely logical that for these thinkers themselves the mechanization of society no longer means something to be feared. They accept it, they rejoice in it and welcome it. They willingly capitulate to the machine. "The machine process," writes one of the acute representatives of the creed, the young sociologist Lawrence K. Frank, "which has captured practically every field of men's behavior, demands group activity."[57] We must learn to live, to work, and to play in groups. We must renounce the illusions of freedom and personality. This is said not in the haughty pessimism of Oswald Spengler but in an attitude of confident optimism, as if on a voyage in a bedecked barge to Arcadia.

Is a Persecution Coming?

Great hatred for the Puritan tradition which so long dominated America's mind has arisen among the younger intellectuals. The chasm that separates them from the circles of the church and conventional morality becomes wider and wider. Compulsory chapel is no longer maintained at the old universities. On the campus of the University of Chicago stands an exquisite chapel for meditation, the gift of a well-

[57] "An Institutional Analysis of the Law," *Columbia Law Review,* 1924, p. 495.

meaning Baptist, in irreproachable Gothic. You never see students in it, our guide assured us. The radical sociologists see with aversion how the old rigid forms of society delay the salvation to be achieved by "social engineering." How beneficial it would be, sighs L. K. Frank, whom we have just quoted, "if we could stop the perpetuation of some of the most ancient habits and customs now recognized in our institutions and laws, so that we would all *be living in the same century at least.*"[58]

That is far from being the present situation. Religious America is getting ready to exterminate the enemy. The fundamentalists have their eye in this respect not on the behaviorists or the new materialism, nor on the science of the professional journals and the laboratories. Most of them probably scarcely know of their existence, not to speak of the intellectual tendencies of these institutions. What they are combatting is the doctrine of evolution in its popular, widespread form in the schools.

It must be remarked that Darwin stands on a more prominent pedestal in the American pantheon than among us. The enthusiasm of modern science and the ideal of education of the people have made almost every museum of natural history in America a place where Darwin's praises are sung in the clearest way as the father of science, indeed of civilization. "Darwin's *Origin of Species* literally created a new civilization," says our old authority Overstreet, placing him in the same row with the Old Testament, Confucius, and Lao Tze. I do not think that we can deny out of hand that a certain danger exists from extremely crude and mythological notions of the doctrine of evolution among the uneducated masses.

But what will the rising opposition to teaching the doc-

[58] "The Emancipation of Economics," *American Economic Review*, March 1924, p. 38.

trine of evolution in the schools bring with it? It is the Protestant churches which have girded up for this struggle. The Catholic church knows that it is safe; it can adapt itself and remain the same. Its foundation is broader than the word of the Bible alone. But the Protestant denominations have to fear decline if their foundations crumble. Their strength lies principally in the South and the West. The common danger brings them into harmony. The renowned Dayton trial[59] does not stand alone. A movement to follow the example of Tennessee with an antievolution law is under way in Mississippi, Arkansas, Washington, Oregon, and California. Louisiana State University refused a petition from students for a course in the theory of evolution. New Jersey and Mississippi have already seen the bonfires of embattled faith in public burning of scientific books. In Texas the state commission supervising teaching materials required that the publishers of all textbooks of biology cut out the pages relating to evolution. In California evolution may only be taught "purely as a theory"; even in private discussions between the teacher and the pupil, it may not be presented as having been proved. The name "The Bible Crusaders and Defenders of the Faith" expresses the attitude in which the campaign is undertaken. More than one dismissed school teacher may already count herself among the martyrs of the new persecution.

This spring Luther Burbank died. He was famous for his experiments in the field of hybridization and was well known to us Dutchmen from the *Reisherinneringen*[60] of Hugo de Vries. He was one of the most noble minds in America, pious in attitude although without belief in any church dogma, and had only recently borne witness to such unbelief. The death of the practitioner in the field of evolution struck the excited fundamentalists as a sign. One preacher told of

59 The "Scopes trial."—H.H.R.
60 "Travel Memories."—H.H.R.

Burbank's descent at full speed to hell; another presented him to the people as an example of God's vengeful justice. A typical American incident makes us see how the fuss raised over Burbank's passing also stirred intellectual circles. At a public meeting Sinclair Lewis, the honored writer of *Main Street*, *Babbitt*, and *Arrowsmith*, declared more or less as follows: "If there is a God who would send death to Burbank because he declared that he was an unbeliever, then I challenge that kind of God to strike me dead within ten minutes." It is only with some difficulty that we can imagine the whole episode transferred to Europe. The newspaper and the pulpit complained loudly about Lewis's atheism. Soon there came well-intentioned preachers of a liberal persuasion to testify that Lewis positively could not be called an unbeliever, any more than Burbank, and that, at the home of a clergyman with whom he was staying, he regularly participated in the morning services.

No doubt the group in the nation which shares neither the antimetaphysical tendencies of the progressive intellectuals nor the narrow-minded fanaticism of the denominations is not only very numerous but also the transmitter of true American ideals. They hold the invisible dear but also science, intellectual culture, and true education of the people. They have to see with anxiety the rise of the threat to science. For the fundamentalists will certainly find the way from the schools to the lecture-halls and the laboratories of the universities. Can the danger be turned aside? The time is not favorable for the middle party. What is worse is that the masses between the extremes do not at all consist only of well-meaning intellectuals. What if the America of the common herd, if ignorance, self-interest, and spiritual emptiness, in a word if Babbitt were to choose the side of fundamentalism? The possibility is not imaginary.

The cultural ideas of America—the true love of humanity,

the building of a better world in which to live that stands before our eyes, the unprejudiced social consciousness—are not held by the crusaders of unshaken faith. The task in which the quintessential America believes is not safe in their hands. An America turning back to puritanism and revivalism is not an imaginary danger.

Finally, we must probably wish that American science will undergo persecution, which will bring to it, with the ardor and the courage which are already its own, the greater depths which it sometimes seems to need.

INDEX

72 73 74 75   12 11 10 9 8 7 6 5 4 3 2 1